Obligations

Essays on Disobedience, War, and Citizenship

Michael Walzer

Obligations
Essays on Disobedience, War, and Citizenship

Harvard University Press
Cambridge, Massachusetts
London, England

© Copyright 1970 by the President and Fellows of Harvard College
All rights reserved
Fourth printing, 1982
Library of Congress Catalog Card Number 70-111489
ISBN 0-674-63000-9 (cloth)
ISBN 0-674-63025-4 (paper)
Printed in the United States of America

Acknowledgments

Most of these essays were once lectures in a course on political obligation that I taught at Harvard University during the years 1966–1969, and my first debt is to the students who listened to them and argued with me about them. I read them also to (mostly critical) groups of colleagues: I am especially grateful to my associates in the Society for Ethical and Legal Philosophy and in the Conference for the Study of Political Thought. Five of the essays were first printed in journals and books whose publishers have kindly allowed me to reprint them here. Several of them appeared in *Dissent,* and many of the political commitments that underlie them are shared (I hope) with the other editors of that magazine.

"The Obligation to Disobey" appeared in *Political Theory and Social Change,* edited by David Spitz, and is reprinted by permission of the publishers, Atherton Press, Inc. Copyright © 1967, Atherton Press, Inc., New York. All rights reserved. This essay was also published in *Ethics,* vol. 77, no. 3 (April, 1967).

"Civil Disobedience and Corporate Authority" is Copyright © 1969 by Random House, Inc. This essay will appear in *Power and the New Polity: Dissenting Essays in Political Science,* edited by Sanford Levinson and Philip Green, soon to be published by Pantheon Books, a division of Random

House, Inc. Reprinted by permission. This essay was also published in *Dissent* (September–October, 1969).

"Political Alienation and Military Service" was published in *Political and Legal Obligations: Nomos XII* and is reprinted by permission of the publishers, Atherton Press, Inc. Copyright © 1970, Atherton Press, Inc., New York. All rights reserved.

"Prisoners of War: Does the Fight Continue After the Battle?" first appeared in *The American Political Science Review*, vol. 63, no. 3.

"A Day in the Life of a Socialist Citizen" first appeared in *Dissent* (May–June, 1968), copyright © 1968 by Dissent Publishing Corporation.

Contents

For J.T.B.W.

הילכו שנים יחדו
בלתי אם נועדו

Amos 3:3

Introduction

It has been said of the theory of political obligation that "originality in this sphere is almost always a sign of error." [1] If this is meant as an endorsement of the conventional wisdom, there is an obvious reply: it is not all that clear anymore what the conventional wisdom is. With regard to civil disobedience, conscientious objection, the conduct of prisoners of war, the meaning of democratic citizenship, and many other subjects that fall within the sphere of political obligation, wise men, and others, disagree. In recent years, the arguments have been intense and the disagreements profound. Nevertheless, and though I hope to join these arguments, my own starting point in all the essays that follow is a piece of conventional wisdom (once revolutionary doctrine) to the effect that governments derive "their just powers from the consent of the governed." These are essays in consent theory, or rather applications of that theory to the political situation of my own contemporaries. I have not sought to be original—it is an old theory—but I have taken "the consent of the governed" to be a very serious matter, and I have never assumed its existence

---

[1] Sidney Hook, *The Paradoxes of Freedom* (Berkeley, 1964), p. 106. Hook refers specifically to obligation in a democratic society and proposes to "vindicate the obvious."

ix

without looking for evidence that it has actually been given. This has sometimes led me to question conventional beliefs about the justice of this or that government's enactments and the obligations of its citizens.

Consent theory suggests a procedural rather than a substantive ethics. It is not, in the usual sense of the phrase, a theory of value (though it does provide certain evaluative criteria that may properly be applied to the procedures of moral life). It is a way of describing how particular men come to have obligations, not what obligations they presently have. It invites us to search out what this or that individual has agreed to do; it provides no information as to what he "should" do or should have agreed to do—except for the single injunction that he honor his commitments. Individual men and women are bound to the limits of their commitments and no further, "there being no obligation on any man," as Hobbes said, "which ariseth not from some act of his own." [2] The paradigm form of consent theory is simply, *I have committed myself (consented): I am committed (obligated).* Committed to what? We can only find out by looking at the history of a particular man's consents, studying him in the setting of his own moral experience, analyzing the character and quality of the groups within which he is set, within which he has set himself. But before trying to do that (in some rough and tentative way), it is necessary to say something about what it means "to consent" or "to give consent"—to a government, but also more generally. I shall not have a great deal to say, for my own views are implicit in the essays and best tested in their applications. Nor do I want to offer a theoretical defense of the proposition that obligations derive only from consent. I am simply going to assume of the many obligations I discuss that they can have no other origin, and the reader must judge for himself whether descriptions and arguments rooted in that assumption are at all helpful. Here I shall only point to some of the problems that arise when we ask: what counts as a

[2] Thomas Hobbes, *Leviathan*, pt. II, chap. 21. In interpreting statements of this sort, I have been helped a great deal by Alexander Sesonske's *Value and Obligation* (New York, 1964).

commitment? How do we know when individuals have consented?

First of all, our consent is signified by "some act of our own," by what we say or do. There is, to be sure, a kind of consent signified by inaction, by silence or passivity, but we do not call this consent without qualification: it is tacit consent, and it raises, as we shall see, many difficulties. Our language reflects the difference between consent and tacit consent with some precision. A silent man is or may be *taken to consent;* the initiative belongs to and the assumption is made by the others, though the man himself must be aware (in some sense) that the assumption is being made or can be made. A man who speaks consents, or does not consent, directly; the moral initiative is his own. I will have to consider later on just how this qualification, expressed in the use of the passive voice, affects what is being signified, but it will be time enough to do that when we have in front of us, as it were, the silent citizen. For the rest, consenting acts can signify a variety of commitments: our sense of ourselves as members of this or that group, our intention to obey this or that rule or set of rules, our authorization of some persons or group of persons to act on our behalf, our belief in or readiness to stake our lives on "these truths," whatever they are. We can signify any or all of these things by saying "yes," or signing our names, or repeating an oath, or joining an organization, or initiating or participating in a social practice. Often the meaning of what we do is implicit not in the action itself, which can be entirely routine, but in its setting. We accept or adopt the routinized signal rather than invent one of our own. The members of secret groups are sometimes very inventive, but the messages they send, it has to be said, are roughly the same as the ones the rest of us send. Only the emotional effects are heightened.

By our acts of consent, we communicate to others that we are persons of a certain sort, who hold certain opinions, and will conduct ourselves in a certain manner. We entitle them to expect things of us, to rely on us, to plan their lives with us in mind as friends, colleagues, allies, or whatever. We give them rights against us and their rights henceforth define our obligations. Consents, then, are commitments to other people, or they are commitments to principles or parties or political institutions that arouse expectations in other people. For this reason, obligations are often compared to debts: they are other people's resources. And all social organizations are funded, as it were, through the commitments their members make to one another. Consents, then, can always be described both as acts of my own and as conveyances to others. I am bound to perform those future acts to which I have committed myself by my past acts; and I am bound to perform those future acts that other men and women (legitimately) expect me to perform. It is always in principle possible to find out what a man's obligations are by asking his friends, but his friends must refer themselves to his own action or inaction in their presence.

Governmental powers derived from consent are "just" not because they are used in benevolent ways or used to insure fairness in the distribution of benefits—though this last is an important sense of the word "justice"—but because we are bound to uphold their exercise. They are a legitimate social resource. In the context of consent theory, we do not say that the government is just, therefore the citizens are obligated, but rather that the citizens have committed themselves, therefore the government is just. This clearly implies a further principle of evaluation: a just government must be one to which or within which consent is possible. But this is a necessary, not a sufficient condition of political justice. Governmental powers are exercised by right only if we have actually granted that right. It should be noted, however, that we do not grant such rights only to those persons who hold office and exercise power. Our fellow citizens may also expect our obedience, and when we authorize certain men to demand obedience or to specify its character, we do not necessarily give them any more than their share of the general expectation. I think, then, that the English philosopher J. P. Plamenatz is wrong when he argues that the consent of the governed can only signify the authorization of some particular persons (governors) to act in certain ways.[3] It can mean many other things: above all, it can communicate our sense of ourselves as citizens, participants in an on-going political system, committed to uphold that system and abide by its rules. When we elect representatives, we certainly consent to their authority (and we do so whether we have supported the winner or not), but that is not all we do; we commit ourselves to our representatives in very limited ways indeed compared to the commitments we simultaneously make to our fellow voters. Plamenatz wants to identify representative government with government by consent, but this identification only holds if the representative system has itself been consented to—that is, if the citizens are pledged to one another to uphold it. This is a pledge they commonly make by participating in elections. It can, however, be made in other ways.

It would be a great mistake to define consent or consenting acts too narrowly. Our moral biographies are constituted in large part by trains of consents—consents of many different sorts, to many different people. Consent itself is sometimes signified not by a single act but by a series of acts, and the determining sign is always preceded, I think, by something less than determining: a succession of words, motions, involvements that might well be analyzed as tentatives of or experiments in consent. In fact, we commit ourselves very often by degrees, and then the expectations that others form as to our conduct are or ought to be similarly graded. We say of certain people, for example, that we can count on them thus far and no further, and no doubt they have given us reason for saying so. I suspect there are citizens who have given us (and the authorities) reason for saying the same thing about them.

Consent is given over time: I will insist on this point often in my essays. Here I want only to stress the extent to which we must take it into account when making judgments about the necessary freedom of consenting acts. It is a commonplace

[3] J. P. Plamenatz, *Consent, Freedom and Political Obligation* (Oxford, 1968), chap. 1. In his "Postscript to the Second Edition," Plamenatz grants that his original definition of consent was too narrow (p. 170).

of consent theory that obligations can only derive from voluntary commitments. The acts that signify my consent must be "my own," freely chosen, freely carried through, not imposed on me by anyone else or coerced or compelled in their course. Not that action unfree in some sense may not bind me in some sense: this too is a matter of degree. But the same qualifications that attach to my freedom attach to my obligation. There may be exceptions even to this general rule, since men whose action is radically circumscribed—oppressed peoples and prisoners of war are considered below—may still have obligations, at least to one another. But these are the limiting cases of consent theory. Ordinarily, men either acquire obligations freely, or they do not have perfect or complete obligations. It is not enough, however, that particularly striking acts of consent be free; the whole of our moral lives must be free, so that we can freely prepare to consent, argue about consenting, intimate our consents to other men and women (and also so that we can reconsider our consents and intimate our withdrawals). Civil liberty of the most extensive sort is, therefore, the necessary condition of political obligation and just government. Liberty must be as extensive as the possible range of consenting action—over time and throughout political space—if citizens can even conceivably be bound to a strict obedience.

When Rousseau and Hegel say that slaves have no obligations, they mean in part that slaves cannot bind themselves for the future because they are presently in bondage.[4] They are not free agents capable of doing what they commit themselves to do. Yet slaves, as Rousseau admits, sometimes come to "love their servitude," and they are perfectly capable of loyalty to their masters even at moments when it is not or cannot be coerced. They are not morally bound to their masters, however, partly because they are in bondage and partly because they *have been* in bondage. Their loyalty has not grown up in what might be called moral time and space. The preparations of their consent to servitude, its beginnings, its

[4] See Jean Jacques Rousseau, *The Social Contract*, bk. I, chap. 4; and G. W. F. Hegel, *The Philosophy of Right*, par. 261.

tentatives and experiments: none of these were free. The history of their (present) loyalty is a history of coercion, even if the loyalty itself is freely given. Now this argument too applies in degrees. Most moral biographies are stories of restraint and coercion as well as of voluntary action. Perfect and complete obligations are rare and perhaps especially rare in political life. I have confined myself in these essays almost entirely to men who have time and space enough, who *can* enter into all the complexities of a moral relation. Mostly, I have considered the problems of citizens of free states, democracies in some degree, whose spheres of moral action are formally, and in large part actually, protected. Even here, however, we must always ask whether they are protected— to take the easiest example—on election day and in the voting booth or all the time and everywhere.

Two practical if not logical consequences follow from the necessary freedom of consenting acts and play a large part in determining the subject matter of these essays: the obligations of individual men and women are unlikely to be either singular or stable. We regularly commit ourselves in more than one direction. We convey to different sets of men and women different senses of our own intentions and beliefs; these senses are not necessarily contradictory, nor are they necessarily devoid of contradiction. We also shift the weight and force of our commitments over time. Friends grow apart, brethren leave the fold, parties and sects divide. These departures and divisions sometimes involve breaches of faith and sometimes do not. That will depend on how they are prepared, on what is said and done in the preceding days, months, even years. Theorists of the liberal state have sometimes argued that citizens are always free to leave, but they rarely argue this without adding or implying some qualification. To specify the qualification, to get it right, seems to me one of the most difficult problems in political theory. I shall return to this problem over and over again, though not always in the setting of the state. Indeed, we experience it most often elsewhere. It is not always the government whose powers are "just" and whose "justice" we sometimes want to repudiate.

The state is not the only or necessarily the most important arena of our moral (or even of our political) life. Churches, movements, sects, and parties can have similar rights and powers similarly derived—as "just" as the state's, though rarely as effective. Here too we sometimes want to withdraw our consent because of conflicting (overriding) obligations elsewhere or perhaps only in defense of ourselves as persons capable of saying yes and no for reasons of our own.

One last point: my decision to write *essays* is connected, at least in my own mind, with the argument of the book. For to say of obligation in general (what I will later say of citizenship in particular), that it comes in kinds and degrees, is to suggest the enormous difficulty of saying anything more. It is only at considerable personal cost and "with a little help from our friends" that we can sort out our own indebtedness. We hardly have sufficient knowledge to do so for other people. So these are literally essays, attempts, nothing more, sketches of the obligations or some of the obligations of factory workers, Negro Americans, conscientious objectors to military service, soldiers, revolutionaries, alienated citizens of the modern state. They are all radically incomplete, and I have chosen the essay form because it seems to permit and proclaim that incompleteness. I hope it has also helped me avoid the presumption that is so common a feature of moral arguments, both when the protagonists claim to be original and when they do not.

Part One: Disobedience

1   *The Obligation to Disobey*

According to liberal political theory, as formulated by John Locke, any individual citizen, oppressed by the rulers of the state, has a right to disobey their commands, break their laws, even rebel and seek to replace the rulers and change the laws. In fact, however, this is not a right often claimed or acted upon by individuals. Throughout history, when men have disobeyed or rebelled, they have done so, by and large, as members or representatives of groups, and they have claimed, not merely that they are free to disobey, but that they are obligated to do so. Locke says nothing about such obligations, and, despite the fact that Thomas Jefferson claimed on behalf of the American colonists that "it is their right, it is their duty, to throw off [despotism]," the idea that men can be obligated to disobey has not played much part in liberal political theory.

"Here I stand; I can do no other"—Martin Luther's bold defiance—is hardly an assertion of freedom or a claim to rights. It is the acknowledgment of a new but undeniable obligation. Nor is this obligation often asserted, as it was by Luther, in the first-person singular. In a recent article on civil disobedience, Hugo Bedau has denied the validity of such an assertion, unless it is supplemented by arguments which reach

3

beyond the moral feelings of the individual. "The force of saying, 'I ought to disobey this law' cannot be derived from 'Obeying this law is inconsistent with my moral convictions.'" [1] Perhaps it cannot, and then we must wait upon Luther's further defense before we judge his defiance. But the first sentence is, in practice, rarely derived from the second. Generally it follows from an assertion of a very different sort: "Obeying this law is inconsistent with *our* moral convictions (on behalf of which we have made significant commitments, organized, worked together for so many months or years, and so on)." And it can be argued that, having said this, one can then go on, without offering additional reasons, to say, "Therefore I ought to disobey." This, at any rate, is the form that disobedience most often takes in history, even though additional reasons are usually offered. Men rarely break the law by themselves, or if they do they rarely talk about it. Disobedience, when it is not criminally but morally, religiously, or politically motivated, is almost always a collective act, and it is justified by the values of the collectivity and the mutual engagements of its members. In this essay I want first to describe the social processes by which men incur, or come to believe that they have incurred, the obligation to commit such acts. Then I want, very tentatively, to say something about the status of the obligations thus incurred.

The process by which obligations are incurred and the process by which they come to be felt are not the same, or not necessarily the same. They are similar, however, in at least one respect: they are both social processes. [2] They occur in groups, and they can both occur simultaneously in different groups of different shapes and sizes. The duty to disobey arises when such processes are more successful (have greater moral impact) in parties, congregations, sects, movements,

[1] Hugo Bedau, "On Civil Disobedience," *Journal of Philosophy,* 57:663 (Oct. 12, 1961).

[2] The best description of these processes is probably still Emile Durkheim's *Moral Education,* trans. E. K. Wilson and H. Schnurer (New York, 1961).

unions, or clubs than in states or churches. This happens often in human history, but precisely what is involved when it does needs to be carefully stated.

Obligations can arise in groups of two, between friends, partners, or lovers. But I am chiefly concerned with those which arise in groups of three or more, groups of a more general social, political, or religious nature. These can be obligations to the group as a whole (including oneself), or to the other members, or to the ideal the group stands for or claims to embody. In practice, none of these occur in pure form; obligations are generally, perhaps necessarily, admixtures of the three. But they are often described exclusively in terms of the last. Thus men announce that they are bound to God or the higher law, and bound "in conscience," which commonly means as morally sensitive individuals rather than as members. In fact, however, the very word "conscience" implies a shared moral knowledge, and it is probably fair to argue not only that the individual's understanding of God or the higher law is always acquired within a group but also that his obligation to either is at the same time an obligation to the group and to its members. "To be 'true to one's principles,'" Robert Paul Wolff has written, "is either a metaphor or else an elliptical way of describing loyalty to other men who share those principles and are relying upon you to observe them." [3] Perhaps this is exaggerated; clearly people feel that their principles embody what is right, and there is nothing odd or metaphorical about saying that one ought to do what is right or what one thinks is right (though it is not clear that this "ought" implies an obligation).[4] All I want to suggest is that commitments to principles are usually also commitments to other men, from whom or with whom the principles have been learned and by whom they are enforced.

This becomes clear, I think, if one examines cases in which ideals are renounced or "sold out." For in all such cases it is

[3] R. P. Wolff, "An Analysis of the Concept of Political Loyalty," in Wolff, ed., *Political Man and Social Man* (New York, 1966), p. 224.

[4] See Alexander Sesonske, *Value and Obligation* (New York, 1964), pp. 20–23 and *passim.*

individuals or groups of individuals who feel, and can plausibly be said to have been, betrayed. To "sell out" is to renounce heretical ideals for the sake of orthodox ones (but actually, it is generally suggested, for the sake of material gain) or to desert a small nonconformist group and join or rejoin society at large. Most likely, as the common descriptions of this common phenomenon suggest, it is to do both. "An affront to God and an injury to His congregation"—this is the way one's former colleagues describe a conversion to religious orthodoxy. And if God alone can judge the affront, they can rightly weigh the injury, taking into account the kind of commitment which had been made, the expectations which had been aroused, the ridicule to which they are (or are not) subjected, the possible weakening of their community, and so on.[5] Similarly, but more loosely, an artist who "sells out" by "going commercial" is not merely giving up an ideal; he is giving up an ideal to which others still adhere, and those others are his former colleagues. His offense, in their eyes, is not only his betrayal of Art but also his betrayal of them. He injures the cause of Art, they would claim, both in its ideal form and in its concrete social manifestation.

The individual involved, of course, may be doing or think he is doing no such thing. He may have changed his mind for good reasons. And he may believe (rightly, I think) that there is or ought to be some due process whereby he can announce this change of mind, explain its reasons, and so escape the charge of betraying his former colleagues. But however far his obligations extend, insofar as he is obligated at all it

[5] Where such judgments cannot be made at all, there is no obligation. And this means that obligations are always shared among men, who must judge one another. "The only obligation which I have a right to assume," wrote Thoreau, "is to do at any time what I think right." But when, in jail, he greeted the visiting Emerson with the famous question, "What are you doing out there?" he clearly implied the existence of a common obligation. Common to whom? Common at least to New England philosophers, one of whom was failing to meet it. Emerson believed the same thing when he spoke in his lecture on the Fugitive Slave Law of the "disastrous defection of the men of letters" from the cause of freedom (*The Complete Essays and Other Writings of Ralph Waldo Emerson* [New York, 1940], p. 867).

is to other men as well as to ideals. Indeed, to think of the
effect of his actions upon the ideal he once espoused, which
is surely a necessary part of any due process of renunciation
or withdrawal, is also to think of its effect upon those who
still hold fast to that ideal.

Obligation, then, begins with membership, but membership
in the broadest sense, for there are a great variety of formal
and informal ways of living within a particular circle of action
and commitment. Membership itself can begin with birth.
Then the sense of obligation is acquired simply through socialization; it is the product and most often the intended
product of religious or political education, of incessant and
unrelenting communal pressure, of elaborate rites of passage,
periodic ceremonial communions, and so on. One does not
acquire any real obligations, however, simply by being born
or by submitting to socialization within a particular group.
These come only when to the fact of membershp there is
added the fact of willful membership. Different groups, of
course, define willfulness in different ways, some in such minimal ways that willful membership becomes nothing more than
continued membership after a certain age, some in such maxi-
mal ways that even formal adherence by an adult is inadequate without a public profession of the faith or a period of
intensive participation in specified group activities. Sixteenth-
and seventeenth-century protests against infant baptism depended upon a maximum definition of individual willfulness,
as did Lenin's attack upon the Menshevik view of party membership. And willfulness can be carried even further. Elaborate tests of would-be members, frightening initiation cere-
monies, solemn oaths: these mechanisms of the secret society
and the revolutionary brotherhood raise to the highest level
the individual's sense of having made a choice of enormous
personal significance and thereby assumed the most profound
obligations.[6]

In general, well-established groups, especially those like the
state, which claim to be coterminous with society as a whole,

---

[6] Eric Hobsbawm, *Primitive Rebels* (New York, 1963), chap. 9; for
some examples of secret oaths, see his appendix 13.

are likely to defend the minimum definition, assume the commitment of their members, and punish those who disobey. Radical or nonconformist groups, precisely because they cannot make the assumption or guarantee the punishment, are likely to require that commitments take the form of explicit and public professions or acts. Through such professions and acts men can and do take on obligations to disobey the rules of the more inclusive group and also accept in advance the risks of their disobedience.

There is also a third sort of group, not sufficiently organized to make any precise determinations as to the character of membership. Disobedient citizens sometimes say that they are obligated by their membership in the "human community" or by their "solidarity with the oppressed." These obligations, if they exist at all, must be said to be universal (and men have indeed been punished for "crimes against humanity"). But they are generally cultivated in relatively small groups, often themselves loosely constituted, whose members can plausibly accuse one another, but not everyone else, of selling out when they fail to live up to their commitments. Since the community which is presumably being sold out is not the smaller but the larger group, which does not have any concrete existence and is only an aspiration, it is difficult to see how or whether anyone else can have made a commitment or what his betrayal would involve.[7] It must be said that efforts to enforce such obligations by individuals against their own states, or by groups of states against individuals, are really efforts to create them. Insofar as these efforts win general support, insofar as an entity like "humanity" acquires some "collective conscience" and some legal and institutional structure, real obligations are in fact incurred by membership. Obviously in such an absolutely inclusive community the willfulness of individuals will play an absolutely minimal part. Humanity can indeed be renounced, but only by becoming a criminal of the very worst sort, by turning oneself into what Locke called a "savage beast." At the present time, since no group exists which can satisfactorily define crimes against humanity, "sav-

[7] Sesonske, *Value and Obligation*, p. 107.

8

age beasts" are necessarily punished ex post facto, not for betraying humanity, but in the hope of creating a humanity whose members are capable of recognizing treason.

The state itself can sometimes be imagined as an ideal or potential community, obligating its members to oppose those authorities who act legally but (it is thought) immorally in its name. Thus those men who disobey the commands of a collaborationist government after military defeat, or of a satellite government after some less formal capitulation, often claim that their state has been betrayed and that they are obligated by their previous membership and driven by their patriotism to resistance. But they cannot claim that all their fellow citizens are similarly obligated. In the aftermath of such struggles, if the resistance is successful, active collaborators may be punished (the legal basis for such punishment is unclear enough), but nothing can be done to those who merely declined to join the fight.[8] They had never incurred any duty to do so. On the other hand, those who did join and subsequently deserted can rightly be said to have broken tangible and morally significant commitments. Thus a leader of the French Resistance, defending the execution of a deserter: "In the Maquis each man had chosen his own lot, fashioned his destiny with his own hands, picked his own name. Everyone had accepted in advance and without question all possible risks." [9] The same obviously cannot be said of Frenchmen in general.

To insist that obligations can only derive from willful undertakings is to restate the theory of the social contract. This has very interesting consequences given the rough typology of groups and kinds of membership just outlined. For contract theory clearly applies best to those sects, congregations, parties, movements, unions, and clubs in which individual choices are made explicit, acted out in some public fashion. It is most useful in discussing what are commonly called sec-

[8] Henry L. Mason, *The Purge of Dutch Quislings* (The Hague, 1952), chap. 2.

[9] Guillain de Benouville, *The Unknown Warriors* (New York, 1949), p. 220.

ondary associations, less useful (though by no means of no use at all) in discussing larger groups like states and established churches or vague and inclusive entities like humanity. Indeed, if the contract is taken at all seriously, it is difficult to avoid the conclusion that groups in which willfulness is heightened and maximized can rightfully impose greater obligations upon their members than can those catholic religious and political associations where membership is, for all practical purposes, inherited. Of course, inherited membership is often seconded by voluntary participation; in such cases the sense of obligation, as well as the obligation itself, is probably strongest of all. But even participation is likely to be more active and willful and so a more satisfactory token of continuing consent in nonconformist than in established and socially orthodox groups. Day-to-day procedures will be less conventionalized, the modes of participation and communion less habitual. In short, it is possible to conclude from contract theory, as Jean Jacques Rousseau did, that small societies are (generally) morally superior to large ones. For is it not the case that obligations incurred within some Protestant sect, derived from an explicit covenant, and sustained by a continual round of activity, ought to take precedence over obligations incurred in society at large, derived from "tacit" consent, and sustained by mere residence or occasional, largely passive, participation? I do not want to attempt an answer to that question immediately; perhaps there are good reasons for the negative answer conventionally given. But I do want to make two points: first, that obligations are in fact incurred within groups of these different sorts; second, that the conventionally assigned relative weights of these different obligations are not obviously accurate.

The duty to disobey (as well as the possibility of selling out) arises when obligations incurred in some small group come into conflict with obligations incurred in a larger, more inclusive group, generally the state. When the small group is called a secondary association, it is being suggested that there is no point at issue here. Secondary associations ought to yield without argument, conflict, or moral tension to primary ones.[10] This is true only of associations clearly secondary, that is, with purposes or ideals which do not bring them into conflict with the larger society. Rotarians cannot sell out.[11] But there exist in every society groups which may be called "secondary associations with claims to primacy." Serious conflict begins when groups of this sort are formed and their claims announced. But here a crucial distinction must be made: these claims can be of two very different kinds. Some groups announce what are in effect total claims. Their members are obligated, whenever commanded, to challenge the established legal system, to overthrow and replace one government with another, to attack the very existence of the larger society. These are revolutionary groups. There are others, however, that make only partial claims. They demand that the larger society recognize their primacy in some particular area of social or political life and so limit its own. They require of their members disobedience at certain moments, not at every moment, the refusal of particular legal commands, not of every legal command.

It is worth insisting upon the great difference between such groups and between the assertions they make, for defenders of state sovereignty often confuse them, arguing that any challenge to constituted authority is implicitly revolutionary and any group which claims to authorize such challenges necessarily subversive. They thus assign the labels "rebel" and "subversive" to all sorts of people who explicitly reject them. When this is done by officials of the state, the labels often turn out to be accurate, since the men who originally chose not to revolt are eventually forced to do so in self-defense. But there is considerable evidence to suggest that the state can live with, even if it chooses not to accommodate, groups with partial claims against itself. The disobedience of the members of such groups will be intermittent and limited; it

[10] S. I. Benn and R. S. Peters, *The Principles of Political Thought* (New York, 1965), chap. 12.

[11] People who accuse trade-union leaders of selling out are, in effect, accusing them of acting like leaders of secondary associations, the implication of their accusation being that the union (or the labor movement generally) is something more than secondary.

is unlikely to be conspiratorial in any sense; it does not usually involve any overt resistance to whatever acts of law enforcement the public authorities feel to be necessary (unless
these are radically disproportionate to the "offense"). Such
disobedience does not, in fact, challenge the existence of the
larger society, only its authority in this or that case or type
of case or over persons of this or that sort. It does not seek to
replace one sovereign power with another, only to call into
question the precise range and incidence of sovereignty. This
is not revolution but civil disobedience, which can best be
understood, I think, as the acting out of a partial claim against
the state.

Limited claims against larger societies can themselves be
of two kinds. They can involve assertions that the larger society cannot make demands of a certain sort against *anyone,*
or they can involve claims for exemptions for the members
(and the future members) of the smaller society. When a man
refuses to register for military service, without challenging
state authority in any other sphere, he may be saying that the
state cannot require anyone to fight on its behalf or to fight
this or that particular sort of war, or he may be saying that
people like himself cannot be so required. The second statement generally accompanies acts of conscientious objection,
which represent only one kind of civil disobedience.

The larger society can always recognize the claims of
smaller groups and so relieve their members from the burdens
and risks of disobedience. Indeed, the historical basis of liberalism is in large part simply a series of such recognitions.
Thus the limited disobedience of religious sectarians was
transformed into mere nonconformity when the state decided
to tolerate the sects. Tolerance required a limit on the power of
the state, a recognition that with regard to religious worship
any church or sect could rightfully claim primacy. Contemporary conscientious objectors are also tolerated nonconformists,
but here the tolerance is of a different sort. It is a recognition
of the claims of a particular type of person (or of particular
groups of people) rather than of the claims of any person (or
group) in a particular area. There is no necessary logical re-

striction on either type of toleration: the state could withdraw all its claims from an infinite number of areas, or it could add to every one of its laws a provision specifying that conscientious disobedience cannot be punished.[12] But few states seem likely to move very far in either of these logically possible directions, doubtless for good reasons.

What is the situation of men who join groups with limited claims to primacy in states where such claims are not recognized? It is a situation which political philosophers have never adequately described—though Rousseau surely understood the possibility of divided allegiance and divided men and bent all his efforts to avoid both. Locke provides a convenient outline of the possibilities more generally thought to be available: (1) A man can be a *citizen;* this involves a full recognition of the primacy of his society and its government. Certain areas are set beyond the reach of the government, but in such a way as to bar any possible obligations against it. There are only rights and ultimately, so far as action goes, only one right, the right of rebellion. Hence, (2) a man can be a *rebel,* seeking to overthrow and replace a particular government and its laws. These are the only two possibilities available to members of the larger society. But Locke suggests two further options for those persons who do not wish to be members: (3) A man can be an *emigrant,* willfully withdrawing from the larger society and physically leaving its territory. Emigration is the only due process through which social obligations can be renounced, for the rebel is still bound, if not to his government, then to society itself. Finally, (4) a man can be an *alien* who, having left the society of his fathers, fails to commit himself to any other and lives here or there at the discretion of the public authorities. An alien, for Locke, has obligations, for he is afforded protection within some particular society and tacitly consents in return to obey its laws. He presumably has rights, at least in theory, since rights are natural. He must even possess, I think, the right to rebel, though it is not clear that he possesses this right as fully as citizens do: he cannot protest if his consent is not asked to government or taxation.

[12] Bedau, "Civil Disobedience," p. 655.

This appears to be the single most important difference between aliens and citizens.

Now the member of a group with partial claims to primacy falls into none of these categories. His loyalties are divided, so he is not in any simple sense a citizen. He refuses to call himself a rebel, and with good reason, for he seeks no total change in the government, no transformation of state or society (though he would surely claim the right to rebel, in Locke's sense, given the conditions under which Locke permits rebellion). He is not an emigrant, since he does not leave, though joining such a group may well constitute a kind of internal emigration. He is not an alien, for while an alien can always leave, he cannot demand to stay on conditions of his own choosing.

Yet the situation of such a man—obligated to obey because of his membership in a larger society, obligated to disobey (sometimes) because of his membership in a smaller one—is, for all its tensions, very common in history and has often been fairly stable over long periods of time. It is the situation of any person who, like Sophocles' Antigone, retains strong tribal or clan loyalties while becoming a member of some (almost any) political order.[13] It is virtually institutionalized in feudal systems.[14] It was lived through with extraordinary intensity by early modern Protestants and has been lived through since with greater or lesser intensity by a considerable variety of religious groups (including Roman Catholics, for Rousseau the visible embodiments of double obligation and moral division)—even in liberal societies, which have recognized some

[13] The conflict in Sophocles' play is, of course, between primary groups. In general, conflicts between groups of relatives or friends and the state take forms similar to those described above, especially in modern times when such alliances tend increasingly to be voluntary. E. M. Forster's statement that "if I had to chose between betraying my country and betraying my friend, I hope I should have the guts to betray my country" is roughly analogous to the sorts of assertions sometimes made on behalf of groups. But it is an extreme statement and has reference to exceptional cases. Most often, the choice is between betraying one's friends (or colleagues) and *disobeying the laws* of one's country. Antigone's act is not treason, in any usual interpretation of that tricky term. Forster, *Two Cheers for Democracy* (New York, 1951), p. 78.

[14] See Marc Bloch, *Feudal Society* (Chicago, 1961), chaps. 9–17.

14

but not all the claims of pious brethren of this or that persuasion. It was the situation of European socialists during the period when their parties and movements had ceased to be revolutionary but had not yet accepted the status of secondary associations. (Otto Kirchheimer describes German Social-Democracy as a "loyalty-absorbing counterorganization." [15]) It is often the situation of trade unionists, especially when their country is at war. It is the situation today of all those persons who object to military service on other than the permitted religious grounds. It is, despite considerable confusion, increasingly the situation of many members of the American civil-rights movement.

What all these oddly assorted people have in common is this: none of them admits without qualification the political sovereignty or moral supremacy of the larger society of which they are members. None of them absolutely denies that sovereignty or supremacy. They are, then, partial members; they are simultaneously partial emigrants, partial aliens, partial rebels. The very existence of such people—even more, their obvious moral seriousness—ought to call into question the conventional description of citizenship as involving an absolute commitment (it is sometimes said, "under God") to obey the laws. Surely such a commitment will never be found among every one of those persons who consider themselves, with reason, citizens of the state. For the processes through which men incur obligations are unavoidably pluralistic. Even or perhaps especially in a liberal society, which allows considerable room for divergent groups and recognizes many of their claims, what might be called the incidence of obligation is bound to be uneven, the obligations themselves at least sometimes contradictory. Unless the state deliberately inhibits the

[15] Otto Kirchheimer, *Political Justice* (Princeton, N.J., 1961), p. 9. Trotsky takes an even stronger position, with regard not to Social Democracy but to the working class, and then draws an important conclusion: "In all decisive questions, people feel their class membership considerably more profoundly and more directly than their membership in 'society' . . . The moral norm becomes the more categorical the less it is 'obligatory' upon all" (Irving Howe, ed., *The Basic Writings of Trotsky* [New York, 1963], p. 378).

normal processes of group formation, and does so with greater success than has ever yet been achieved, it will always be confronted by citizens who believe themselves to be, and may actually be, obligated to disobey. As J. N. Figgis wrote: "The theory of sovereignty . . . is in reality no more than a venerable superstition . . . As a fact it is as a series of groups that our social life presents itself, all having some of the qualities of public law and most of them showing clear signs of a life of their own." [16]

Many political philosophers have insisted that there exists a prima facie obligation to obey the laws of the most inclusive organized society of which one is a member, that is, for most men, the state.[17] This is not unreasonable, so long as the state provides equally to all its members certain essential services. It is not unreasonable even though the state maintains a monopoly of such services and tolerates no competition, for it may be that the monopoly is itself essential to the provision of the services. But the existence of a prima facie obligation to obey means no more than that disobedience must always be justified. First explanations are owed to those of one's fellow citizens who do not join in, who remain obedient. I think it can be argued that membership (that is, morally serious membership) in groups with partial claims to primacy is always a possible explanation.

But I want to attempt a somewhat stronger argument than this, loosely derived from the preceding discussion of the uneven incidence of obligation in any larger society. I want to suggest that men have a prima facie obligation to honor the engagements they have explicitly made, to defend the groups and uphold the ideals to which they have committed themselves, even against the state, so long as their disobedience of

[16] J. N. Figgis, *Churches in the Modern State* (London, 1914), p. 224. See also G. D. H. Cole, "Conflicting Social Obligations," *Proceedings of the Aristotelian Society*, n.s., vol. 15 (1915), and "Loyalties," *ibid.*, n.s., vol. 26 (1926).

[17] See, e.g., W. D. Ross, *The Right and the Good* (Oxford, 1930), pp. 27–28; and discussion in Richard Wasserstrom, "Disobeying the Law," *Journal of Philosophy*, 57:647 (Oct. 12, 1961).

laws or legally authorized commands does not threaten the very existence of the larger society or endanger the lives of its citizens. Sometimes it is obedience to the state, when one has a duty to disobey, that must be justified. First explanations are owed to one's brethren, colleagues, or comrades. Their usual form is an argument that physical security or public health or some other such necessity of the common life— which the smaller groups cannot supply, which is actually supplied by the state—is being threatened or is likely to be threatened by particular acts of disobedience, however limited their scope. This, of course, is precisely what is asserted (usually by an official of the state) in every case of disobedience, but it is not necessarily asserted rightly. Indeed, there is very little evidence which suggests that carefully limited, morally serious civil disobedience undermines the legal system or endangers physical security.[18] One can imagine situations in which the acting out of partial claims might encourage or inspire the acting out of total claims. But the two sorts of action remain distinct. It may be necessary for a man contemplating civil disobedience to worry about the possibilities of revolutionary violence, but only if such possibilities actually exist. It is by no means necessary for him to reflect upon the purely theoretical possibility that his action might be universalized, that all men might break the laws or claim exemptions from them. For his action implies nothing more than that those men ought to do so who have acquired obligations to do so. And the acquiring of such obligations is a serious, long-term business which is not in fact undertaken by everybody.

[18] It is often enough said that disobedience even of bad laws undermines the habit of law abidance and so endangers that fundamental order upon which civilized life depends. But I have never seen this argued with careful attention to some particular body of evidence. In the absence of such an argument, I would be inclined to agree with David Spitz that there are clearly *some* laws obedience to which is not required for the maintenance of social order. Even more important, perhaps, there are many laws which can be disobeyed by *some men*, without prejudice to social order (Spitz, "Democracy and the Problem of Civil Disobedience," *Essays in the Liberal Idea of Freedom* [Tucson, Ariz., 1964], pp. 74–75).

The state can thus be described as a purely external limit on group action, but it must be added that the precise point at which the limit becomes effective cannot be left for state officials to decide. For them, the law must be the limit. At the same time, it must be the claim of the disobedient members that the law is overextended, that its sphere ought to be restricted in some fashion, that this activity or this type of person should be exempted, at this particular moment or for all time. There can be no possible judge of this disagreement. All that can be said is that the moral seriousness of the disobedient members is evidenced in part by their respect for those genuine goods the state provides not only to themselves but to everyone. To argue that the state does not provide such goods at all, or that it denies them entirely to particular sections of the population, is to justify, or to try to justify, unlimited and uncivil disobedience, that is, revolution. Revolution always requires (and generally gets) some such special justification.

There are two other ways of describing the state which appear to argue against the claim that disobedience can ever be a prima facie obligation. The first is to insist that the state is itself a group, that its members too are willful members who have incurred obligations of the most serious kind. It was the original purpose of social-contract theory to uphold just this conception of the state. But there are serious problems here. Since for many men there are no practical alternatives to state membership, the willfulness of that membership seems to have only minimal moral significance. A theory like Locke's requires the argument that one can always leave the state; residence itself, therefore, can meaningfully be described as a choice. That argument has some value—it may even be true that more people move across state frontiers now (though not always voluntarily) than in Locke's time—yet one cannot always leave, and so we would be wrong, I think, to base the weightiest political obligations on the non-act of not-leaving. There is a better way of describing the willfulness of state membership: that is to take very seriously the possibility of joining secondary associations with limited claims to primacy. Such engagements represent, as I have already suggested, a kind of internal emigration, and so long as the processes of group formation are open, and whether or not the frontiers are open, they offer real (though partial) alternatives to state membership as it is conventionally described. It is not the case, of course, that whoever fails to seize upon these alternatives thereby declares himself a member of the state and accepts all the attendant responsibilities. But membership is established as a moral option by the existence of alternatives. Thus, the possibility of becoming a conscientious objector establishes the *possibility* of incurring an obligation to fight in the army. But if the groups within which men learn to object are repressed by the state, that possibility disappears, for in one important sense at least the state is no longer a voluntary association.[19] Only if the possible legitimacy of countergroups with limited claims is recognized and admitted can the state be regarded as a group of consenting citizens.

But the obligations of citizens to the state can be derived in yet another way: not from their willfulness but from its value. "If all communities aim at some good," wrote Aristotle, "the state or political community, which is the highest of all, and which embraces all the rest, aims, and in a greater degree than any other, at the highest good."[20] Obviously, groups which aim at the highest good take priority over groups which seek lower or partial goods. There are two major difficulties, however, with Aristotle's description. First of all, it is not the case that the state necessarily embraces all other communities. A state with an established church and no legal provision for religious toleration obviously excludes a dissenting sect. Groups with universalist or international pretensions, like the Catholic church or any early twentieth-century socialist party, necessarily exclude themselves. Political or religious communities which oppose war are in no simple sense "embraced"

---

[19] I argue for the pluralist basis of conscientious objection in the sixth of these essays, and of citizenship in the tenth.

[20] Quoted in Benn and Peters, *Principles*, p. 315, and discussed, pp. 315–325.

by states which fight wars. It is precisely the nature of secondary associations with claims to primacy that they cannot and do not exist wholly within the established political or legal frame. Second, while the state may well provide or seek to provide goods for all its members, it is not clear that these add up to or include the highest good. Perhaps they are goods of the lowest common denominator and only for this reason available to all, for it may be that the highest good can be pursued only in small groups—in pietist sects or utopian settlements, for example, or, as Aristotle himself suggested, in philosophic dialogue. In any case, men do not agree as to the nature of the highest good, and this fact is enormously significant for the processes of group formation. Groups are formed for a great variety of reasons, but one of the chief reasons is to advocate or act out ("without tarrying for the magistrate," as a late sixteenth-century Puritan minister wrote) a new conception of the highest good, a conception at which the state does not aim, and perhaps cannot. To form such a group or to join one is to reject Aristotle's argument and renounce whatever obligation is implied by it. I fail to see any reason why this is not an option available to any morally serious man.

In the argument thus far, I have attached a great deal of weight to the phrase "morally serious." Obviously, the term is not easy to define, nor the quality easy to measure. Yet frivolous or criminal disobedience cannot be justified by membership in a group. There are obligations among thieves, but not prima facie obligations against the state. This is true, first of all, because the activities of thieves endanger the security of us all. But it is also true because a robbers' gang does not make claims to primacy. Thieves do not seek to limit the authority of the sovereign state; they seek to evade it. But there is nothing evasive about civil disobedience: a public claim against the state is publicly acted out. This willingness to act in public and to offer explanations to other people suggests also a willingness to reflect upon and worry about the possible consequences of the action for the public as a whole. Neither of these by themselves legitimate the action; but they do signal the moral seriousness of the group commitment that legitimates it.[21]

Frivolous disobedience can also never be a duty, and so groups that do not encourage an awareness in their members of the purposes and actions to which they may become committed cannot commit them. Awareness of this sort would appear to be required by social-contract theory; even the notion of tacit consent implies that there exists some knowledge of the duties being incurred. Nor, it seems to me, are the requirements of the theory entirely satisfied if such knowledge is but glimpsed at one brief moment in time. Continued awareness, a kind of shared self-consciousness, is necessary before the consent and participation of individuals carry sufficient moral weight to establish obligations—or, at any rate, to establish such obligations as I am trying to defend. A morally serious member of a group with partial claims may, then, be described as follows: he joins the group voluntarily, knowing what membership involves; he devotes time and energy to its inner life, sharing in the making of decisions; he acts publicly in its name or in the name of its ideals. Such a person—not any person—is obligated to act as he does, unless he is given good reasons why he ought not to do so.

The problem of civil disobedience needs to be placed squarely in the context of group formation, growth, tension, and conflict. There is a sociology of disobedience, which has greater relevance for philosophy than has generally been thought; it helps establish the proper units of analysis. Now these units doubtless have their limits, for it is true that there come moments when individuals must make choices or sustain actions alone—or rather, and this is not at all the same thing, when they must endure the anguish of loneliness. The state always seeks to isolate its disobedient citizens, because it is far more likely to bend their wills to its own if it can break the cohesion of the group which initially planned the disobedience and convince its members that they are mem-

---

[21] Secret societies, if they are not criminal, are implicitly revolutionary; the moral seriousness of their members must be signaled differently.

bers no longer. But this only suggests that the men who run prisons are always very much aware of the sociology of disobedience. Surely philosophers should be no less so.

The heroic encounter between sovereign individual and sovereign state, if it ever took place, would be terrifyingly unequal. If disobedience depended upon a conscience really private, it might always be justified and yet never occur. Locke understood this very well, for even while he proclaimed the right of individuals to rebel, he recognized that "the right to do so will not easily engage them in a contest, wherein they are sure to perish." [22] Rebellion, he thought, is only possible when it engages "the whole body" of the people. But clearly, rebellion and, even more, civil disobedience are most often the work of groups of much more limited extent. Clearly, too, it is not the mere individual right to rebel, unchanged in groups large or small, that sustains the enterprise but, rather, the mutual undertakings of the participants. Without this mutuality, very few men would ever join the "contest"—not because of the fear of being killed but because of the greater fear of being alone. "This is what is most difficult," wrote Jean Le Meur, the young French army officer who was imprisoned for refusing to fight in Algeria, "being cut off from the fraternity, being locked up in a monologue, being incomprehensible." And then: "Do tell the others that this is not a time to let me down." [23]

All this is not to suggest that there is anything unreal about individual responsibility. But this is always responsibility *to someone else* and it is always learned *with someone else*.[24] An individual whose moral experiences never reached beyond "monologue" would know nothing at all about responsibility and would have none. Such a man might well have rights, including the right to rebel, but his possession of the right to

[22] John Locke, *The Second Treatise of Government*, par. 208.

[23] Jean Le Meur, "The Story of a Responsible Act," in Wolff, *Political Man*, pp. 204, 205.

[24] Individual integrity, honor, or "authenticity" is different from this, though it is sometimes described, metaphorically, as responsibility to oneself. In the ninth of these essays, I discuss possible conflicts between obligation and personal honor.

rebel would be purely theoretical; he would never become a rebel. No political theory which does not move beyond rights to duties, beyond monologue to fraternal discussion, debate, and resolution, can ever explain what men actually do when they disobey or rebel, or why they do so. Nor can it help us very much to weigh the rightness or wrongness of what they do.

2 Civil Disobedience and Corporate Authority

Civil disobedience is generally described as a nonrevolutionary encounter with the state. A man breaks the law, but does so in ways which do not challenge the legitimacy of the legal or political systems. He feels morally bound to disobey; he also recognizes the moral value of the state; civil disobedience is his way of maneuvering between these conflicting moralities. The precise requirements of civility have been specified by a number of writers, and, while the specifications vary, they tend to impose a similar discipline on the disobedient persons. Above all, they impose the discipline of nonviolence. Civility, it is generally said, requires first the adoption of methods that do not directly coerce or oppress other members of society, and second, it requires nonresistance to state officials enforcing the law. I want to argue that there is a kind of disobedience that does not meet either of these requirements, and yet sometimes falls within the range of civility.

Perhaps the actions I am going to describe should not be called civil disobedience at all; I do not want to quarrel about names. But it is arguable, I think, that narrow definitions of civil disobedience rule out certain sorts of unconventional yet nonrevolutionary politics which should not be regarded as attacks on civil order. These may well involve both coercion

24

and violence, though always in severely limited ways. It is important to recognize the significance of such limits when making judgments about civility. The insistence on the absolute nonviolence of civil disobedience is, in any case, a little disingenuous, as it disregards, first, the coercive impact disobedience often has on innocent bystanders, and second, the actual violence it provokes, and sometimes is intended to provoke, especially from the police. I don't doubt that it is preferable that no one be coerced and that police violence be met with passive resistance, but there may be occasions when neither of these is politically possible, and there may also be occasions, not necessarily the same ones, when they are not morally required. Such occasions, if they exist, would have to be described and delimited precisely. One of the dangers of a narrow definition of civil disobedience is that it simply rules out the effort to do this. By setting rigid limits to civil conduct, it virtually invites militants of various sorts to move beyond the bounds of civility altogether, and it invites the police to respond always as if they were confronting criminals. (Sometimes, of course, the police are confronting criminals, but it is important that we know, and that they know, when this is so and when it is not.)

The limits of civility are a matter of academic interest in more than the usual sense just now, and I do want to speak to the problems of university radicalism and to help mark out the moral space within which students (and faculties) can legitimately, if not legally, pursue their demands. My more immediate focus, however, will be on the past—for the sake of clarity and dispassion. There are historical cases in which the coercion of innocent bystanders and resistance to police authority have in fact proven compatible, or so it seems to me, with a kind of civility. The sit-down strikes against General Motors in 1936–1937 provide a classic example, to which I will later refer in some detail. For now it is enough to indicate the general principles under which such cases may be justified. They *may* be justified when the initial disobedience is directed against corporate bodies other than the state; when the encounter with these corporations, though not with the state that protects them, is revolutionary or quasi-revolutionary in character; and when the revolution is a democratic revolution, made in good faith. I will suggest later on just what these principles involve and argue very briefly that some (at least) of the recent student sit-ins, though they have been defended by reference to the 1936 strikes, cannot be justified in the same way.

Americans today probably have a greater number of direct contacts with state officials than ever before. We continue, however, to have many contacts, perhaps more, that are mediated by corporate bodies. These corporations collect taxes on behalf of the state, maintain standards required by the state, spend state money, and above all, enforce a great variety of rules and regulations with the silent acquiescence and ultimate support of the state. Commercial, industrial, professional and educational organizations, and, to a lesser degree, religious organizations and trade unions all play government roles—yet very few of these reproduce the democratic politics of the state. They have official or semiofficial functions; they are enormously active and powerful in the day-to-day government of society, but the authority of their officers is rarely legitimized in any democratic fashion. These officers preside over what are essentially authoritarian regimes, with no internal electoral system, no opposition parties, no free press or open communications network, no established judicial procedures, no channels for rank and file participation in decision-making.[1] When the state acts to protect their authority, it does so through the property system, that is, it recognizes the corporation as the private property of some

[1] The list is adapted from Robert Pranger, *The Eclipse of Citizenship: Power and Participation in Contemporary Politics* (New York, 1968), esp. pp. 73–76. See also the excellent discussion in Grant McConnell, *Private Power and American Democracy* (New York, 1966), chap. 5. I should say at this point that I am not considering public corporations and civil services in this essay, though their employees may also be deprived of the benefits of internal democracy. Many of the arguments that I make later on may well apply to them, but their special position vis-à-vis a democratic government raises problems I cannot cope with here.

determinate group of men and it protects their right to do, within legal limits, what they please with their property. When corporate officials defend themselves, they often invoke functional arguments. They claim that the parts they play in society can only be played by such men as they, with their legally confirmed power, their control of resources, their freedom from internal challenge, and their ability to call on the police.[2]

Neither of these arguments justifies or requires absolute power, and some of the subjects of corporate authority have managed to win rights against it, rights which generally come to them as citizens and are also protected by the state. I am thinking of such things as the right to work no more than a specified number of hours, the right to work in at least minimally safe surroundings, and so on. The right to strike is of the same sort, though it was for a longer time unprotected. The claim of workers to shut down a factory they did not own was once widely regarded as a denial of the sanctity of private property and a threat to the efficient running of the economy. For years the strike (in the face of one or another court injunction) was the most common form of working-class civil disobedience, but it has long since been allowed, and the strikers legally protected, by the state. I should note that the right of students to strike is not similarly allowed, since students cannot, so far as I know, claim state protection against expulsion after an unsuccessful strike. In any case, such rights, even if securely held, would still not be comparable to the rights a citizen has in a democratic state, and just how far they can or ought to be extended remains unclear, a matter of continuing public debate. By and large, the subjects of corporate authority are . . . subjects, and state citizenship does not generate corporate citizenship even when it guards against the worst forms of corporate tyranny.

There is one argument in support of this subjection that at

[2] These are the implicit assumptions, for example, of Peter Drucker's *The Concept of the Corporation* (New York, 1946). In chapter 3 Drucker describes the suggestion box as a crucial channel for worker participation in corporate management, and suggests no other channels.

least falls within the realm of democratic theory. This is the argument from tacit consent, which holds that corporate subjects are, in some morally significant sense, voluntarily subject. By their willing entry into, and acceptance of the jurisdiction of, one or another corporate body, they commit themselves, on this view, to obey rules and regulations they have no part in making. They join the firm, go to work in the factory, enter the university, knowing in advance the nondemocratic character of all these organizations, knowing also who runs them and for what purposes. They are not deceived, at least no one is trying to deceive them, and so they are morally bound for the duration of their stay. However subject they may be during that time to authoritarian pettiness and to oppressive rules and regulations, they are never the captives of the authorities. Their citizenship guarantees their ultimate recourse: if they don't like it where they are, they can leave.

This is a serious argument and deserves some attention. Residence in a democratic state does, I think, generate a prima facie obligation to obey the laws of that state—in part because of the benefits that are necessarily accepted along with residence, in part because of the expectations aroused among one's fellow residents, and finally because of the universality of obligation in a democracy, from which no resident can easily exclude himself. The effects of residence in a nondemocratic state, however, are very different. There the right of resistance and revolution may well be widely shared, and there is no reason why a new resident should not associate himself with the rebels rather than with the authorities. It is not obvious that the same distinction applies to the corporation, since the strict forms of political democracy are often said to be impractical in corporate bodies organized for industrial or educational purposes. But this is precisely what is at issue in most cases of corporate disobedience, and I see no reason to prejudge the issue by agreeing that tacit consent to nondemocratic corporations establishes any greater degree of obligation than tacit consent to nondemocratic states. In any case, arguments about the possible reaches of democracy are carried on almost continuously within both the corporation and the state; surely no one can bind himself not to join them; and it is one of the characteristics of political arguments in nondemocratic organizations that they will often take "illegal" forms. Such forms may even be necessary if the arguments are to be carried on at all. So there can be no binding commitment not to break corporate rules and regulations, or at least, there can be no binding commitment until the best possible democratic procedure for establishing rules has been adopted.

There is another reason for rejecting the argument from tacit consent: corporate bodies do not offer anything like the same range of benefits that the state provides. Membership in corporations in no sense replaces citizenship in the state. A man may well provide himself with new benefits and even incur powerful, perhaps overriding, obligations by joining a corporate body, but he cannot be conceived as having yielded any of the legal rights he has as a citizen. Corporate officials may offer him a trade: we will pay you so much money, they may say, if you surrender the right to strike. That agreement, whatever its moral force, is not legally binding so long as the right to strike is recognized by the state. But the legal rights of a citizen are also matters of dispute, and so it is always possible for a corporate subject to break the rules and regulations, appealing to the laws of the state or to the established rights of citizenship as his authority for doing so.[3]

It is when such an appeal is not recognized by state officials that civil disobedience may begin. But for the moment, I want only to suggest that disobedience of corporate rules is probably justified whenever it is undertaken in good faith as part of a struggle for democratization or for socially recognized rights. By the phrase "in good faith," I mean to limit the occasions of justifiable disobedience to cases in which four conditions hold: when the oppressiveness of the corporate authorities can be specified in some rational way; when the so-

---

[3] Perhaps there is a moral as well as a legal basis for such appeals: it can be argued, I think, that in discussing rights and obligations, one can always appeal from less to more democratic bodies. Obviously, this can work against the state as well as in its favor.

cial functions of the corporation have been taken into account in judging the rights its participants might enjoy; when concrete proposals for corporate reorganization have been brought forward; and when a serious effort has been made to win massive support for these proposals. I would assume also that whatever channels for "legal" reform are available within the corporation have been tried. It is important, however, to stress the fact that such channels do not always exist in the sorts of bodies I am considering here. Indeed, in many of them any serious demand for democratization may plausibly be called revolutionary, for it involves an attack upon the established authority system of the corporation. This was certainly true, for example, of the demands of the labor movement, as one of its historians has noted: "If revolution is defined as a transfer of power from one social group to another, all forms of union activity which involve a challenge to the power of owners and managers are revolutionary." [4]

If this is so, then all the forms of revolutionary politics that we know from the history of authoritarian states may now be re-enacted on a smaller stage. In these kinds of situations, in fact, we ought to anticipate this kind of politics and not be shocked or surprised when it comes. Thus the presence of corporate police and spies (as in the auto plants before 1936) and the pervasive atmosphere of fearfulness generated by unlimited power will often impose secrecy and a severe discipline upon the revolutionary organization. At critical moments, initiatives may be seized by small minorities of militants who claim to represent their fellow subjects, but who also force them to make choices they did not anticipate and might well prefer not to make. Those who refuse to join the revolution may be threatened, mocked, perhaps beaten, their right to work systematically denied. Finally, the militants and their new supporters, now embattled and exposed, will often resist corporate countermoves, and may do so even if these countermoves have state support. All this, secrecy, discipline, coercion, resistance, still falls or may fall, I want to argue, within the limits of civility—so long as the revolution is not

[4] Robert Brooks, *When Labor Organizes* (New Haven, 1937), p. 112.

aimed at the state itself and so long as the corporate authorities really are as oppressive as the rebels claim.

There is another condition, of course: that the corporate revolution not take the form of a violent coup, an attempt to blow up the central offices of the corporation or to murder or terrorize its personnel. It is crucial that violence on this scale, if it occurs, does not occur at the initiative of the rebels. In fact it rarely does occur at their initiative; in almost all the cases I can think of (there may be some recent exceptions), the rebels have followed a different course. Their strategy is almost always to shut down the corporation, to curtail its operations or to stop them altogether, until some new distribution of power is worked out. It is important to note that this first shutdown is different from all those that come later. Once the authority and cohesion of the corporate subjects have been recognized, strikes may become a permanent feature of the power system. The simple withdrawal of workers from their routine activities will then be sufficient to close the corporation, and even the threat to strike will be a valuable bargaining point in its on-going politics. But this is not so earlier on, and the first strikes may have to take more direct and coercive forms. Generally, they involve the physical occupation of the corporate plant and the expulsion of nonstrikers. Occupation is preferable to withdrawal, because it can be achieved successfully without majority support, or immediate majority support, and majorities are not readily organized under authoritarian conditions. Occupation is also preferable because it precludes, at least for a time, the effective dismissal of the strikers and the resumption of corporate activity with new subjects. For these reasons, the sit-down or sit-in is a typical form of revolutionary activity in nondemocratic corporations.

The state then comes into the picture not to enforce the laws against assault and murder, but to enforce the property laws. This is the paradox of corporate revolution: the revolutionaries encounter the state as trespassers. However serious their attack on corporate authority, they are guilty of only minor crimes in the eyes of the state, though one would not

31

always guess this from the response of state officials. In fact, violence often, perhaps most often, begins with law enforcement. "A large proportion of the . . . disturbances we have been surveying," writes Charles Tilly in a report on European strikes and riots, "turned violent at exactly the moment when the authorities intervened to stop an illegal but nonviolent action . . . the great bulk of the killing and wounding . . . was done by troops or police rather than by insurgents or demonstrators." [5] The case is the same, I believe, in the United States.

In suggesting how disobedience to corporate rules and regulations might be justified, I have treated the corporation as a political community within the larger community of the state. I have discussed its government and the rights of its subject population. This is obviously not the way, or not the only way, the officials of the corporation and the state regard the matter. They see the corporation also as a piece of property, protected as property by the law. When corporate officials find "their" buildings occupied, their first response is to call on the police to clear them. The police sometimes come and sometimes do not. They are pledged to enforce the law, but they also take orders from the political leaders of the state, who may (and, I would suggest, ought to) see in the corporate revolution something more than a mere violation of the property laws. What is at issue here is not who owns the corporation, but what such ownership entails, above all, what, if any, governmental powers it entails. It is one of the characteristic features of feudal regimes that the ownership of property always entails governmental powers (and responsibilities): public functions such as war-making, tax-collecting, and adjudication are dispersed among a class of landlords and the right to carry out such functions is literally owned along with the land. Clearly no modern state, even more clearly no democratic state, can permit or tolerate such a dispersal of

[5] Charles Tilly, "Collective Violence in European Perspective," in *Violence in America* (A Report to the National Commission on the Causes and Prevention of Violence), ed. Hugh Davis Graham and Ted Robert Gurr (New York, 1969), p. 39.

powers. Corporate officials who carry out governmental or quasi-governmental functions (even the simple maintenance of social order within the corporation) must be responsible to the larger community, whose citizens they and their subjects are. This means that the state has an interest in the internal politics of the corporation, an interest that may or may not be served by police intervention on behalf of private property. It is not far-fetched, I think, to suggest that the interests of a democratic state are best served by corporate democratization —at least so long as this process does not seriously interfere with the social functions of the corporation, in which the larger community also has an interest.

It is important, in any case, for state officials to realize that when they enforce the trespass laws against strikers, they are also doing something else. They are acting to restore not merely the "law and order" of the state, but that of the corporation as well. They are enforcing another set of rules in addition to their own. And while they can argue that the strikers have every right and opportunity to work in public and try to change the first set of rules, they must recognize that the second set can, perhaps, only be changed by the very revolutionary action they are repressing. When police resist efforts to overthrow the state, they are behaving in a perfectly straightforward way, but the case is not straightforward when police resist efforts to overthrow corporate authority. Corporate authority is not the same as the authority of the property laws—it does not have their democratic legitimacy—and the differences between the two may require the police to use some discretion in moving against men who violate the laws of the state solely in order to challenge the authority of the corporation. The corporate rebels may, for example, be defending rights they actually have as citizens. Their violation of the law may be a means of bringing to the attention of their fellow citizens other, more important violations of the law.[6] Then the police must choose the laws they

[6] This is the way the 1936–37 strikes are justified in Joel Seidman, *Sit-Down*, League for Industrial Democracy pamphlet (New York, 1937), p. 38.

will enforce and may reasonably choose to do as little as possible for the time being. Police inaction may even be justified if the rebels are wrong, or if the courts hold that they are wrong, about their rights as citizens, for the size and scope of the strike may suggest changing communal values which the political leaders who command the police may choose to respect, if only in order to avoid violence.

The rebels may, of course, be wrong in other ways: the militant minority may not have even the silent and fearful sympathy of the others; its demands may be inconsistent with the continued fulfillment of important social functions. But corporate authorities always claim that these two conditions hold, and have done so in many cases where they clearly did not. Because the truth is often difficult to discover, especially in the early hours or days of a rebellion, state officials must keep an open mind as long as they can. Police action may be necessary, but it is rarely necessary immediately. It is, however, almost always the demand of the corporate authorities that the police act quickly. If there is any hesitation, their subjects, they think, will rally around the militants—though it is obviously also possible that they will desert the militants, leaving them helpless and isolated. Time is the best test of the support the strikers actually have among the passive majority, but this has not, historically, been a test the authorities are willing to risk. Delay, moreover, pushes them toward negotiations with the strikers, and the beginning of talks is itself a victory for democratization even if no other demands are allowed. Hence any refusal to enforce the law probably constitutes a kind of indirect intervention by the state against the corporation. It would be naive to deny this; I can only suggest that the interests of a democratic state are sometimes served in this way.

If the police do enforce the law, then they must expect that the strikers will respond in the context of their own revolutionary situation. They are not at war with the state, but they are (or they may be) caught up in a political struggle of the most serious sort, and direct police intervention, whatever its supposedly limited purposes, brings the police into that struggle and into what may well appear the closed circle of its strategic necessities. The more desperate the struggle, the less likely they are to meet with either obedience or a merely passive resistance. Even active resistance in such circumstances, however, does not necessarily constitute an attack upon the law and order that the state represents. It may do so, of course, if state officials are totally committed to the maintenance of corporate authority in its established forms and if their interference on behalf of that authority is not merely occasional but systematic. Clearly there have been governments so committed, and to their officials corporate revolution must look like (and may actually be) revolution *tout court*. But the history of liberal government is a history of retreat from such commitments, retreat from the total support, for example, of church prelates (ecclesiastical authority, and above all the right to collect tithes, was once protected by the property laws), of industrial magnates, and so on. The occasion for such retreats has generally been an act or a series of acts of corporate rebellion which state officials decided they could not or discovered they need not repress.

Continuous repression, if it were possible, would virtually force the rebels to expand their activity and challenge the state directly. There are always some militants among the rebels who assume that such repression is inevitable. Like the corporate authorities, they see civil order and corporate authority inextricably intertwined. But this is rarely the case. Law and order is indeed always law and order of a particular sort; it necessarily has a specific social content. But law and order is also a universal myth; the liberal state is at least potentially a universal organization; and in the name of its myths its leaders can always or almost always dissociate themselves from some particular piece of social oppression. For this reason, corporate rebellion is potentially a limited form of political action and potentially a kind of civil disobedience. The violation of property laws is not in itself an act of revolution against the state, and state officials acknowledge this and confirm it when they give up on such things as collecting tithes or clearing the factories.

35

If they intend to be civil and hope to be treated civilly, the rebellious subjects of corporate authority must in turn be careful not to make revolutionary claims against the state. Doubtless the occasion calls for a certain rhetorical extravagance, but that can be ignored so long as the actions of the rebels bespeak a concern for the appropriate limits. In general, this is the case: the rebels argue by their actions that the commitments they have made to one another (their new-found solidarity) establish an obligation to disobey not all laws, but only *these* laws, for example, the trespass laws. They claim for their revolutionary organization not that it replaces the state or is a law unto itself, but only that it wins primacy in this or that limited area of social life. It requires its members to violate state laws *here*, not everywhere, and insofar as it justifies the use of violence against state officials, it does so only if they intervene against the revolution. The justification is local and temporary and does not challenge the general authority of the police to enforce the law. In fact, the rebels will often demand law enforcement—against the corporation—and explicitly pledge themselves to obedience, as they should do, whenever obedience is compatible with corporate democracy.

All the arguments I have thus far made are illustrated by the autoworkers' sit-down strikes of 1936–1937, and I think the illustration is worth presenting in some detail since so little has been written about this form of civil disobedience. The right of workers to strike has come to be so widely accepted that its illegal and semi-legal history and all the philosophical issues raised by that history have been forgotten. The sit-down, moreover, was not only called illegal by the local courts in 1937, it eventually was called illegal by the Supreme Court. Indeed, the strike that went so far to establish the right of corporate subjects to organize and defend themselves remains illegal today. Yet it is not the case that all corporate systems have been democratized, nor do all corporate subjects have the same rights. The questions raised in 1936–1937 still have to be answered.

I do not think that I need to describe at length the kind of oppression that existed in General Motors plants before the victory of the autoworkers. Corporate officials possessed absolute authority over hiring and firing, the conditions of work, the pace of work, and the rates of pay. They used this power not only to maximize production and profit, but also to maintain the established authority system. In effect, they ran a miniature police state in the factories, and the organization of the workers, their incipient union, took on in response the features of an underground movement.[7] This movement claimed a kind of legality not within the corporation but within the state: its spokesmen insisted that they were acting in accordance with the National Labor Relations Act, which made the encouragement of union organization a matter of public policy, and in defense of those legal rights that workers were said to have in their jobs.[8] But though they might argue that the activity of union organizers was democratically authorized outside the factories, inside it necessarily took revolutionary and sometimes nondemocratic forms.

There can be no doubt that the union enjoyed widespread sympathy among the workers, but union members did not make up anything like a majority at any of the struck plants, and in some of them this was true not only of members but even of supporters. Majority rule does not operate very well in the early stages of the struggle for democracy when the majority is likely to be both passive and frightened, justifiably anxious for its jobs, and often resentful of militants who do not share that anxiety or repress it in the name of possibly distant goals. Hence the way is always open for vanguard initiatives which are dangerous both practically and morally.

[7] See Henry Kraus, *The Many and the Few: A Chronicle of the Dynamic Auto Workers* (Los Angeles, 1947), chap. 1, for an account of what organizing was like before the sit-downs. Kraus was editor of the *Flint Auto Worker,* the local union newspaper, during 1936–1937. Sidney Fine, *Sit-Down: The General Motors Strike of 1936–1937* (Ann Arbor, 1969), appeared too late for me to consult it in preparing this essay.

[8] Solomon Barkin, "Labor Unions and Workers' Rights in Jobs" in Arthur Kornhauser et al., eds., *Industrial Conflict* (New York, 1954), p. 127. These claims were eventually rejected by the courts.

Militants who seize the initiative always run the risk of finding themselves alone, deprived not only of effective support
but of moral justification. In 1936, the risks paid off; the basis
of a democratic movement did in fact exist, though this was
not known, and could not be known with any certainty, in
advance.

It is important to stress the risks the militants accepted and
had to accept if they were to undertake any political action
at all, but it is also important to stress all they did to minimize
those risks. A long history of struggle and failure preceded the
dramatic victory of 1937. The commitment of the union militants to corporate democracy is best evidenced by their
months and years of work in the factories, building support,
searching for activists, adjusting their own proposals to meet
the interests of the men on the job. A strike might have been
attempted without all that; angry men were never lacking in
the auto plants. But there is a kind of legitimacy that can only
be won by hard work. Without a disciplined base the civility
of the strike would have been precarious at best, and
it is not difficult to imagine isolated militants, faced with
certain defeat, setting fire to a factory or shooting at the
police.

A successful strike requires not only that the militants find
majority support, it also requires that they coerce minorities,
and often that they begin to do so before they have demonstrated the extent of their support. This is not a usual feature
of civil disobedience against the state, but it has to be remem-
bered that what is going on in the corporation is not civil disobedience at all but revolution. Exactly what this involves can
be seen most clearly in the seizure of Chevrolet Plant No. 4,
the turning point of the General Motors strike. The union was
relatively weak in Plant No. 4, and its seizure required careful planning. Company police were lured away by a demon-
stration in another factory; several hundred union militants
from Plant No. 6 were brought in during a change of shifts;
and these men together with union supporters already inside
succeeded in forcing the shutdown of No. 4. Before the strikers carried the day, however, there was a time when uncom-

mitted workers were attacked from both sides. Here is the account of a union official:

A few of the staunchest unionists got into the aisles and be-gan marching around shouting . . . "Strike is on! Come on and help us!" Many of the workers stood waveringly at their posts . . . And meanwhile the superintendents and foremen . . . tore about, starting the conveyors up again, yelling to the men to "get back to work or you're fired" . . . Some of the men began working again or at least made a desperate effort to do so under the tumultuous circum-stances as they were still anxious to differentiate themselves from the strikers. But the ranks of the latter grew inexor-ably . . . There was practically no physical violence. The men would merely act fierce and holler threats. There was huge Kenny Malone with wrench in hand tearing down the lines and yelling: "Get off your job, you dirty scab!" Yet he never touched a man.[9]

This is a graphic description of a revolutionary moment, the decisive overthrow of the absolutism of superintendents and foremen. It is clear, I think, that one can justify the coercion of the "wavering" workers only by reference to that end and to the legitimate expectation that it was widely shared. For the moment, however, the militants could only assume that the end was widely shared, and such assumptions may have to be sustained without proof for some time. In Plant No. 4 the political battle was won, but the moral outcome, so to speak, remained inconclusive:

The fight was over; the enormous plant was dead . . . The unionists were in complete control. Everywhere they were speaking to groups of undecided workers. "We want you boys to stay with us. It won't be long and everything will be settled. Then we'll have a union and things will be different." Many of the workers reached their decision (for the union) in this moment. Others went home, undeterred

[9] Kraus, *The Many and the Few*, pp. 214–215.

by the strikers. About two thousand remained and an equal number went off.[10]

I do not mean to suggest that *any* degree of coercion of un-decided or neutral persons can be defended by reference to the end of corporate democracy, but it is likely that, given the limits I have already sketched, virtually any degree of necessary coercion can be defended. Surely it would be dishonest for those of us who value democracy in corporations as well as in states to pretend that we would judge the GM strike differently if Kenny Malone had actually hit somebody with his wrench—though we are certainly glad (and should be glad) to be told that he did not. However, in discussing violence against state officials, somewhat different standards apply, at least they apply if we believe the state to be so constituted that attempts on its authority are not easily justified. Within the corporation, revolutionary initiatives may well be appropriate; within the larger democratic community, they are inappropriate, and the corporate rebels demonstrate their civility only insofar as they make clear, as the autoworkers did, that they intend no such initiatives. During the GM strike, for example, a number of workers were arrested, and the union leaders ordered mass demonstrations in front of the local police station. They thus used against the police legal forms of protest that they had declined to use against the corporation.

On the day after the seizure of Plant No. 4, a Michigan court issued an injunction against the strike, and the strikers began discussing among themselves what they would do if confronted by police or National Guardsmen. There were a few men in the factories and among the union's leaders who urged passive resistance. They thought the workers should allow themselves to be carried out of the factories. But a much larger group favored active resistance, on the pragmatic grounds that there was no working-class tradition of passivity and no religious or ideological foundation for a politics of nonviolence. The spectacle of strikers being carried, limp and

[10] Kraus, *The Many and the Few*, p. 216.

unresisting, in the hands of the hated police would have, they argued, a profoundly disillusioning effect on the families of the strikers and on all the men who had so far refused to join the revolution. It would seem a terrible defeat rather than a moral victory, an incongruous and humiliating end to a period of heroic action. This argument carried the day, and the strikers publicly committed themselves to fight back against any effort to use force to clear the factories.[11]

At the same time, they did everything they could do, short of leaving the factories, to avoid such an outcome. They established their own law and order, a strikers' discipline far stricter than that of the foremen; they banned liquor from the occupied plants, worked out informal agreements with the police which permitted workers to come and go and food to be brought in, and carried out all necessary repair and maintenance work on factory machinery.[12] Above all, they repeatedly stressed their willingness to negotiate a settlement. This last is a crucial token of civility. However radical their demands, and even if those demands imply that the corporate authorities ought not to be authorities at all, the rebels can never deny to their opponents the recognition they themselves seek. The call for unconditional surrender may sometimes be appropriate in time of war and civil war, but it is never a political demand, nor is it compatible with civil peace.

The argument in the factories indicates some of the problems of any absolute commitment to nonviolence. Men who live in a democratic state can plausibly be said to be obligated to preserve its peace, to accept the forms of its law and order. But the strikers did not live only in the state. They were members, as all of us are, of overlapping social circles, and within the spheres specific to them—General Motors, the auto industry, the capitalist industrial system generally—they did not enjoy the benefits usually associated with the words law and order. These were worlds of oppression and struggle, in which the mutual forbearance necessary to civil disobedi-

[11] In a letter to Governor Murphy. On the arguments within the union, see Kraus, *The Many and the Few*, pp. 220, 231–233.

[12] Seidman, *Sit-Down*, pp. 32–36.

ence did not exist. In these worlds, state police had all too frequently played a role no different from that of company police, implicating themselves in the oppression and compromising their own authority. The point where the two circles overlapped had thus been dominated by the violence of the corporate world. It was only the refusal of Michigan's Governor Frank Murphy to enforce the court injunction—his own civil disobedience—that re-established the state as a universal organization and a sphere of nonviolence, within which autoworkers could conceivably incur serious obligations to the public peace.

Most of the criticisms of the strikers were simply refusals to recognize the pluralism of their social lives and the possible pluralism of their moral commitments. When A. Lawrence Lowell, President-Emeritus of Harvard University, said that the sit-downs constituted "an armed insurrection . . . defiance of law, order, and duly elected authorities," he was suggesting that the spheres of corporate and state authority coincided perfectly.[13] I have already argued that this is sometimes true, and, when it is, civility on the part of corporate rebels is almost impossible. But it was not true in Michigan in 1937. Governor Murphy, who had only a few months before become a "duly elected authority" with the support of the autoworkers, symbolized this fact. His affirmation of the independence of the state recognized that the primary focus of the strike was on General Motors and not on Michigan or the United States, and so ended the threat to civil order. By forcing negotiations between the corporate authorities and the union leadership, he began the long (and as yet incomplete) process of bringing some kind of legitimacy to General Motors. Until that process was well begun, I see no reason to deny to the workers the right to use (limited) force within the corporate world, against their oppressors and against any allies their oppressors might call in. But I do not mean to state a general rule; the argument depends upon the specific character of the overlapping social circles.

[13] Quoted in J. Raymond Walsh, *C.I.O.: Industrial Unionism in Action* (New York, 1937), p. 182.

Even if the police had gone in, the resistance of the workers would not have constituted an "armed insurrection," though it is not difficult to imagine an insurrection growing out of such an encounter. Particular, limited acts of resistance, coupled with appeals to community laws and values, do not necessarily break through the bounds of civil order. There was, in fact, an action of this sort early in the strike, a short, sharp battle between police and strikers (known, among the strikers at least, as the Battle of Bulls' Run) which took place at the initiative of the police.[14] I do not believe that incidents of this sort detract in any serious way from the double description of the strike that I have attempted to sketch: revolution in the corporate world, civil disobedience in the state. Obviously that dualism breeds difficulty; neither label is precise. Together, I think, they capture something of the social and moral reality of the sit-down.

Civil disobedience has often been divided into two types: direct disobedience, in which state laws thought to be unjust are openly defied; and indirect disobedience, in which state policies thought to be unjust are challenged by the violation of incidental laws, most often trespass laws. I have tried to describe a third type, more indirect than the second, in which the state is not challenged at all, but only those corporate authorities that the state (sometimes) protects. Here the disobedience takes place simultaneously in two different social arenas, the corporation and the state, and in judging that disobedience different criteria must be applied to the two, though I have tried to show that the two sets of criteria are not entirely unrelated. When revolution is justified in the corporation, then certain limited kinds of resistance, even violent resistance, may be justified against state officials protecting corporate property. I assume a strong presumption against

[14] Kraus, *The Many and the Few,* pp. 125ff. It should be noted that compared to previous strikes in American history, "the sit-down strikes were exceptionally peaceful." Philip Taft and Philip Ross, "American Labor Violence: Its Causes, Character and Outcome," in *Violence in America,* p. 363. This was true largely because the workers were in the buildings, disengaged from company agents and the police. In labor disputes, violence most often erupts on the picket line.

43

such violence, however, and I would want to justify the use of force only when the oppression of the corporate subjects is palpable and severe and the interference of the police of such a kind that leaves the rebels no alternative but resistance or defeat. At the same time, it seems to me that state officials, recognizing the oppression, ought not to interfere, ought to refrain, that is, from enforcing the property laws, and so avoid even limited violence.

The character of private governments obviously varies a great deal, and so the argument I have developed on the basis of the General Motors strikes will not apply in any neat and precise way to all other sit-downs. The student rebellions of the sixties, for example, are very different from the labor rebellions of the thirties. But I do believe that the same criteria can be used in framing our judgments in these two, and in many other, cases. This suggests the sorts of questions we must ask student militants: what is the nature of the oppression you experience? have you worked seriously among your fellow students (and among your teachers) to build support for your new politics? do you have, or potentially have, majority support? what are your specific proposals for university reform? and so on. By and large, I think, these questions have not been adequately answered—chiefly for two reasons that I can only mention here. First of all, contemporary universities are very different from the General Motors plants of 1936 (or even of 1969). However authoritarian their administrations, their students enjoy personal and civil liberties undreamt of in the factories, and these liberties open the way for a great variety of political activities short of the sit-in, or at least, short of the sit-in as I have described it, with its attendant coercions. Yet, and this is the second point, contemporary student movements have rarely been able, in fact, they have rarely attempted in any politically serious way, to win and hold majority support. Their militants have often rushed into adventures that cannot hope to win such support, in part because they have nothing to do with corporate democratization, in part because they call into question the very functions of the university the militants profess to value.

It is, nevertheless, not difficult to imagine universities so rigidly authoritarian and student movements so committed as to justify the sorts of politics I have been examining. There have certainly been justified sit-ins during the past several years, sit-ins that actually moved this or that university closer to whatever form of democracy is appropriate to the academic community. There have also been sit-ins justified in part, open at the same time to severe criticism, that resulted or might have resulted in similar movements. The theoretical model I have tried to elaborate permits us, I think, to defend such movements and their necessary methods—but always in a way that reveals to the participants themselves the nature and limits of their action.

The problems of university government indicate clearly the great importance of arguing about the possibilities of democracy in every institutional order and not only in the state. I do not mean to prejudge these arguments—at any rate, I do not mean to prejudge them absolutely. A government of equals may be possible in one setting; weighted voting, or some such recognition of inequality, may be necessary in another; collective bargaining between employees and managers may be appropriate in a third. The range of political decision-making or of bargaining may have to be limited in this way or that, or it may not be limited at all.[15] There is no single desirable system of internal adjudication. Nevertheless, I think it can be said flatly that some kind of democratic legitimacy is always necessary to corporate authority. Insofar as corporations lack this legitimacy, their very existence breeds revolt, and the more private and autocratic their government is, the more angry, perhaps violent, the revolt will be. If democratic states choose to shelter corporate autocrats, then they must learn to shelter corporate rebels as well. And if the rebels are asked, as they should be, to maintain civility, then the authorities must see to it that civility is a genuine option for them and not merely a convenience for the autocrats.

[15] Democratic decision-making in the university does, I think, have to be limited: it is appropriate, for example, in the organization of day-to-day student life; in the classroom, not so.

3 The Obligations of Oppressed Minorities

I had reduced everything to the simple theory that the oppressed are always right and the oppressors are always wrong: a mistaken theory, but the natural result of being one of the oppressors yourself.—
GEORGE ORWELL

Majority rule is the hardest question in democratic theory. There are certainly good arguments to be made for allowing the people to rule—if only the people had some collective identity or general will and did not always demand to be counted! What can possibly be said for allowing 51 percent of the people to rule? Mostly we fall back on a practical argument, morally rooted in the idea of a political community, a single unified order which is temporarily represented or activated, in lieu of anything better, by a majority of its members. Thus John Locke: civil society is *one body;* one body can only move in one direction; so it must move "whither the greater force carries it." [1] The greater force is, however, not always the force of numbers. Political bodies can be moved, and generally are, by relatively small numbers of men who possess wealth, offices, inherited status, or a monopoly on the means of violence. The defense of majority rule requires something more: a theory of equality stipulating that every man ought to have and must be provided with the same po-

[1] John Locke, *The Second Treatise of Government,* par. 96.

litical force as every other man. Then the "greater force" can only be discovered by counting heads.

There are, then, two moral reasons for a minority to yield to majority rule. First, because it too is a part of the community and acknowledges the unity of the state; second, because it too has been counted. Then an overriding practical reason: some decision there must be; the state must act; there is no option; and how else but by "greater force"? If we assume further that the adding up of individual wills takes place at the end of a political process during which all citizens are equally free to make arguments, we can add another moral and another practical reason for minority obedience. By participating in the process, knowing in advance its regular course and the possibility of an adverse outcome, individuals agree to the legitimacy (though not to the rightness) of the eventual decision. If they lose out, they defer to the majority, hoping that one day they will not lose out and will be deferred to in turn. The only alternative is war, but by joining the argument they have committed themselves to politics, and politics, given their minority position, remains their safest choice. Hence, even if they are outraged by the majority decision and feel morally bound to disobey, they will choose, if they are wise, to disobey in political ways, which do not call into question the survival of the democratic system.

This describes an ideal case, however, and its three crucial assumptions are rarely realized in practice. So we must ask, what is the status of majority rule if (1) the unity of the state is not universally acknowledged, (2) all citizens are not, in fact, politically equal, and (3) the political process is not absolutely open and free? The question can be put more directly: what if there exists a minority group which either is or regards itself as separate from the political community and whose members are or feel themselves to be oppressed? Obviously there are such groups in more than one modern democratic state. Sometimes their members occupy a single piece of territory within the larger community, and then their politics is likely to take separatist or secessionist forms. They will not challenge majority rule so much as the political integrity of the state within which a particular majority rules. They claim the right to be a majority in their own state. I am inclined to concede the right, though sometimes there are other claims to be considered. It is not difficult to imagine a situation in which a right (in the minority) to secede or attempt secession coexists with an obligation (in the majority) to defend the original union. In many cases, however, and these are the ones I want to discuss, the minority is geographically dispersed. Then the issue is not the integrity of the union, but the legitimacy of majority rule. What are the obligations of an oppressed minority in a state where only the members of the majority are entirely free and equal? That is not a question that can be answered until something more is said about the nature of the oppression, but for the moment let it stand as this: members of the minority, for whatever reason, do not "count" in the same way as everyone else.

The case is not difficult where they do not count at all. Then the oppressed persons simply have no political obligations, or rather, no obligations to the state. Slaves owe nothing to their masters and nothing again to the ruling committee of their masters. Nor do the relative numbers of slaves and masters make any difference, except in the strategic considerations of the two groups. Cases where the oppressed are recognized as citizens are much harder. Their votes are honestly counted, let us assume, but as it turns out they never win. They are free to organize, but they face a thousand petty difficulties and their attempts to sustain large-scale organizations regularly fail. Patterns of social and economic discrimination reinforce their minority political status (and their political weakness reinforces the social and economic patterns—it hardly matters which way the causal connections are worked). The pressure they can bring to bear within the political system is limited. Their day-to-day lives offer them little hope. They are trapped in a moral and political ghetto—in a country that is still in some serious sense open and democratic. Obviously the situation I am sketching is something like that of American black people, though the sketch is formal in character and hardly suggests their long years of humiliation and outrage. It also ignores the problems of elite domination in the modern state. I am simply assuming what many blacks believe and what seems plausible, that they confront a unified, though not a monolithic, white majority, that they are the victims of *popular* oppression. What obligations can they possibly be said to owe to the (more or less) democratic state?

On this issue, liberal and democratic theorists have had very little to say, but what they have said is clear enough and, it must be admitted, very radical. They have argued, in effect, that oppressed minorities have no obligations at all within the political system. "And where the body of the people, or any single man," writes Locke, "is deprived of their right . . . there they have liberty to appeal to heaven [that is, to rebel, to make war against the government], whenever they judge the cause of sufficient moment." [2] Of course, Locke's conception of "right" did not explicitly include a right of political participation. That is a later extension, but it is one that would today be difficult to deny. For oppression can never be limited to the political sphere: it endangers a man's "life, liberty and property" as soon as it diminishes his political force, and so it cuts away his (Lockeian) reasons for consenting to government and obeying the law. The seriousness of Locke's commitment to consent theory is best revealed by the last phrase in the passage I have quoted: the crucial judgment about oppression must be made by the "oppressed" themselves. Feeling oppressed, then, yields the same "liberty to appeal to heaven" as being oppressed. Rousseau characteristically suggests a more objective judgment, but the essential point is the same. The social contract "would in point of right be dissolved" if a single citizen were treated wrongly. [3] The victims

---

[2] *Second Treatise,* par. 168. Locke specifies that this liberty only exists when the oppressed "have no judge on earth," but he seems to believe that they have "no judge" and so no appeal short of heaven (that is, war) whenever the government designs or participates in their oppression.

[3] Jean Jacques Rousseau, *A Discourse on Political Economy,* in *The Social Contract and Discourses,* trans. G. D. H. Cole (New York, 1950), p. 303.

of injustice are released from every social bond; they are free in society, or they are free out of it, for they can never rightly be oppressed.

It might be argued that Rousseau did not really believe this, since he defends the legitimacy of states, like that of ancient Rome, where more than one citizen, indeed, many more than one, were treated wrongly. I am going to do the same thing, though with less resolution, since it is difficult to regard the United States today with anything like the admiration Rousseau felt for the Roman republic. But I want first to grant the moral force of the argument: where justice is not done, there is no legitimate state and no obligation to obey. I also want to deny the force of the easiest response: that all human creations, and states especially, are imperfect, hence to be endured as long as possible. This is no response at all, for, if it condones anything, it condones equally the imperfect justice of the government and the imperfect obedience of its subjects. If oppression is to be accepted as an inevitable feature of the political condition, then why not violent rebellion? Isn't the arrogance of the oppressor a far greater human imperfection—to say the least—than the rage of the oppressed?

When oppressed men exercise their "liberty" and act out their rage, they do so in relation to two social groups, and therefore the extent and limits of that liberty must be twice specified, each time in a different way. They act first with or on behalf of the group that they themselves constitute and (sometimes) bring to self-consciousness by their action. Not their rights as individuals but their connection to the mass of the oppressed is their reference point in explaining to themselves and to each other what they can and cannot do. They act secondly within the larger community and against their oppressors. Here the democratic state and their own ambiguous citizenship is the reference point of their arguments and justifications. Both these references can best be explicated, I think, by looking closely at all that is implied by words like "on behalf of" and "within," and this is what I shall try to do in the rest of this essay. My discussion will necessarily ignore

50

much else that ought to be taken into account; I shall have to justify its emphases as I go along. There are few guidelines, for political philosophers have not dwelt at any length upon the moral life of the oppressed.

I have already suggested that oppressed individuals rarely experience their oppression as individuals. Their suffering is shared, and they come to know one another in a special way. They have an understanding among themselves—by no means founded on mutual admiration—which no one outside the circle of oppression can readily share and which no one inside the circle can easily escape. From this understanding obligations follow, their contents determined by the specific interactions of the oppressed, their force determined by the intensity of those interactions and their almost suffocating closeness. It is the fate of the oppressed that the whole of their moral lives be mediated by their common situation.[4] For this reason, something must be said about the obligations they owe to one another before anything can usefully be said of their "liberty" within the state.

I cannot specify the procedures through which patterns of recognition and solidarity or definitions of loyalty and betrayal are worked out. The procedures are informal; it is not the case that they are constituted by a succession of voluntary acts, any more than the group of the oppressed is constituted by a series of individual contracts. Members of the group do form voluntary associations, at least partly to make the patterns and definitions as precise as possible and to enforce them. And they form different associations because they disagree as soon as they try to be precise. Yet there is a sense in which the possibility of acting faithfully and the possibility of breaking trust pre-exist all voluntary acts. This is part of what it means to be oppressed, and it suggests the two ways in which oppression marks the limit of the consensual universe. "It is the anti-Semite who makes the Jew," writes Sartre, and that means, first, that the Jew does not make himself and, sec-

---

[4] This argument does not relate only to politics, but also to art and culture: see Irving Howe, "Black Boys and Native Sons," *Dissent* 10:353–368 (Autumn 1963).

ond, that he must make himself an (authentic) Jew.[5] The same thing is true of the black man: he did not choose blackness; now he must choose blackness.

These are not conventional or easy moral assertions, perhaps they are not moral assertions at all, though Sartre's insistence that inauthenticity is never "morally blameworthy" is belied by the tone in which he writes about it. One ought never agree too quickly to match the coercion of the oppressor (all black men must defer) with the coercion of the oppressed (all black men must resist). Individuals do escape, or at least they seem (sometimes to themselves, sometimes only to the others) to escape. They pass or assimilate, or they hide. They choose to be inauthentic Jews or blacks. Such men are surely not traitors, not in any literal sense of that word. But they are not quite faithful either. They have moved into a world of deceit and self-deceit, where trust and mutuality are lost ideals.

Obligations in the strict sense are established when the more active members of oppressed groups form organizations for mutual defense or political struggle. The precise content of these obligations, the political or social creed to which the activists commit themselves, the relative intensity of the commitment—all this has to be negotiated and is negotiated with very different results in different organizations. There is no single correct result that I or anyone else can stipulate. Nevertheless, I do think that certain general things can be said about the obligations of activists, given the claim they commonly make: to speak or act on behalf of oppressed men and women.[6] It is important to try to do this, since the activists

[5] Jean-Paul Sartre, *Anti-Semite and Jew*, trans. George J. Becker (New York, 1960), p. 69.

[6] In the paragraphs that follow, I have been helped a great deal by Hannah Pitkin's discussion of what it means to "act for" someone else, *The Concept of Representation* (Berkeley, 1967), chap. 6. I should note as she does (p. 127) that the *Oxford English Dictionary* distinguishes the phrases "on behalf of" and "in behalf of." The first indicates a representative function (acting in someone else's name, with his authorization); the second has the sense which I have singled out: "in the interest of, as friend or defender of, for the benefit of," but the phrase is no longer in common use. "On behalf of" is now used in both senses.

are rarely authorized to speak or act on behalf of anyone (I do not mean that they have no right to do so), nor is it easy for the mass of the oppressed to repudiate them because of what they say or do. A certain responsibility to the mass is sometimes enforced within particular organizations of activists or, more often, through competition among different organizations. Whenever this enforcement is attempted, arguments are made about political obligation, arguments that focus, consciously or not, on the problem of the unauthorized agent. It is easy to be outraged at the plight of others, especially easy (perhaps) for a man who shares or has shared that plight, but it is not easy to act for them when they are unable to act for themselves. Many men claim to do so; other men question their good faith. Despite endless variations in theory and rhetoric, these arguments have a recurrent form. We encounter them often in the history of the Left: action on behalf of others is the Left's version of virtual representation and shares the same difficulties and dangers. I want to examine these, first with occasional reference to their classic exposition in the work of Marx and Trotsky, then with specific reference to an example drawn from the recent history of black militancy.

The basic principle of arguments about responsibility is simply that the activists, when they commit themselves to work on behalf of the oppressed, also commit themselves to work as effectively as they can and actually to help the oppressed whenever they can. But what does it mean to work "effectively" or "actually to help" the oppressed? Who shall judge the effects or the helpfulness? I should think that the immediate goals of the activists must be set by the general consciousness of the oppressed group rather than by their own ideology. The effects can only be judged by those who will feel them. "Helping" someone usually means doing something for him that he regards or seems likely to regard (given his present state of mind) as helpful. There are exceptions to this rule, but each exception requires justification; it usually requires some plausible claim to special knowledge on the part of the active persons—such as a doctor or a lawyer might

53

make. But this is an especially implausible claim for political activists to make, so long as they wish to maintain that they are struggling for equality.[7] Not that they must acquiesce in the established forms of deference and passivity; then they would not be activists at all. They may and they often should seek "to raise the level of consciousness" among the oppressed through various sorts of educational and political work, even, sometimes, by setting an example of boldness and militancy. But they win the "liberty" that oppression confers only if they respond to the felt needs of their putative constituents and represent these to the larger community. Otherwise they are not acting for the oppressed at all, but for themselves (not necessarily in their own interests, perhaps for the sake of their own ideals). Then the moral rules relevant to their activity are not those we derive from the situation of oppressed minorities, but rather those we derive from the experience of sect life in a democratic society. Sectarian activists, in contrast to the oppressed groups from which they sometimes come, are likely to be both free and equal, even to be counted in ways that exaggerate their numbers.

One might go further and suggest that sectarian activists often stand to the oppressed group in rather the same relation as does the oppressor government, even though they are without the same power. They are a competing elite. They make similar claims to esoteric knowledge. They replace the general struggle for freedom and equality with their own struggle for recognition and power. This replacement can take different forms depending on the ideology that rationalizes it,

[7] Pitkin quotes a contemporary political scientist who argues that "The true representative obeys the people by doing the things they would want done if they possessed his knowledge . . . as a physician when he prescribes things disliked by his patient, nevertheless represents the patient's real will to get well." She proceeds to criticize this view of representation in ways that seem to me entirely right (*Concept of Representation*, pp. 135–139). We do, of course, say or assume that a doctor works "in the interests" of his patient. But we cannot assume even this in the case of a professional politician (or revolutionary) and the people. The politician does not simply apply his skill to reach an agreed-upon end. He joins in the on-going debate as to what that end is, and he cannot be said to act in the people's interests unless he accepts their view or wins their agreement to his.

and though it is often self-serving, I do not want to suggest that it is always that or merely that. Nor is the pride a man may take in having worked his way through to a coherent ideological position necessarily a false pride. But there is a great difference in the moral position of a would-be leader who finds his warrant for action in his ideology alone and one who finds his warrant in the fact that he can give his ideology currency among the oppressed themselves. Only the second is a leader *of* the oppressed, defining their interests in terms they, or many of them, can and do accept. But it might be argued that the first man, given his ideology and assuming his good faith, is nevertheless bound to act as he does, for how else can he honestly help the oppressed? Perhaps this is so, but to whom is he bound? Not to the oppressed men and women whose consciousness he rejects: surely he takes their name in vain. Then he is bound only to himself, if that is possible, and to the small band of militants who share his commitments. And the militancy of such a group, whose members necessarily act on their own behalf whatever else they do or think they are doing, easily degenerates into one or another kind of elitist conspiracy. Marx's description of the relation of Blanquist sectarians to the working class as a whole points to just such a degeneration:

> These *conspirateurs* do not limit themselves to the mere task of organizing the proletariat; not at all. Their business lies precisely in trying to pre-empt the developing revolutionary process, drive it artificially to crisis . . . For them, the only necessary condition for a revolution is an adequate organization of their conspiracy . . . Hence their deepest disdain for the more theoretical enlightenment of the workers about their class interests.[8]

Marx is not making a moral but rather a tactical argument here—or so he would say—and his hatred for the *conspirateurs* hangs on his conviction that there is a revolutionary process. If such a process cannot be, or if it is not discerned, or if it

---

[8] Quoted in Shlomo Avineri, *The Social and Political Thought of Karl Marx* (Cambridge, Eng., 1968), p. 201.

proceeds or seems to proceed at too slow a pace to offer any hope for those who are oppressed *now,* then there may well be arguments for creating a crisis artificially or hastening a crisis that seems likely to come only in the distant future. What this means is that the activists put themselves into some radically exposed position (they seize a building, begin an armed struggle, and so on), expecting a repressive response from the state, and calling on the mass of the oppressed to come to their rescue. Indeed, they may try to force people to come to their rescue by choosing a course of action that endangers not only themselves but everyone else on whose behalf they claim to be acting. If this strategy works, if support is forthcoming, and if major concessions are won, the activists will be called heroes. Yet there is a kind of self-sufficiency, an ability to take risks for oneself alone, implied by the classic idea of the hero, that they seem to lack.[9] Perhaps the real heroes are the men who come to their rescue. In any case, the action can be successful only if they do come, and that means it should be undertaken only if they can be expected to come. Hence "the mere task of organizing" the oppressed must precede the adventures of the activists. And that task, if it is carried forward with energy and seriousness, is very likely to begin a political process, a long revolution, to which contrived crises are superfluous. There will be crises enough in the normal course of things. The whole of the long revolution is a collective adventure, which will have its resonances in the lives of many men and women, but which no small group can rightly claim for itself. Thus Trotsky's argument against terrorism, a personal adventure generally undertaken, or so it is said, on behalf of others: "To the terrorist we say . . . only in the mass movement can you find expedient expression for your heroism."[10]

[9] It is not easy to be a hero when acting for someone else; sometimes action in good faith requires the repression of all impulses to personal heroism: ". . . we are expected to be more cautious when we act for others, less willing to take risks. What is courage or daring on our own behalf becomes irresponsibility when committed on behalf of another" (Pitkin, *Concept of Representation,* p. 118).

[10] Irving Howe, ed., *The Basic Writings of Trotsky* (New York, 1963), p. 397 (hereafter referred to as *Trotsky*).

It is never possible to know in advance the course of the mass movement or the historic shape of the long revolution. The easiest visual image is one of gradual linear advance, but that image is often deceptive or deceitfully employed. I do not mean to commit the activists to an incremental politics. If they are "actually to help the oppressed whenever they can," however, they have no right to reject any possible improvements in their condition. The argument is sometimes made that all such improvements, short of full liberation, reduce the incentives for further struggle. Men can be partially satisfied, it is said, often at no significant sacrifice by the ruling majority or the established elite, and then the oppression is stabilized, at least for a time, and the activists effectively isolated from their base. Whatever its historical plausibility —the evidence is not easy to assemble or weigh—this argument suggests what seem to me morally impermissible risks. It suggests that the activists give up present and certain gains for the oppressed in the name of a future and impalpable triumph—and a triumph, most likely, in which only they entirely believe. It amounts to saying what has in fact been said more than once in the recent past: the worse, the better. These words probably have to be read: the worse for the mass of the oppressed, the better for the activists. I should add, the better for the *activity* of the activists, for the risks they themselves run may also be heightened. (Once again, I am not suggesting that their politics is necessarily self-serving.) Even put that way, the maxim may well be false. Its possible falseness is less important, however, than the fact that the choice it implies will never be made by the men certain to be most affected by it. So it can never rightly be made in their name.

Actual improvement in the condition of the oppressed is most likely in the special circumstances I am considering, that is, when the larger community is at least formally democratic and when real possibilities exist for open organizational and agitational activity. This is a proposition often disputed, especially in periods of political failure and frustration, but I do not think there are many, even among the activists, who would choose to work underground and live in hiding so long

57

as they had alternatives. It is important, of course, not to exaggerate the value of democratic rules (as distinct from democratic practice): the mere existence of an *oppressed* minority suggests forcefully that the rules are being worked, twisted, and manipulated, often brutally so, in the interests of the majority or of its leaders. But that only means, I think, that men acting in the name of the minority ought to insist upon the real meaning of the rules and upon the practices that follow from them.

Given the formalities of citizenship and suffrage, oppression is enforced in large part by the incapacities of the oppressed themselves—their economic helplessness, lack of education, inarticulateness, self-hate, and above all, their political dispersion, disunity, incompetence, and isolation—incapacities at which the whole society more or less openly conspires and which can only be overcome through equally open political struggle. If this struggle is actually being fought on behalf of the oppressed, it must eventually broaden to include them. This is one of the oldest maxims of the Left: "the liberation of the workers can come only through the workers themselves." [11] The same thing can be said about minority groups, though the word "only" is more ambiguous in their case. Thus, it remains a crucial test of all those who claim to work for the oppressed that the action they choose activates as well as benefits other men and women and that it does nothing to lower their faith (low enough already) in the possibility of their own democratic participation. Conspiracy and terrorism never, I think, meet this test; they are the politics, as esoteric ideology is the consciousness, of a competing elite. "Bureaucratism has no confidence in the masses and endeavors to substitute itself for the masses," wrote Trotsky. "Terrorism [functions] in the same manner; it wants to make the masses happy without asking their participation." [12] Oppressed minorities do not find participation easy; that is why the activists must act on their behalf; but in more or less democratic conditions it is a great deal easier to "ask" their participation, to seek it,

[11] *Trotsky,* p. 398.
[12] *Ibid.,* p. 296.

58

to work for it. And that means (though Trotsky at this point might not agree) that anyone who really hopes to initiate a liberating politics must exploit the democratic hypocrisy of the majority, conniving at every chance the laws allow for public agitation and largescale action and breaking the law, whenever necessary, only to increase the chances. "Let them calmly and resolutely improve the opportunities of republican liberty, for the work of their own class organization."[13] So wrote Marx of the French workers in 1870, warning against an insurrectionist adventure that might undermine liberty. That is a warning worth repeating, though it can hardly be delivered with the same assurance by a white man today as by a bourgeois intellectual then.

I have used the words "ought" and "should" in the preceding paragraphs because I believe I have been elucidating the moral commitment implied by the phrase "acting on behalf of the oppressed." I have not been exploring questions of tactics, or not these alone. The principles I have put forward are not, nor are they intended to be, tactically specific. That activists must pay attention to and be guided by the consciousness of the oppressed (even if they hope to change that consciousness); that they must not despise concrete improvements in the condition of the oppressed (even if such improvements make their own work harder); that they must act so as to open up (or keep open) the possibilities of democratic action: these seem to me moral injunctions. They follow from commitments that political activists make and reiterate in the course of their struggles. Perhaps I should say, that they generally make, for it is at least possible to imagine a vanguard of militants that acted explicitly on its own behalf and whose members were entirely honest about their hope to exploit the misery of the oppressed. The "liberty" of such men is not at issue; they have none at all, despite their ideology, beyond the common liberty of every other citizen. Activists on behalf of the oppressed do have further rights, but their exercise of these rights is or ought to be restrained by the moral responsibility they have accepted.

[13] Quoted in Avineri, *Marx*, p. 199.

I want to complete my description of that responsibility by looking at a recent case in which one black activist called another to account. The exchange is not of great historical significance, but it is worth examining because it is typical in its content and classical in its form. In 1964 Robert Williams, then living in exile in Cuba, issued a call (echoed many times since) for urban guerilla warfare by Negro Americans:

> The new concept of revolution defies military science and tactics. The new concept is lightning campaigns conducted in highly sensitive urban communities with the paralysis reaching the small communities and spreading to the farm areas. The old method of guerilla warfare, as carried out from the hills and countryside, would be ineffective in a powerful country like the USA. Any such force would be wiped out in an hour.[14]

Thus Williams makes a tactical argument which suggests some sense of moral responsibility to the black community: fewer of its members would die if they fought in this new way. But that is not his primary consideration:

> Of course, there would be great losses on the part of our people. How can we expect liberation without losses? Our people are already being admonished by the nonviolent forces to die for Freedom . . . If we must die, let us die in the only way that the oppressor will feel the weight of our death. Let us die in the tried and proven way of liberation. If we are going to talk about revolution, let us know what revolution means (p. 391).

Behind these words lies a vision of revolution as a grand moment of retribution, when the last shall suddenly and violently be first. I would be surprised if that were not a fantasy savored by many American blacks. But Williams offers it as a political program, and as a program it has been sharply criticized by Harold Cruse in his book *The Crisis of the Negro*

---

[14] Robert Williams in *The Crusader* (monthly newsletter published by Williams while in Cuba), February 1964, quoted in Harold Cruse, *The Crisis of the Negro Intellectual* (New York, 1967), pp. 386–387.

Intellectual. I will summarize Cruse's criticisms in terms of my own three principles, but in doing so I do not mean to suggest that he would endorse the principles as they stand. His own argument is in the service of a particular politics and not of a moral theory.

Cruse begins by insisting (1) that "the masses of our people have not yet said they want a revolution. They want equal rights." [15] This is a goal to which Williams was (in 1964, at least) publicly committed. But equal rights cannot be won by a revolutionary attack upon the social and political structures within which equality is being sought. Perhaps new structures are necessary—Cruse apparently believes this to be the case—but then Williams must say so and try to convince the men he is inviting to die that their death would have some meaning. As it is, the violent methods he advocates bear no relation to the ends he says he shares with other American blacks. They amount to little more than "a grand act of . . . directionless defiance of the power structure" (p. 401). Moreover, this is a defiance that can only be acted out by a conspiracy of "young warriors." It hardly requires, nor can it evoke, a mass movement. Williams is the advocate, Cruse suggests, of a "one-sided activism" that not only denies the value, but actually blocks and frustrates, political, economic, and cultural work within the larger black community. (2) Guerilla warfare, if it ever began, would not make things any better for the men and women on whose behalf it presumably was being fought. Cruse argues that "it is not enough to say . . . 'How can we expect liberation without losses?' It must be added that life is not so cheap that great losses should be bought and paid for by . . . illusory objectives" (p. 400). Or worse: that the losses should be paid for by still greater losses—not only the immediate "death, waste, and destruction," but also the more general effects of an exclusive commitment to insurrectionary politics: the anti-intellectualism, the strain toward nihilism, the failure to explore alternative strategies, the a priori rejection of peaceful advance. Cruse's

[15] Cruse's argument is presented, none too clearly, in pp. 302–401 of *The Crisis of the Negro Intellectual.*

critique of "young warrior adventurism" strikes precisely at its most vulnerable point: that its votaries are often as contemptuous of the immediate needs of the oppressed as they are, with far greater reason, of the "rights" of the oppressors. Finally, (3) Cruse points to the long-term effect of guerilla warfare on Negro life in America. Given an urban insurrection or a series of insurrections, and given the sort of response from the white community and from the state that Williams himself anticipates, the result can only be a repression so severe that it blights all hopes for a genuinely democratic politics. "Race war in the United States would probably mean the end of any hope for the Negroes' democratic inclusion in the American scheme of things" (p. 390). Nor is Cruse thinking here only of integration: he means something else, or at least, he thinks that something else might be meant. Whatever is meant, however, "democratic inclusion" requires a politics committed to democracy.

Now Williams or some other supporter of an insurrectionary politics might reply to this argument in a variety of ways and with more or less force. I am less concerned to insist that Cruse has made his case than that there is a case to be made. This is the form that arguments about responsibility take and should properly take. But I must stress that these arguments reveal to us only the structure or possible structure of obligations among the oppressed. They tell us nothing directly about obligations to the state or, generally, to its citizens.

There is a sense in which oppression makes men free, and the more radical the oppression the more radical the freedom. Thus slaves have a right to kill their masters, subject peoples their tyrants. They are set loose from the normal restraints of social life, because any violence they commit against masters and tyrants can plausibly be called defensive. "Democratic" oppression is more subtle and confusing, in large part because of the way in which the oppressed people are within the democratic system, enjoying the formal and some of the real benefits of membership. They cannot be reduced to mere objects, and though they are still attacked and injured in a multitude of particular ways by particular other people, their greatest injury derives from the fact that they are inferior (less powerful) subjects within the system. Hence it is especially difficult to identify in any plausible way the agents of their oppression. It seems that everyone is guilty, or everyone but a handful of righteous men, and then the appeal of the oppressed to heaven might well be answered with a second Flood. Since the oppressed must pursue their appeal in this world, whom should they attack? Cruse poses this question clearly: "If Negroes are to 'die in the tried and proven way of liberation,' precisely whom must we take along with us to oblivion? Is it white people—without distinction? Or is it a certain class of white people located in the power structure? Would it be the army or the National Guard or the police? Or . . . the organized aggression of the radical right wing? Perhaps it would be the Federal or state power?"[16] For reasons I will discuss later, the answer is likely to be the first. The war of an oppressed minority, if it comes to that, will almost certainly be terrorist in character.

But a kind of intermittent defensive violence is also likely, directed against particular members of the oppressive majority, marauders, vigilantes, sadistic policemen, and so on. This has little to do with war (or revolution), however it is described, and it requires no general view of oppression to justify it. The state exists to protect its members, the democratic state to protect *all* its members, and whenever people are not protected, for whatever reasons, they have every right to protect themselves. In the case of an oppressed minority, this principle may well justify a large number of defensive acts and a considerable range of preparations for defense. It can also be expected that one or another of the bands of activists will construe it as an obligation that they join in the preparations or recommend or initiate them.[17] So long as they are

[16] *Ibid.*, p. 391.
[17] Thus A. Philip Randolph, writing in the socialist monthly *The Messenger* (1919) on "How to Stop Lynching," urged physical resistance to white mobs in accordance with "the law of self-defense." Quoted in August Meier and Elliott Rudwick, "Black Violence in the Twentieth Century: A Study in Rhetoric and Retaliation," in *Violence*

welcomed by the people they profess to be joining or helping that too seems justified. But self-defense and mutual defense are also limiting principles. They apply within the immediate context of violence and not more generally. They do not set people free to engage in preventive or pre-emptive violence. Nor do they set people free to become marauders or vigilantes on their own account. The question is, does oppression itself generate this kind of freedom? Are oppressed men free to become terrorists?

Terrorism has often been called the weapon of the weak, and for a very good reason that needs to be stated clearly: terrorism is also a weapon against the weak, that is, against members of the majority as individual, isolated, helpless *men*. The terrorist does not risk a head-on battle with the police or the army. He does not challenge the state directly, but only through the commitment of the state to defend the everyday security of its citizens. This is extraordinarily difficult to do when even a small group of terrorists set out to make it so. The state is vulnerable at this point, if at no other: majorities are made of men and men are easy to kill. It has to be added that the terrorists do not always mean to coerce only the majority. Terrorism invites violent repression, and this necessarily reaches far beyond the (unknown) murderers and arsonists who are its first targets. So it tends and is often intended to provoke a general crisis in the relation of the oppressed minority and the democratic state, forcing the oppressed into a revolutionary posture. Since the effects of this crisis are often disastrous for the oppressed themselves, as well as for the larger community, its protagonists must be judged in terms of the principles I have already outlined. But I want now to consider terrorism from the standpoint of that larger community and from the standpoint of the state, and to ask whether the "liberty to appeal to heaven," given the form it is likely to take, actually exists.

It has to be said first that this appeal is not always intentionally political and not always the work of men who claim

in America, ed. Hugh Davis Graham and Ted Robert Gurr (New York, 1969), pp. 382–383.

to be acting on behalf of others. There is a kind of spontaneous terror, generally concealed in the crime statistics, occasionally exploding in riot and *jacquerie,* which expresses only the inchoate rage of oppressed men.[18] About this, there is painfully little that a moral theorist can say, and much that has been said suggests only that silence is sometimes the most appropriate form of moral discourse. I think it is wrong to attach any honor to such violence or to attempt to justify it (it is not wrong, obviously, to try to understand it). Apolitical murderers and arsonists do not, after all, ask to be justified. They are not claiming a "liberty" and it would be sheer masochism for any of us—their possible victims—to make the claim on their behalf. Nevertheless, the claim has been made. Thus John Thompson in a recent review of William Styron's novel *The Confessions of Nat Turner:*

> We made a community here, agreeing to practice violence only minimally against one another, while reserving the right to practice it totally against others. Negroes . . . were not members of the community. Their nonviolence was imposed, not agreed upon. Now, uninstructed in the unconscious taboos that guard the rest of us from one another, they are free to commit random acts of aggression, pure aggression quite without other aim.[19]

Styron has brilliantly evoked the meaning of black slavery as a historically specific oppressive system. The reviewer's "now" is his own, and I am not sure it points to anything more specific than the general guiltiness we all feel. But we must try to say more clearly what we feel guilty about. Black Americans do not experience "total" violence today, for reasons I hope I have already suggested, nor does anyone today reserve the right to practice such violence against them. Nor again can it be said that they are incapable of consenting to (else

18 Richard Wright's *Native Son* (New York, 1940), is the best description I have seen of the rage of the oppressed exploding in violence. That the recent riots are similar explosions is suggested by most of the recent accounts and need not be documented here.

19 John Thompson, "Rise and Slay!" *Commentary,* 44, no. 5 (November 1967), 85.

they would be incapable of participating in) the everyday peacefulness of the political community and of the social life it organizes. If their occasional violence, like that of other oppressed groups, is not unexpected, it remains true that large numbers of specific men and women (Mr. Thompson among them, I should guess) have entirely legitimate expectations as to their ordinary nonviolence. Nor, finally, are black people "uninstructed in the unconscious taboos" of social life. Many among their militants would say they are "instructed" all too well. They are inhibited even in their self-defense; their random aggression is directed most often against other black people. There is a kind of moral hysteria in the suggestion that such violence is "free." Indeed, it is utterly wrong to say that anyone's random aggression is "free." The victims of "total" violence cannot by definition be aggressive: wherever they strike, they strike someone who has struck them first. And the men who endure more subtle sorts of oppression must look to their "aim." If in their rage they are incapable of doing that, it is likely that the word "free" cannot be applied to them, in any of its senses.

I do not want to suggest, however, that the spontaneous terrorist is simply a criminal. His violence is done *without right,* yet it expresses a rage which may well be justified. It warns us of the existence of a class of men, in whose condition we are implicated, whom we cannot easily judge. They are neither wholly within nor wholly outside the political community; they are estranged but not strangers, our fellow citizens and our nearest enemies. Since we cannot grant their freedom to kill us, we must face up to the causes of their rage.

Political or programmatic terrorism is very different: it is random aggression *with* another aim, and so to be judged at least partly in conventional means-ends terms. The political terrorist is also to be judged, as I shall try to show, by the way he is within the political community, the precise forms of his membership and his estrangement. In this sense, terrorism seems almost appropriate to secessionist movements, since it serves to shatter the minimal moral cohesion of the community, and this is precisely what the secessionists want to do and claim a right to do. That is a right they may have, and can only have, if the community has already failed to include them, if they are within it only as objects of radical exclusion, brutality, and humiliation. It is at least possible to imagine oppression so severe that terrorism aimed systematically at political division might be morally defensible. The price is high, however, for the use of terror is likely to have divisive and demoralizing effects upon the oppressed men and women whose interests it supposedly serves as well as upon the larger community. It undermines their confidence in mass action, that is, in their own action, and invites them passively to watch what must be called a degrading spectacle—degrading especially if they vicariously enjoy it. Nor will it be easy for the oppressed to free themselves from the activists whom their passivity enfranchises: an elite of assassins who may one day claim to have set them free.

These arguments apply as well to a dispersed minority seeking a different sort of liberation, except that now there is no possibility at all of a symmetry of moral and political division. Whenever it is intended that oppressed and oppressor groups live together as equals and that political unity be preserved, terrorism must be rejected out of hand. And it is usually the position of activists on behalf of oppressed (and dispersed) minorities that coexistence of some sort is possible, once freedom and equality have been won. They commit themselves, then, to the political community, not as it is, but as it might be, *with its present population.* That commitment can take as many forms as there are projects for a new state. Whatever its form, it seems to me to preclude the murder of randomly selected, specifically innocent men and women. For these are potential citizens, with whom the terrorist is, or pretends to be, or plans to be united, and their murder echoes in the consciousness of other potential citizens and makes that union impossible.[20]

[20] It has been asserted, by Frantz Fanon and by various American epigones, that violent action is the only way for the oppressed to regain their manhood and so to associate with other men as equals. Fanon never tells us whether this method works only for those who actually use violence or also for those who watch. But I know of no evidence

But I want to argue more than this, beginning again with the special condition of the people I am considering: they are oppressed *citizens;* they are *formally* free and equal. I have suggested that activists working on their behalf ought to exploit the formal rules of the democratic system. Now insofar as they do this, or rather, insofar as they do it with some success, they begin the process of transforming their citizenship into something real (something valuable as well). That means also that they begin acquiring obligations within the democratic state where they work and to its citizens among whom they find allies and supporters. At the same time, however, their obligations continue to be mediated by the patterns of responsibility that exist within the world of the oppressed. The result is a situation of extraordinary complexity, sometimes of deep personal agony, which I can only outline here. The activist takes advantage of democratic rules in order to expose their hypocrisy. But if the rules yield advantages, they are not entirely hypocritical. Then they must be respected, and first of all by the activist. If he respects them too much, however, if he settles comfortably into the political community, he forgets the men and women on whose behalf he is working; he is accused, perhaps rightly, of selling out. He must frequently move beyond the range of actions normally sanctioned by democratic rules in order to extend their application to the whole of the oppressed group. He may move far beyond the normal range, accepting whatever risks this involves. Yet if he acts to undermine the rules themselves, he benefits no one; he makes future action more difficult. Then he breaks faith simultaneously with the oppressed and with his (and their) fellow citizens.

The "liberty to appeal to heaven" exists only when heaven

---

that it in fact works for either group. In the socialist tradition similar effects have often been claimed for the political struggle against oppression, but not for particular acts of violence against members of the oppressor class. Marxists especially have always understood, as Hannah Arendt remarks, "that revolutions are not the result of . . . violent action" ("Reflections on Violence," *New York Review of Books,* 12:4 [February 27, 1969], p. 30). See Fanon's *The Wretched of the Earth,* trans. Constance Farrington (New York, 1963), pp. 65–74.

is the only appeal. So long as activists on behalf of the oppressed appeal in fact to other men and find channels available to do so, they incur obligations within the political community that makes the appeal possible. This is what it means, the least that it means, to act within a democratic system: that one is bound to respect the general freedom to act and the lives of all possible actors. It does not mean, however, that one is bound to obey every law, or pay every tax, or ever to defend the state. For these are the obligations of free and equal citizens and also, perhaps, of men who freely choose not to be free and equal citizens, who do not ask to be counted, but receive all the other benefits of the political community. The oppressed do not receive all the other benefits because they are not counted equally. They are in a special and very difficult position that may best be defined by suggesting that they possess within the state the liberty to refuse, to say no to the laws they have not been able to join in making. They possess the liberty to refuse because they have themselves been refused full participation in the democratic community. The activists, however, begin to say yes, and I have tried to elucidate the moral consequences of a struggle against oppression that utilizes (successfully) the possibilities of an open political system. But so long as oppression persists, oppressed men and women retain the right, not to destroy the democratic state or to make war against it, but to deny it what they have to give: their loyalty, service, and obedience. Activists on their behalf are free to repeat this refusal and to organize it in the struggle against oppression.

There are options open to them, then, that are closed to every other group of political men. If I have stressed the fact that these are limited options, I have not meant to deny their reality, but only to respond to the "mistaken theory" and common cant, that the oppressed are right whatever they do. In fact, of course, the oppressed may rightly do more (and differently) than I suggest. For the liberty that is theirs belongs to them as a group, by virtue of their oppression, while the obligations belong only to those among them who choose to be active in the political community. Liberty is passively "enjoyed," while obligations are incurred through action. And this suggests the possibility of a kind of action that avoids the obligations I have described by avoiding any use of democratic politics. Thus an honest revolutionary, though he may not "work effectively for the oppressed" and so may fail in his duty to them, never breaks faith with the other citizens of the state. He is simply and avowedly their enemy (and his war may or may not be just). It cannot be said that the "liberty to appeal to heaven" exists only when heaven is the only appeal *that can be made*. It exists only when heaven is the only appeal *that is made*.

But the honest revolutionary is an unlikely and in fact a rare figure in a democratic state. More common is the man who uses the open arena of political life to express his terrible anger, to talk loosely of violence and revolution. Of him it must be said that he has a right to talk—that is what the arena is for—but if he ever acts out his words, he will act wrongly. Most of the time he just talks, for he does not have the power to act. Then people like myself worry about what he is saying and, hopelessly and perhaps presumptuously, try to tell him what he should and should not do. The important question, of course, is what we should and should not do. That, however, is much easier to answer.

Appendix: On the Responsibility of Intellectuals

The argument that the oppressed are right whatever they do has as its practical corollary the argument that they cannot be criticized whatever they do. So men who otherwise speak and write a great deal are sometimes led to keep silent, and sometimes, perhaps, silence is our best choice. I have already urged this choice in the case of the spontaneous violence of the oppressed: we neither praise nor blame someone like Richard Wright's Bigger Thomas. With regard to premeditated action or to literary or ideological creativity (not Bigger Thomas, but *Native Son*), we cannot so easily be silent. And if we speak at all, we can hardly refrain from criticism. Criticism, in all its senses, is simply the mode of our speech. The implicit pledge any intellectual makes to his readers is that he will criticize, is criticizing, freely and honestly. This pledge may be mediated by a variety of agencies, magazines, publishing houses, theaters, and so on, that promise their audience something more: relevance, propriety, fashion, this or that political creed. But no one buys a magazine or comes to the theater expecting to be deceived, whatever his other expectations; he does not read a book in order to see important questions avoided. He expects writers and artists to tell whatever truth they know. He is counting on their judgments as a guide to his own thought and action. If they lie or conceal what they know or decline to commit themselves at all (even in the complex and ambiguous ways that are their prerogative and perhaps their necessity), they are breaking faith. They are breaking faith however noble the reasons they have or give for what they are doing.

Two of the most common reasons do not seem to me noble at all. It is often said, first, that criticizing the politics or ideology of the oppressed plays into the hands of their oppressors. In fact, the precise opposite is true. The best pos-

71

sible movement of the oppressed requires the best possible criticism, dispassionate, tireless, utterly honest. "There is no greater crime," wrote Trotsky, "than deceiving the masses, palming off defeats as victories and friends as enemies . . . fabricating legends." [21] When new mystifications replace the old, there is no end to oppression.

The second argument requires not that we lie but that we refrain altogether from criticism: only the oppressed, it is said, can understand their own condition and judge the appropriateness of their own response. Here the intellectual of the "oppressor" culture defers to his "oppressed" colleague. He candidly confesses his moral incapacities. But candor in this regard is something less than faithfulness. Thus Richard Gilman in a review of Eldridge Cleaver's *Soul on Ice:*

> in its victories of understanding, its blindness and incompletions, its clean or inchoate energies, its internal motives and justifications, [Cleaver's] writing remains in some profound sense not subject to correction or emendation or, most centrally, approval or rejection by those of us who are not blacks . . . We want to be able to say without self-consciousness or inverted snobbery that such and such a Negro is a bastard or a lousy writer, but we are nowhere near that stage.[22]

If Gilman means that Negroes are free to write badly, the point is indisputable; they are as free as any of us are. If he means that we (white intellectuals) cannot tell when they do write badly, he must speak for himself; they are, after all, writing in a language they share with the rest of us, choosing words and phrases whose meanings we know. They do not have or even claim to have a private language.[23] If he means that we

[21] *Trotsky*, p. 398.

[22] Richard Gilman, "White Standards and Negro Writing," *New Republic* (Mar. 9, 1968), pp. 28–29.

[23] Cf. Sartre on Fanon: "An ex-native, French-speaking, bends that language to new requirements, makes use of it, and speaks to the colonized only . . ." *The Wretched of the Earth*, "Preface," p. 9. But he speaks French; and if he did not, he would be translated (his language is available for translation). No writer who publishes his work can choose his readers—or his critics.

cannot judge what they say, then he is evading his responsibility as a critic. A writer like Cleaver is not discussing esoteric issues, but common and vital issues that have been discussed before, well and badly, by whites and blacks alike. If he means, finally, that we have no right to criticize black writers (even if we are able), then he has a strange idea of the commitment of an intellectual. I should have thought he had no right to publish an uncritical review. Surely a reviewer owes to his author the most sympathetic reading he is capable of and to his readers the clearest possible description of his literary and moral response.

When an intellectual writes about the oppression of others, he must imitate the Jews at the Passover *seder* and imagine that he too was a slave in Egypt. When he writes about an oppressive government, however committed he may be against it, he must imagine that he too was an Egyptian. Such imaginings are hard (I suspect the second is easier for most intellectuals), and we must be suspicious whenever the result is a merely facile empathy or "understanding." For it is not just the feelings of the others, but their situation, ideology, arguments, and choices, that must be imaginatively entered into and intellectually joined. The possibility of doing this, for all the difficulties involved and the likely failures, establishes the right of criticism. Having made the effort, the intellectual must report the results, revealing his own "victories of understanding . . . blindness and incompletions." His readers are waiting, and they need to know.

Part Two: War

4 The Obligation to Die for the State

Men have been said to be obligated to die or to risk their lives for a great variety of reasons. Religion and philosophy have claimed their martyrs, as have family, friendship, and office. Parents have thought themselves bound to die for the preservation of their children; soldiers have sacrificed their lives for the sake of civilians, officers have done so for their men, crew members for the passengers on a ship, captains for their crews. It has never been difficult to teach men to die, or rather, to *die well,* before their time, at an appropriate moment, and for appropriate purposes. But surely there has never been a more successful claimant of human life than the state. It is the obligation to die when the state commands it and for the sake of the state's security or welfare that I want to consider here.

We assert a political obligation to die only when we describe the reason for the obligation in one or more of three ways: as a function of the state's foundation or of the individual's act of adherence, or as a deduction from the collectively affirmed or (it is said) universally recognized ends of the state, or, finally, as a necessary consequence of the citizen's relations with the political community as a whole. Socrates' duty to drink the hemlock, as described by the Laws of

Athens in Plato's *Crito,* is political in all these ways. "Tell us, Socrates, what are you about? Are you going by an act of yours to overturn us—the Laws, and the whole state, as far as in you lies?" He must not do so, Socrates is told, because he has consented to obey the Laws, because he approves of the ends of the Athenian state, and because both his consent and his approval have been publicly expressed, manifest in his participation in the life of the political community. He is obligated to die because he can live only by so acting as to contribute to the (possible though remote) overthrow of the state. What is more, he is obligated to die willingly and *for this reason,* even though he also has other reasons.

The precise nature of political obligation may become more clear if I consider, briefly, some marginal cases. First, the obligation to die rather than to kill an innocent man, in cases where the state enforces the obligation. There are, for example, several court cases which conform more or less to this model: A holds a pistol to the head of B and threatens to kill him unless he kills C; B then kills C. The courts have generally called this murder, often referring to a decision by Justice Hale in the seventeenth century: "If a man be desperately assaulted and in peril of death and cannot otherwise escape unless, to satisfy his assailant's fury, he will kill an innocent person then present, the fear and actual force will not acquit him of the crime and punishment of murder, if he commit the fact, for he ought rather to die himself than kill an innocent." [1] Other judges have based a similar decision on the argument that death, in the situation described by Hale, is not certain but only probable and ought to be risked—thus at least suggesting that certainty of death, if it could be established, might be a mitigating circumstance. Whatever the precise limits of the duty involved, it is quite certainly not a political duty, even though enforced by the state, but rather a moral duty which the courts have attempted to make into a legal duty. The courts may well have a political motive for the attempt: they may intend the safety of the city and its in-

[1] Quoted in Jerome Michael and Herbert Wechsler, *Criminal Law and Its Administration* (Chicago, 1940), p. 54.

78

habitants.[2] But no one, to the best of my knowledge, has suggested that individuals "desperately assaulted" ought to die for the sake of the city. The clear implication of the court decisions is that they ought to die for the sake of the innocent person they are being asked to kill.

Second, the obligation of a would-be martyr to accept death quietly and without resistance at the hands of the state. The martyr may, of course, die willingly because he believes the state to be necessary in this world, even though he also believes himself obligated to refuse certain of its commands. He may be committed to the ends of the state, but not only to those ends. If so, his death is not very different from that of Socrates, who was, I suppose, a martyr to philosophy as well as to citizenship. But the martyr usually has reasons very different from those suggested by the Laws of Athens. If he is a Christian, the primary reason for his death is that God has commanded him to die (and to die quietly) rather than perform certain idolatrous acts; he dies, then, not to save the state, but to glorify God and vindicate his faith. He may also die in order to win eternal salvation and the joys of heaven, but the effect of this motive upon religious obligation is a problem I must leave to the theologians.

Third, I do have to consider the analogous case of the political hero who risks his life and accepts death for the sake of the state, but also because he too seeks immortality, that is, personal glory. The state promises glory to its heroes whenever it can, but it must insist that citizens are equally obligated to die, if commanded to do so, in ignominious circumstances or even (and this is harder) in total obscurity. This suggests very forcefully what it means to die *on behalf of* the state: the citizen must make the reason for his obligation the motive of his voluntary obedience. "To be a good man," wrote Montesquieu (talking about political virtue), "a good intention is necessary, and we should love our country not so much on our own account, as out of regard to the community."[3] No

---

[2] See James Fitzjames Stephen, *History of the Criminal Law,* II, 107–108, cited in Michael and Wechsler, *Criminal Law,* p. 64.

[3] Montesquieu, *The Spirit of the Laws,* bk. II chap. 6.

other motives are sufficient, for they can provide nothing more than accidental reinforcement of the obligation, whereas the proper motive follows necessarily from the obligation and insures its fulfillment.

The question then is: can an individual citizen be obligated to make the safety of the state the motive of his voluntary death? Can a prisoner be obligated to wait quietly for his executioner or a soldier to stand in the breach or march up to the cannon's mouth, when neither man has any conceivable reason for waiting, standing, or marching except the safety of the state? Or rather, except the *alleged* safety of the state, for this proviso must be added to what has so far been said: if any obligation exists, the prisoner and soldier are obligated (within certain limits) to accept public definitions of public safety and danger and to die when they are commanded. One cannot be obligated to die sometimes, at one's own discretion. No more can one be obligated to die a little bit. The question must be answered with a yes or a no. One may want to qualify the answer by referring it to a particular state or kind of state, or to a particular group—or kind—of citizens. But the situation of a given man in a given society is necessarily simple: he is either obligated or not. Afterwards, he is either dead or not. As to the obligation, all sorts of equivocations are possible in practice: public authorities may grant that no obligations exist and then presume upon their subjects' sense of obligation, as a captain does when he asks for volunteers; or they may insist upon the obligation, but never presume upon it, as when they load a prisoner with chains or encourage religious fervor among soldiers. These are practical and perhaps necessary confusions, but theorists must try to clear them up and offer one or the other answer. I want now to describe and comment upon two of the answers that have been proposed by two of the major theorists of consent: Hobbes's no and Rousseau's yes.

Hobbes begins by examining one of the practical equivocations. In chapter 14 of *Leviathan*, "Of the First and Second Natural Laws and of Contracts," he writes:

A covenant not to defend myself from force, by force, is always void. For . . . no man can transfer or lay down his right to save himself from death, wounds or imprisonment (the avoiding whereof is the only end of laying down any right) . . . For though a man may covenant thus, *Unless I do so, or so, kill me;* he cannot covenant thus, *Unless I do so, or so, I will not resist you when you come to kill me.* For men by nature chooseth the lesser evil, which is death in resisting, rather than the greater, which is certain and present death in not resisting. And this is granted to be true by all men, in that they lead criminals to execution and prison, with armed men, notwithstanding that such criminals have consented to the law, by which they are condemned.

Now Hobbes's illustration does not really make his point, for the prison authorities need not admit that criminals necessarily and by nature will fight or escape if they can; they only presume that some of them will do so and that it is not possible to know which ones. Nor are prison authorities likely to grant Hobbes's argument that criminals have a right to try to escape. They would surely be uncomfortable with that idea, for their claim to be "authorities" implies that right is on their side alone. But that is not Hobbes's view. He would argue both that the prisoner has a right to escape if he can and that the guards have a right to stop him if they can. Prisoner and guard are simply at war with one another; they are no longer members of the same state. The decision to punish a criminal is, for Hobbes, his effective expulsion from the political community; he is no longer protected but actively endangered; hence he is free from his contract and under no obligations whatsoever. More than this, he is not merely free to resist or escape, he is physically or psychically bound to do so. Given Hobbes's theory, the behavior of Socrates is literally inexplicable; Hobbes would have to say that the man was mad. That is not at all the view of prison authorities. When they find a passive, resigned, quiet, and obedient prisoner, they do not call him mad, they call him good—which suggests, I think, both the inappropriateness of Hobbes's example and the radicalism of his theory.

The foundations of the theory can be briefly described. For Hobbes, the end of the state is individual life. That is both its primary purpose as an institution and the primary aim of each and every man who participates in its foundation and preservation. The brief moment of political creativity and the subsequent eternity of obedience both have a purely instrumental significance: the goal toward which both are directed is survival, or rather, security, which is survival along with freedom from the terrible fear of violent death. A man who dies for the state defeats his only purpose in forming the state: death is the contradiction of politics. A man who risks his life for the state accepts the insecurity which it was the only end of his political obedience to avoid: war is the failure of politics. Hence there can be no political obligation either to die or to fight. Obligation disappears in the presence of death or of the fear of death.[4]

Fighting, however, is not the same as dying and therefore Hobbes's discussion of the obligation of soldiers poses difficulties not present in the discussion of prisoners—difficulties which need to be examined in some detail. When war begins, the political authorities, instead of protecting their subjects, invite their subjects, in Hobbes's words, "to protect their protection." [5] This request is an admission of failure and can best be described by paraphrasing a line from Brecht's *Mother Courage:* only a bad sovereign needs brave subjects. Nevertheless, Hobbes argues that subjects are obligated to defend their society as long as they are able. They may not be "able" for very long, of course, since "by nature" they will choose to defend themselves first. Indeed, when they protect their protection they are doing nothing more than defending themselves, and so they cannot protect their protection after their protection ceases to protect them. At that point, it ceases to be

---

[4] These negative assertions can be sustained I believe, whatever positive view one takes as to the place of moral obligation in Hobbes's philosophy.

[5] Thomas Hobbes, *Leviathan,* pt. II, chap. 29; compare the more careful formulation in the "Review and Conclusion."

their protection. The state has no value over and above the value of the lives of the concrete individuals whose safety it provides. No man has a common life to defend, but only an individual life. And so Hobbes's injunction has very narrow limits and obligates men to a very narrow range of actions. An individual can be obligated to contribute financially to the defense of the state; he may be obligated to engage in military exercises and demonstrations for the sake of deterrence, or even to march bravely off to battle, still hoping to frighten the enemy by his stalwart and resplendent appearance. But it is difficult to see how, in Hobbes's terms, he can be obligated actually to fight. For, if he loses his life while protecting his protection, he loses everything there is to lose and saves nothing.

Once again, however, risking one's life is not the same as losing it, and it might be said even of Hobbesian men that they can be bound (can bind themselves) to take certain limited and foreknown risks for the sake of a secure social life. The difficulty here is that the limits of such risks, expressed as the statistical probability of dying or of facing death in battle, have a timeless and general application: they describe the individual as a nameless member of society living at no particular moment. But then there comes a more precise time when a particular man finds himself or thinks he finds himself face-to-face with death. Hobbes insists that whatever the commitments made earlier such a man at such a time is morally free to do whatever he is driven to do by his fear. He cannot foreswear that freedom (in any degree) because he cannot know in advance the point at which the fear of death will strike him. Now many of us in everyday life and discourse make "special allowances" for individuals who run or hide or surrender under the strain of battle and imminent death. Soldiers normally are expected to surrender rather than be killed. But Hobbes makes this "special allowance" into the central theme of his philosophical system. Recognizing the power of the fear of death (or of physical pain) is not for him a way of excusing actions that violate previous commitments; it is a way of delimiting the moral world: beyond

this point there are no commitments. Still, the practical consequences of the two positions are not so different, and the
extent to which "special allowance" has become a cultural
imperative suggests the triumph of Hobbesianism in the modern world.

When a frightened man refuses to fight or runs away when
battle begins, then, he does not break faith with the state; he
does nothing unjust. The crucial passage is this one:

> A man that is commanded as a soldier to fight against the
> enemy, though his sovereign have right enough to punish
> his refusal with death, may nevertheless in many cases re-
> fuse, without injustice . . . When armies fight, there is on
> one side, or both, a running away, yet when they do it, not
> out of treachery, but fear, they are not esteemed to do it
> unjustly, but dishonorably.[6]

It is important to stress immediately that Hobbes does not
say that all men will run away. Only some men ("of feminine
courage") will do so. The others are presumably bound to
fight since they have not been moved by their fear to refuse.
This is the only difference I have been able to discover in
Hobbes's theory between the acceptance of death and the acceptance of the risk of death: the first is automatically void;
the second is subject to private re-evaluation of the risks involved and to unilateral annulment. Such an annulment may
in fact be morally wrong if it has any other reason than the
fear of death. Only God, however, can know its reasons; men
must grant the rights of the fearful to all who claim them.
The use of the word "punish" is therefore technically incor-
rect, for a man cannot be punished for acting "without injustice." As in the case of the prison guard and the escaped prisoner, the cowardly soldier and his sovereign are simply re-
turned to the state of nature. This is the radical argument that
Hobbes makes: faced with death or with the spectre of death,
any man may reclaim his natural rights.

He immediately suggests two exceptions to this far-reaching assertion, however. First, he argues that individuals who

[6] Hobbes, *Leviathan,* chap. 21.

84

have enlisted in an army or accepted press money (a kind of enlistment after the fact) are obligated to fight. The obligation here is not really political, since the individual is presumably bound by his military oath, and this is an ordinary contract, subsequent to and different from the social contract. Nor is the mercenary or impressed soldier obligated by Hobbes to make his oath the motive of his fighting. Plunder and pay, presumably his original motives, will suffice to motivate the fighting. Nevertheless, this first exception does not seem consistent with Hobbes's general theory, and it is worth suggesting just why it is not. If a soldier admitted that the acceptance of money or even the taking of an oath obligated him to kill and be killed, he would be turning himself into a mere instrument of the state or of the mercenary captain who hires him and utterly destroying himself as a Hobbesian person, that is, as a man who fears death. An individual can sell his labor to another, and a soldier can also, but he can neither sell nor give away his right of self-defense. That is an inalienable right, and it must include the right, under certain circumstances, to run away. Individual bodily security is the only ultimate in Hobbes's system and the search for that security can never be forsaken or transcended. In fact, then, for Hobbes there can be no obligation to die of any sort. The critique of political obligation is also a critique of all forms of ultimate obligation, though by no means, as we have just seen, an unequivocal critique.

Hobbes's second exception is more precisely political in character and brings us to the very heart of the whole problem of political dying. After asserting the obligation of enlisted soldiers, he writes (chapter 21):

> when the defense of the commonwealth requires at once the help of all that are able to bear arms, everyone is obliged; because otherwise the institution of the commonwealth, which they have not the purpose or the courage to preserve, was in vain.

The most obvious, the most Hobbesian, response to this is simply: if a man dies defending the commonwealth, its institution, from his point of view, was equally in vain. Only if the destruction of the commonwealth involves the certain death of all its citizens could it be said that those citizens should (or perhaps better, must) risk their lives in its defense. Hobbes, however, seems to say more than this; he seems to say that unless men are actually willing to fight, even when defeat would not involve certain death, the commonwealth will not long survive. Either a man obligates himself to risk his life when contracting to form society or in the act of contracting he contradicts himself. Society must be an agreement to die if necessary in order to live together in safety as long as possible, for otherwise it is not possible to live in safety at all. Now that is palpably not what the Hobbesian contract is. Instead, it is an agreement to live together in safety as long as possible and to disband whenever group safety is no longer possible and allow each individual to face the risks of nature alone. Hobbes's second exception is so obviously inconsistent with his general theory that it would hardly be worth considering if it did not raise, indirectly, a very crucial question: can a man be morally bound to take into account the possible long-term consequences of such an act as running away? More important, can a man be morally bound to consider what would happen if every other man acted as he did?

Hobbes is here very close, I think, to a more explicit argument of Spinoza's, put forward in *The Ethics* as proof of the proposition: "The free man never acts fraudulently, but always in good faith." [7] Spinoza goes on:

> If it be asked: What should a man's conduct be in a case where he could by breaking faith free himself from the danger of present death? Would not his plan of self-preservation completely persuade him to deceive? This may be answered by pointing out that, if reason persuaded him to act thus, it would persuade all men to act in a similar manner, in which case reason would persuade men not to agree in good faith to unite their forces, or to have laws in common, that is, not to have any general laws, which is absurd.

[7] Spinoza, *The Ethics* (trans. Elwes), pt. IV, proposition lxxii, proof.

If one man breaks faith, all will do so, and the commonwealth will collapse. Hobbes's argument is weaker, since he is really not talking about breaking faith. His argument would go like this: one man's cowardice leads to cowardly behavior on the part of all men, and so destroys the commonwealth. Therefore, a man ought to control his fearfulness and so maintain his obligations and preserve the commonwealth which he helped to found, and if he is unwilling or unable to do this, he has no business founding commonwealths in the first place. It is not, perhaps, a moral argument (given Hobbes's psychology it is barely a comprehensible argument), yet it is common enough in the history of theory and may well have a point. In any case, it suggests the great difficulty of Hobbes's political philosophy. One man's cowardice kills society, and yet, by virtue of the instinct for self-preservation and the fundamental law of nature, all men have a right to be cowards. The very existence of the state seems to require some limit upon the right of self-preservation, and yet the state is nothing more than an instrument designed to fulfill that right.

"The essence of the contradiction inherent in patriotism," writes Simone Weil, "is that one's country is something limited whose demands are unlimited." [8] But not all states are limited in the same way or to the same degree. The contradiction so apparent in Hobbes is missing entirely in the *Crito*, chiefly, I think, because the Athenian state had other, more extensive purposes than the preservation of individual life. Socrates was asked to die for the common life, or rather, he was told to die because he had no right to do any damage whatsoever to the common life: "are you going . . . to overturn us . . . *as far as in you lies?*" His escape would be criminal even if the overthrow of the Athenian state did not lie within his power—as it certainly did not. But Hobbes and Spinoza cannot say that citizens are forbidden to damage the common life; they are driven to the logically extremist argument that any individual's breach of faith or cowardly flight in some sense *entails* every-

[8] Simone Weil, *The Need for Roots*, trans. Arthur Wills (Boston, 1955), p. 157.

one else's breach of faith and cowardly flight and then the collapse of society, and therefore contradicts his own previous political acts and endangers his own life. The breach and the flight, motivated presumably by terrible fear of death, are wrong because they eventually lead to death or to terrible fear. But the obvious reply to this is Hobbes's own: "for man by nature chooseth the lesser evil, which is danger of death . . . rather than the greater, which is certain and present death."

If society is indeed an agreement to die, then Hobbesian men can form society only through a kind of mutual deceit. The commonwealth may not endure if its citizens all run away in battle, but that only means that it would be irrational for them to tell one another that they are likely to run away. Kant's requirement of publicity might well turn the Hobbesian contract into an absurd contradiction. Nevertheless, in a moment of personal crisis, faced with the danger of violent death, each individual legitimately makes his own decision, without consulting either the public authorities or his fellow citizens, since neither government nor society offers him any salvation. There is no reason for him to assume, he is in fact most unlikely to assume, that his cowardly flight entails the cowardly flight of all other men. But what if it does? What fears can the breakdown of society hold for an individual faced with immediate danger—an individual moreover who came into society only to avoid such danger? The empirical fact (I am not at the moment questioning it) that society will not endure unless men risk their lives on its behalf cannot obligate a particular man to risk his life at a particular time. Only if something more is said than either Hobbes or Spinoza say about the nature of political society will the obligation conceivably follow.

Much of what I have just argued about Hobbes is true also of all those later liberal theorists who retain his individualist foundations—even when they give up, as Spinoza had already given up, his narrow emphasis upon bodily security and the fear of violent death. John Locke, because of the peculiarly collectivist formulation he gives to the fundamental law of nature, is able to reassert an obligation to die, but the reassertion seems inconsistent with the general pattern of his political thought.[9] For any theory which, like Locke's, begins with the absolute independence of freely willing individuals and goes on to treat politics and the state as instrumental to the achievement of individual purposes would seem by its very nature incapable of describing ultimate obligation. This is certainly true when individual purposes reach no further than bodily safety or physical welfare or the appropriation and enjoyment of physical objects. Then "the preservation of the city," as the young Hegel wrote, "can only be important to [its citizens] as a means to the preservation of their property and its enjoyment. Therefore, to expose themselves to the danger of death would be to do something ridiculous, since the means, death, would forthwith annul the end, property and enjoyment." [10]

Once they have freed themselves from Hobbesian fearfulness, liberal writers can, of course, describe various kinds of ethical (not political) dying. Moved by love, sympathy, or friendship, men in liberal society can and obviously do incur ultimate obligations. They may even find themselves in situations where they are or think they are obligated to risk their lives to defend the state which defends in its turn the property and enjoyment of their friends or families. But if they then actually risk their lives or die, they do so because they have incurred private obligations which have nothing to do with politics. The state may shape the environment within which these obligations are freely incurred, and it may provide the occasions and the means for their fulfillment. But this is only to say that, when states make war and men fight, the reasons of the two often are and ought to be profoundly different. Indeed, the great advantage of liberal society may simply be this: that no one can be asked to die for public reasons or on behalf of the state.

[9] John Locke, *The Second Treatise of Government*, pars. 6 and 139. The argument is by no means clear.
[10] G. W. F. Hegel, *Early Theological Writings*, trans. T. M. Knox (Chicago, 1948), p. 165 (*The Positivity of the Christian Religion*).

A good society might, however, be defined in precisely opposite terms: as one worth dying for, whose citizens actually are obligated to risk their lives for public reasons. This, I think, is Rousseau's definition, and it represents a return to the argument of the *Crito*. At first glance, however, Rousseau seems to offer only a rather obtuse version of the Hobbesian position.

> The social treaty has for its end the preservation of the contracting parties. He who wills the end wills the means also, and the means must involve some risks, and even some losses. He who wishes to preserve his life at others' expense should also, when it is necessary, be ready to give it up for their sake. Furthermore, the citizen is no longer the judge of the dangers to which the law desires him to expose himself, and when the prince says to him: "It is expedient for the State that you should die," he ought to die, because it is only on that condition that he has been living in security up to the present, and because his life is no longer a mere bounty of nature, but a gift made conditionally by the state.[11]

This is surely untenable as it stands, for several reasons. First, a man fundamentally interested in self-preservation can never give up the right to judge the peril to which he is exposed, for that would be to surrender his interest in self-preservation. Second, men who associate solely to preserve their individual lives cannot then be obligated to die on each other's behalf. What a man does when he signs the social contract is to turn the others into means to his own safety. If he makes any moral commitment at all, it is simply to obey the sovereign as long as they do and as long as *his* life is not endangered. Finally, by his contract the citizen has exchanged his natural freedom for his security in society. His obedience is now the price of his security, and he pays, so to speak, as he goes. He cannot be obligated to make a further exchange and give his

[11] Jean Jacques Rousseau, *The Social Contract*, bk. II, chap. 5. (All quotations from *The Social Contract* are from the G. D. H. Cole translation [New York, 1950].)

life for such security as he has already enjoyed—and already paid for.

But Rousseau's politics is not really based upon self-preservation or upon any absolute interest in security, property, welfare, or happiness. Indeed, he rejects interests of this sort precisely because they cannot serve as the basis of an obligation to die.

> Self-interest, so they say, induces each of us to agree for the common good. But . . . does a man go to death from self-interest? No doubt each man acts for his own good, but if there is no such thing as moral good to be taken into consideration, self-interest will only enable you to account for the deeds of the wicked.[12]

Nor is Rousseau's politics in any simple sense contractualist. What he calls the social contract represents less an exchange than a moral transformation, and this transformation depends less on the separate wills of the individuals involved than on the quality of the collective will that they together create. All this is suggested, I think, by the words with which Rousseau concludes the long defense of voluntary death which I quoted above: "because his life is no longer a mere bounty of nature, but a gift made conditionally by the state." The reference here might be to nothing more than that Hobbesian security that the state provides, but in the light of the body of Rousseau's work, it is more plausible to argue that the words "bounty" and "gift" refer to two different kinds of life and that a qualitative change has occurred in the transition from nature to the state. Into the state, according to this interpretation, a man brings the life which he has received from the bounty of nature and which is wholly his own. From the state, that is, from the shared experiences and general will of the political community, he receives a second life, a moral life, which is not his sole possession, but whose reality depends upon the continued existence of his fellow-citizens and of their association. Thus Rousseau: "At once, in place of the

[12] Jean Jacques Rousseau, *Emile*, trans. Barbara Foxley (London, 1950), p. 252.

individual personality of each contracting party, [the] act of association creates a moral and collective body." [13] And again:

> The passage from the state of nature to the civil state produces a very remarkable change in man by substituting justice for instinct in his conduct [that is, the obligation to die for self-preservation] and giving his actions the morality they had previously lacked.[14]

A good society is one in which the new man, a moral member of a moral body, achieves his fullest development. The very instincts of pre-social man are overwhelmed and above all the instinct for self-preservation. When the state is in danger, its citizens rush to its defense, forgetful of all personal danger. They die willingly for the sake of the state, not because the state protects their lives—which would be, as Hegel argued, absurd—but because the state is their common life. So long as the state survives, something of the citizen lives on, even after the natural man is dead. The state, or rather, the common life of the citizens, generates those "moral goods" for which, according to Rousseau, men can in fact be obligated to die. The character of the political community obligates the citizen who participates in it to die on its behalf and it simultaneously provides him with a motive for dying. Once again, Hegel has stated the point most clearly: in the society of egotists, he argued,

> death, the phenomena which demolishes the whole structure of [the individual's] purposes and the activity of his entire life, must . . . become something terrifying . . . But the republican's whole soul was in the republic; the republic survived him, and there hovered before his mind the thought of its immortality.[15]

I want to stress those last three words: of *its* immortality— and not his own. The republican citizen may well dream of

[13] *Social Contract*, bk. I, chap. 6.
[14] *Ibid.*, chap. 8.
[15] *Early Theological Writings*, p. 157.

glory and eternal renown, but that is not his most important dream. Many of Rousseau's contemporaries among the *philosophes* were as eager as he was to produce citizens loyal unto death, patriotic soldiers on the model of the Spartans at Thermopylae or the Roman Horatio. But since they believed that society had been formed, to quote Diderot's friend, Paul Holbach, only in order to maintain its members "in the advantages of their nature," they could not admit an obligation they thought so obviously against nature. "To overcome the instinct for self-preservation," wrote Holbach, ". . . a special courage is necessary, and not all citizens are capable of such courage." The state must seek to persuade its soldiers to risk their lives by "feeding the ardor" of its young men and promising glory to its heroes. But it cannot with justice force men into the army or soldiers into battle.[16] As I suggested earlier, the hope for glory generates no obligation. Men cannot be bound to seek a secular immortality, nor would such a search necessarily lead them to serve the state. The Rousseauian republic does not claim, then, to be an eternal shrine to the memory of its heroes; it claims something more: to be the totality of their present existence. Its collapse does not merely deprive them of glory, nor of bodily security, nor even of life itself; it is literally a fate worse than death, a fate undreamt of in Hobbes's philosophy. "If the citizen is alone," writes Rousseau, "he is nothing; if he has no more country, he has no existence; and if he is not dead, he is worse than dead."[17]

Now this is, even in Rousseau's terms, overstated. For Rousseau knew very well that the transformation of natural man into citizen is never complete. Instinct and nature survive; the ego defends and aggrandizes itself. The general will of the community, which speaks for the common life, is always in conflict with the particular wills of the individual members. Rousseau's political theory is designed to give the communal being supremacy over the natural egotist, while recognizing

16 Paul Holbach, *La Politique naturelle* (London, 1773), I, 190.
17 Jean Jacques Rousseau, *Considerations on the Government of Poland*, chap. 4, in *Political Writings,* trans. Frederick Watkins (Edinburgh, 1953).

that in fact a tension always exists between the two. This supremacy is most dramatically manifest when the state says to the natural man: die! He ought then to die, and if he does not, he can be forced to die, just as he can be "forced to be free." Obviously, however, he cannot be forced to die, though he can be put to death, *for the sake of* the state. The resort to punishment is an admission of the failure of political transformation: "in putting the guilty to death we slay not so much a citizen as an enemy." [18]

Hobbes might have said the same thing, but there is a crucial and revealing difference here between the two theorists. For Hobbes, the guilty man would be killed as an enemy of the sovereign and of the sovereign only, and he would be killed by natural right, that is, by the right of self-defense. There is no political right to punish in Hobbes, no right generated by the social contract, no right of collective defense vested in the community as a whole.[19] In Rousseau, on the other hand, a guilty man is an enemy of the state, an enemy of the people. But perhaps "enemy" is not the best word for Rousseau's purposes. The domestic criminal and the wartime deserter were once citizens of the state, themselves committed to its preservation. They have "broken the social treaty," they are "rebels" and "traitors," fallen members. They can now be put to death (as enemies cannot be) by virtue of their own previous consent, and they can only rightfully be put to death because they have previously consented.[20] The right to punish derives from the universally recognized need to defend the common life. This, at any rate, is Rousseau's claim, and I think it suggests the great difficulty of his theory of ultimate obligation. Let me approach that difficulty cautiously.

In general, the political obligation to die implies the political right to punish, though it need not imply the vesting of

[18] *Social Contract,* bk. II, chap. 7.

[19] See *Leviathan,* pt. II, chap. 28: "For the subjects did not give the sovereign that right; but only in laying down theirs, strengthened him to use his own."

[20] Captured enemies cannot be put to death; they are "merely men, whose life no one has any right to take" (*Social Contract,* bk. I, chap. 4).

that right in any man or group of men. One can imagine a society so confident of the moral transformation of its members that it leaves their punishment to themselves: it patiently awaits the suicide of its criminals and traitors, certain that their actions are only temporary aberrations and that they will return to reason and then die by their own hand. In his study of crime in primitive Melanesia, Malinowski describes such a society. There individuals publicly accused of certain crimes, chiefly violations of the sexual taboos, and knowing themselves to be guilty, actually commit suicide. They do so, however, only if they have been publicly accused, and their suicide is more a socially expected response to personal dishonor than it is an example of political obligation—though Malinowski does insist upon the element of self-punishment in the act.[21] In a way, the Greeks with their hemlock were closer to that primitive society than to us with our guillotines and gas-chambers. Here Rousseau is a modern. He anticipates that there will be traitors and rebels who will have to be put to death, and this is to admit that the moral transformation of the citizens is not entirely successful. If we go just a step further and imagine a case where it is not successful at all, then there is a very obvious defense that a man might offer when he refuses to die at the state's command.

"Look at me," he might say, "an unreconstructed egotist. I have lived among you, but never shared in your common life. I do not attend your meetings; I do not rejoice at your festivals. The image of the immortality of your state never dances before my eyes. If this state should collapse, I am certain that I will make out well enough in the next; but I am less sure about this world and the next, and so I have determined to save my skin at all costs. I shall not fight in your wars, and if I am driven into battle, I shall hide or run away. If you come to kill me, I shall struggle against you with all the force at my command."[22]

[21] Bronislaw Malinowski, *Crime and Custom in Savage Society* (London, 1926), pp. 85–100.

[22] This same response might plausibly be offered to the argument Simone Weil made on behalf of political obligation in 1943, when

Now Rousseau argues at one point in *The Social Contract* that any man who lives in the state must be regarded as a member.[23] But this seems a woefully inadequate criterion for moral membership; it is surely not obvious that every resident shares in the "moral goods" of the political community, even if he shares in the material goods that the state provides.[24] If we insist upon anything more than residence, however, then the unreconstructed egotist that I have just quoted must be called a noncitizen (a resident alien, perhaps, though not necessarily in the strict legal sense), and it follows necessarily that he cannot be called a traitor or rebel if he refuses to die on behalf of the state. Since he has never shared in civic life, the state has no right to kill him (unless the political authorities claim a natural right to do so) and he has no obligation to die. He is, so to speak, a Hobbesian man loose in a Rousseauian society.

This will surely be the condition of many men in Rousseau's

France was occupied by the Germans. "Today every Frenchman knows what it was he missed as soon as France fell. He knows it as well as he knows what is missing when one is forced to go hungry. He knows that one part of his soul sticks so closely to France, that when France is taken away it remains stuck to her, as the skin does to some burning object, and is thus pulled off. There is something, then, to which a part of every Frenchman's soul sticks, and is the same for all, unique, real though impalpable, and real in the sense of something one is able to touch. Hence, what threatens France with destruction—and in certain circumstances an invasion is a threat of destruction—is equivalent to a threat of physical mutilation for all Frenchmen, and for their children and grandchildren . . . to the end of time. For there are peoples which have never recovered after having once been conquered. This is sufficient for the obligation owed to one's country to impose itself as something evident" (*The Need for Roots*, p. 159). No, it is not sufficient, for it is not the case that every legal member of the French state is obligated to have a "Frenchman's soul" and to feel this near-physical sense of attachment to France. Any man is free to announce that he doesn't and to live as if he doesn't. Weil suggests that such men should be banished—a good Rousseauian punishment—but it is not clear that that is a feasible solution to the problem of ultimate obligation in a modern mass society. Imposed in 1945, it would have left a France inhabited only by *résistants*, a moral community, certainly, but a small one.

[23] Bk. I, chap. 5.

[24] In the next essay I draw a distinction between two kinds of membership in the political community which closely parallels this distinction between the different "goods" that citizens can share.

or in any other society and especially of many of those who refuse to defend the political community in time of war. They are not fallen members, but political strangers. Such men are not necessarily without any obligations at all. They need not be *moral* strangers, like the anti-hero of Camus's novel, for it may be that they are egotists only with regard to the political community, not with regard to every other community. They may share in some other common life. Insofar as Hobbes is describing an association of such men (loyal, perhaps, to their families, but literally devoid of any more extensive commitment, self-consciously exchanging limited obedience for benefits received in the political world), he is perfectly correct to insist that there can be no ultimate obligation. A political stranger can never be morally bound, or rightly forced, to risk his life for the state.

How, then, do men cease to be strangers? How do they create and recognize those moral goods for which political dying is conceivable? I am not sure, but I am sure that no man can be obligated to die unless he admits or has at some time in the past admitted that such moral goods actually exist. There is a crucially important sense in which the obligation to die can only be stated in the first person singular. For this reason, both Plato in the *Crito* and Rousseau in all his major works are driven to contractualist arguments. The individual's contract is obviously not a founding act; nor, I think, is it simply a solemn promise upon which all subsequent obligation is based—for that would not meet Hobbes's argument that the promise to die is different from all other promises. Rather, the contract must involve some acknowledgment of the reality of the common life and of the moral transformation which it makes possible. I think, also, that the contract must be acted out, the common life must be lived, before it can be said to generate ultimate obligation. Consent must be given over time. Thus Socrates' contract includes all his politically relevant actions right up to the moment of his condemnation, and these actions are listed by the Laws: born in the city and educated there, when he came of age he chose to stay; he married and raised children in the city; he fought in the army, participated in the assembly, argued in the streets, held public office. At any point he could have left, renouncing his accumulating obligations.[25] Even after his condemnation, he could have chosen exile as his punishment. Now he can no longer choose, now he is bound to die, but his whole life has been a choice.

All this comes dangerously near to suggesting that a man is obligated to die only if he feels or thinks himself obligated. That seems to be the consequence of arguing first, with Rousseau, that there are moral goods for which a man might well be bound to die, and arguing secondly, against Rousseau, that it is never possible to say that a particular man is bound to die for a particular moral good (unless he has said so himself). But it is surely not the case that being and feeling obligated are the same. It is not enough that a common life be felt or thought to exist; there must *be* a common life. I do not mean to defend all those nationalistic or ideological mystifications that lead men to believe they are living in a community when in fact they are not. Men are bound by their significant actions, not by their feelings or thoughts; action is the crucial language of moral commitment. Socrates is bound because he chose to act like a citizen in a world where citizenship was morally significant. Up to some point in the history of his actions, he might have changed his mind. After that, he had "spoken" and egotism was no longer his right. This suggests that, when men are called upon to face death for the state, an assertion is always being made, and when young men are called a presumption is being made (both of which are subject to critical examination) about the very character and quality of their lives. The assertion or presumption is that they have chosen or will choose, and also that they *can* choose, to live like citizens.

[25] Perhaps not at *any* point, for Socrates' life as an Athenian citizen spanned the years of the Peloponnesian War. Rousseau argues that a man may always renounce his citizenship by leaving the country, "provided, of course, he does not leave to escape his obligations and avoid having to serve his country in the hour of need" (*Social Contract*, bk. III, chap. 18 [note]).

5 *Political Alienation and Military Service*

Despite the conventional claims of the authorities, it is not at all easy to determine the precise extent of the obligations owed by an individual citizen to the modern state. The authorities claim what they have, as far as I can tell, always claimed: that citizens must, if necessary, fight and die for the state. But this view of every citizen as a potential soldier, rushing to arms at his government's call, has its origins in states and societies very different from our own; above all, very much smaller than our own. It was in the polis of ancient Greece and in the medieval commune that the notion of the citizen-soldier was born, and the idea was elaborated by theorists like Rousseau who still thought in terms of small participant communities. The extraordinary transformation in social scale which has occurred in the past century and a half has created a radically different kind of political community— one in which relations between individual and state are so attenuated (at least their moral quality is so attenuated) as to call into question all the classical and early democratic theories of obligation and war. The individual has become a private man, seizing pleasure when he can, alone, or in the narrow confines of his family. The state has become a distant power, captured by officials, sometimes benevolent, sometimes not, never again firmly within the grasp of its citizens. If this is so, what do these citizens owe to this state?

In an important sense, only liberal (I mean, chiefly, Lockeian) theory is capable of answering this question, for only the liberals have been entirely accepting of the transformation in scale and of the new individualism it has generated. I want to argue that the liberal concept of tacit consent provides a key to understanding the new relations between citizens, or rather, some citizens, and the state. Because the man most often described as having yielded tacit consent and no more is the resident alien, I want to examine the (limited) obligations such a man incurs. It is a commonplace of contemporary social thought that the modern state breeds aliens, whereas older political societies could only import them. We can learn something about this modern alienation, I think, if we begin with the older notion of alienage.

All the philosophers of consent have realized what their critics have in any case told them quickly enough, that the possibility of express consent to a political system—even a democratic system—is rarely available to all men and sometimes is available only to a few. If consent theory is to be taken seriously, it must suggest some way of submitting oneself to a government other than by pledging allegiance to it, taking out naturalization papers, or becoming an active participant in its politics. Liberal writers have generally argued that there is such a way; there is a kind of silence that may be construed as consent. This is the silence of the unsworn, inactive resident, who enjoys the benefits conferred by the state and lives amidst its citizens without ever publicly acknowledging its authority. The acceptance of benefits, even if their rejection would require such extreme courses of action as emigration or hermitic retreat, involves, we are told, an unspoken agreement to maintain the conditions that make the benefits possible, for oneself and others. That means, most importantly, to obey the laws and keep the public peace. This seems to me a reasonable doctrine; I would only add that the obligations incurred by silence are not owed exclusively to the state but to society as well, that is, to the population in whose midst the resident resides. They have their origin not only in the acceptance of benefits but also in the daily round of social activities and the expectations of peaceful conduct which that round inevitably produces in the minds of all the other residents.

The immediate difficulty with this merely tacit consent is, as Locke wrote in his *Second Treatise,* to know "how far it binds." It was Locke's view that any "enjoyment"—of property, lodging, or the bare freedom of the highways—bound a man to an obedience no different in character from that of a full-fledged citizen. A visitor to England or a resident alien was as committed as any "denizen," as any natural-born or legally sworn subject of the king. Tacit consent produced a temporary bond, while express consent made a man "perpetually . . . and unalterably a subject," but the nature of the obligation for the respective durations is, according to Locke, precisely the same.[1] This is a curious view, and, as Locke's expression of it is casual and cursory, it need not be taken as an important feature of his political theory. Surely the moral situations of a mere visitor and a long-term resident are different in significant ways, and one might say the same thing about a resident alien and a citizen—especially in a liberal society. The citizen, after all, participates in his government and shares to some degree in the making of decisions about such crucial matters as taxation, conscription, and war. A resident alien does not participate: how far can he be bound to pay taxes, to serve in the army, to risk death in battle?

Before attempting to answer this question, it will be useful to consider an older distinction between temporary and perpetual obligation, made by the English common lawyers and summarized in Blackstone's *Commentaries.* Blackstone distinguishes the allegiance owed by a natural-born subject, which "cannot be forfeited, cancelled, or altered by any change of time, place, or circumstance," and the allegiance of an alien and stranger which "ceases the instant such a stranger transfers himself from this kingdom to another." A natural-born

---

[1] John Locke, *The Second Treatise of Government,* pars. 119–122.

subject can, of course, "transfer himself" as easily as can an alien, but not with the same results. "An Englishman who removes to France, or China, owes the same allegiance to the king of England there as at home and twenty years hence as well as now." [2] This is a view that makes a good deal more sense than Locke's, since it is founded on a whole set of ideas about birth that lend themselves to talk of perpetual obligations. A man does not choose and cannot change his native land as he can chose a political system and later change his mind about its merits. A natural-born subject is like a son or daughter—a comparison implicit in Blackstone's discussion— whose parents are his willy-nilly and who has permanent commitments. If this comparison is rejected, as it explicitly is by Locke, it would seem that the notion of perpetual obligation must also be rejected. Perpetuity is an awkward notion when intruded into a consensual universe. The possibility of reconsideration is surely inherent if not in the idea of consent itself, then in the idea of government by consent. In the latter phrase both terms refer to series of acts over time (possibly, in the case of a radical democracy, to the same series), and the two together do not suggest an agreement made at some single moment or for all time. A theorist may reasonably want to make reconsideration a similar series of acts, prescribing some lengthy process for terminating consent and so making the bonds established by consent as firm as he can. However, he cannot bar entirely the possibility of a political divorce.

If this is so, then Locke's effort to distinguish tacit and express consent must be called a failure. It is not in the duration of the bond established but in its character for whatever duration that the difference must be sought. In fact, a difference of precisely this kind has been worked out, once again by the lawyers, and it is of enormous relevance to political theory, though it has not, so far as I know, been discussed by political theorists. In the course of the eighteenth and nineteenth centuries, it became a principle of international law that resident

[2] William Blackstone, *Commentaries on the Laws of England*, bk. I, chap. 10.

aliens were obligated differently than citizens: they were bound to a more narrow range of actions.

> Until a foreigner has made himself by his own act a subject of the state into which he has come, he has politically neither the privileges nor the responsibilities of a subject . . . He is merely a person who is required to conform himself to the social order of the community in which he finds himself, but who is politically a stranger to it, obliged only to the negative duty of abstaining from acts injurious to its political interests or contrary to its laws.[3]

This is a far-reaching assertion. It suggests that tacit consent produces only "negative" duties, and it might require a political society to include within its territorial confines men whom it could neither tax nor conscript for any public service whatsoever. When stated more concretely, however, the argument is also more limited, and it tends to focus on the issue of military service. The same writer I have quoted above argues that "aliens may be compelled to help maintain social order, provided that the action required of them does not overstep the limits of police, as distinguished from political, action."[4] This is the common distinction: because they enjoy the benefits of social order, aliens may be required to maintain that order, to pay taxes, to serve as police deputies, to join a fire brigade, and so on. But they cannot be bound to fight in either a civil or an international war (unless the country where they live is "threatened by an invasion of savages . . ."). The distinction is nicely illustrated by the behavior of the British government during the American Civil War:

> The British government in 1862 [insisted] that as a general principle of international law neutral aliens might not be compelled to perform any military service . . . [but] in 1864 the British government saw no reason to interfere in

[3] William Edward Hall, *International Law* (Oxford, 1880), p. 43.
[4] *Ibid.*, pp. 171–173; he is following J. C. Bluntschli, *Le Droit international codifié* (Paris, 1874), section 391, but the argument is common to virtually every writer on international law since Emerich de Vattel's *Droit des gens* (1758).

the case of neutral foreigners . . . enrolled as a local police for New Orleans.[5]

This argument by the international lawyers has a double rationale, only the first part of which is of interest to us, though the second may well be of greater interest to them. The resident alien is conceived both as an individual who has made a limited commitment and so incurred only limited obligations, and also as the subject of another state which retains, so to speak, rights in his person. Hence the precise limits of his obligation to the state within whose jurisdiction he resides is often a matter of negotiation between that state and his own (and so not merely of his "own acts").[6] He is protected in his residence *here* by his citizenship *there*, and this protection is often confirmed by explicit bilateral treaties. It is important to stress, however, as an American Secretary of State did in 1918, that the existence of treaties exempting subjects of the contracting parties from military service abroad does not constitute "evidence of a practise among nations to draft aliens into their forces." [7] The treaties do not, in this regard at least, create a right, but merely protect a right already established. Aliens cannot be compelled to serve (though they can be subjected to considerable pressure to do so, as we shall see). Nor is the condition of a stateless person any different from that of a foreign citizen, though such a person, unprotected by treaty, is all too often treated differently.[8]

[5] Francis Wharton, *A Digest of the International Law of the United States* (Washington, 1886), section 202.

[6] Thus the phrase "neutral aliens" in the statement of the British government cited above; *allied* aliens have often been conscripted with the consent of their governments. See Ministry of Labor and National Service, *The Obligations of Allied and Other Foreign Nationals in Great Britain* (London, 1943).

[7] G. H. Hackworth, *Digest of International Law* (Washington, 1942), vol. III, section 282.

[8] International meetings held before and after World War II attempted to guarantee to stateless persons the status and privileges of neutral aliens. See the *Convention on the Status of Refugees* (1938) and Geneva Convention IV (1949). These are discussed in F. Lafitte, *The Internment of Aliens* (Hammondsworth, England, 1940), p. 221; and Morris Greenspan, *The Modern Law of Land Warfare* (Berkeley, 1959), p. 51.

The condition of a resident alien in international law suggests two distinctions of major importance to political theory. The first is a distinction between ultimate obligation—the obligation to fight and risk death—and all other, lesser duties. The second is between obligations owed to society and those owed to *political* society or to the state. International law seems to suggest that a man can incur ultimate obligations to society, he can bind himself to defend its population against devastation and destruction even at the risk of his own life, simply by residence and daily intercourse. But he cannot commit himself to the polity, he cannot bind himself to risk his life for "ordinary national or political objects," except through those expressions of consent and participation (which may, of course, be variously defined) that make him a citizen. So tacit and express consent have different moral consequences, and the difference suggested by the lawyers, it seems to me, illuminates the precise character of political membership far better than Locke's *Second Treatise*. To be a citizen is to be committed to a political system, not merely to the survival of the society that system organizes, but to the survival of the particular organization and also to all those purposes beyond survival that the organization sets for itself. Residence alone cannot and does not generate such a commitment.

I do not doubt that this is a difficult distinction to apply in practice, for the "ordinary" purposes of the state are not necessarily political in the narrow sense of that term, concerned, that is, with power manipulation and aggrandizement or with the fostering of some secular ideology. One of the purposes of any state is the defense of "its" society, and it is probably true that certain sorts of societies can only be defended by certain sorts of states. There are likely to be moments, then, when all residents, aliens and citizens alike, are morally obligated to defend the state that defends their everyday social life—against barbarian invasion, as the lawyers have suggested, and conceivably against any invasion likely to entail serious disruption and devastation. If this is so, it is not difficult to imagine a variety of borderline cases—which I cannot even attempt to resolve here—when the invasion is only threatened and the state takes one or another kind of preventive action. But it is important to stress that the existence of borderline cases does not call the original distinction into question, since it is only by making such distinctions that we know which are the borderline cases. The cases on either side of the line are clear enough.

Because the rights of hospitality and asylum are also established in international law, though not necessarily in the practice of nations, it would appear that the lawyers intend that any given state at any given time include men who have only limited obligations toward its own survival and its "ordinary political objects." And it is not difficult to imagine a state that includes a large number of resident aliens—as Athens did, for example, after the days of Solon. In 434, when the Peloponnesian war broke out, Athens had a population of one resident alien for every two citizens; one-third of the free men of the city were foreigners. The Athenian case is especially instructive, because citizens and aliens were treated differently with regard to military service: the aliens were organized into separate military units and used only for the defense of the city and its immediate environs.[9] But the condition of Athenian aliens was different from that of aliens in a modern nation-state in that it was virtually impossible for them to become citizens; they constituted something very near a hereditary political caste, with carefully limited rights and duties. The opening up of the possibility of naturalization, and the steady pressure of modern governments to establish a uniformity of obligation among their subjects, raise moral issues which, so far as I know, never arose in the classical polis. These issues can be seen clearly in the history of conscription in the United States.

Consent theorists have one fundamental problem with the obligation to perform military service: the young men con-

---

[9] There is some disagreement about this among historians. I am following Michel Clerc, *Les Métèques athéniens* (Paris, 1893), p. 48; for another view, see H. H. M. Jones, *Athenian Democracy* (New York, 1958), p. 164.

scripted for that service are often below the age of consent. They are asked not so much to fulfill their obligations as to anticipate them. There are some good reasons for this strange request, beyond its obvious practical reason. Ideally, wars ought to be fought by old men—they might then be less bloody as well as less frequent—but young men perform with markedly greater efficiency and have always been required to serve. It can be said that these young men have already enjoyed years of peace, as well as all the other benefits their state confers, and moreover that their parents, who are presumed to love and protect them, have had a say in determining the policies of their country. This last cannot be said of the young resident alien, even if he has been resident for all or most of his life. Still, he can only serve when he is young, and if he is exempted now on the grounds of his alienage and later becomes a citizen, as he may well do or try to do, he will have escaped military service altogether.

This is the calculation that led U.S. officials, beginning in 1863, to require military service of any alien who had formally declared his intention of becoming a citizen, that is, who had taken out first naturalization papers.[10] This requirement was sharply protested by the treaty nations, on the reasonable grounds that intentions, even declared intentions, do not make a man a citizen and that many of the draftees were in fact citizens elsewhere and so not liable for conscription in the U.S. As a result of these protests, new procedures were adopted which permitted "declarant" aliens (whether citizens of treaty nations or not) to withdraw their declarations, provided they had not exercised political rights under state law and provided also that they left the country within sixty-five days. Both these conditions are of interest. Many states at that time permitted residents of one year to vote in state elections even if they were not yet U.S. citizens. The federal government claimed the right to draft all persons who had exercised this suffrage and so illustrated nicely the close connec-

[10] For the following paragraph I am relying chiefly on Wharton, *A Digest*, section 202, and John Houck, "Comment," *Michigan Law Review* 52:265–276 (December 1953).

tion between express consent and military obligation. Clearly, the voting aliens of 1863 were thought to have committed themselves to the U.S. in some more significant way than any other declarant aliens had done. Hence the others could leave rather than serve; the voting aliens were given no option. The requirement that the others leave if they wished to escape service (this did not apply to nondeclarant aliens, who were exempt in the first place) was unusually harsh and so far as I know without precedent. It was not repeated in the World War I regulations, which went through an evolution similar to that just described. Once again, an effort was made to draft all declarant aliens; once again, there were protests from the treaty nations; once again, the U.S. yielded and established procedures for the discharge or exemption of aliens who withdrew their declarations, with the provision that such men would be "forever . . . debarred from becoming citizens of the U.S." [11] They were not, however, required to leave the country. Efforts to bar from future citizenship all nondeclarant aliens who refused military service failed in Congress in 1917. In 1941, however, the distinction between the two kinds of alienage was dropped. After that, no resident aliens were automatically exempt; they could claim exemption only by forswearing U.S. citizenship.

Like the native-born young, then, aliens were required to anticipate their obligations, even though they might not have enjoyed two decades of benefits and even though neither they nor their parents had any political rights. If this seems unfair, however, aliens had one striking advantage over the native-born: they were required to serve only if they hoped one day to become citizens. They could refuse to serve if they were willing to accept a perpetual alienage. This last has never been an option open to the native-born, at least not in their "own" country. If they wish to be aliens, they must go somewhere else.

In 1952, during the Korean War, a law was adopted requiring military service of every male alien admitted to perma-

[11] Hackworth, *Digest,* section 282, amendment of July 9, 1918, to Selective Service Act of May 18, 1917.

nent residence (that is, holding an immigrant's visa) and actually resident in the U.S. for more than one year.[12] The same rule has held during the war in Vietnam. This effectively turns conscription into a kind of enforced naturalization, since it requires an alien to assume the same burdens as a citizen whatever his own hopes and intentions with regard to citizenship. Clearly it lies within the power of Congress to do this, but it may be argued that it does not lie within its right. The present legislation represents a sharp break with the established rules of international law and also with the legal traditions of our own country.[13] It is particularly strange and disturbing, though also perhaps revealing of the motives of the legislators, that this dramatic shift should have come during the Korean and Vietnamese wars. For these are precisely the kinds of war—distant struggles in which the safety of the country and the lives of its inhabitants are not at stake—that the rule against alien service was most clearly intended to bar. Indeed, the bar was first expressed in terms of a simple, no doubt an overly simple, distinction between external and internal service—the first (as Americans once were more ready to admit than they are today) being likely to have some political motive beyond mere survival. Thus Secretary of State Madison in 1804 said: "Citizens or subjects of one country residing in another, though bound . . . to many common duties, can never be rightfully forced into military service, *particularly external service.*"[14]

I want to fasten for a moment on this anomaly: according to international law and American legal tradition, foreign-

---

[12] Houck, "Comment," p. 275.

[13] I have been unable to discover any court cases under the new law. This is probably because it affects so many fewer people than did previous legislation with regard to alien service, the number of resident aliens having fallen sharply during the past thirty years. I should add that many recent immigrants are from Puerto Rico, and they are not regarded as aliens at all. They are, strangely enough, equally subject to conscription at home and in the U.S., before and after they have become citizens.

[14] Quoted in Ernst W. Puttkammer, "Alien Friends and Alien Enemies in the U.S.," *Public Policy Pamphlet* No. 39 (Chicago, 1943).

born residents of the U.S. can refuse that express consent which provides the only moral basis for conscription, while native-born residents cannot. It would appear that the distinction between tacit and express consent is meaningful only in the life of an alien. But this was surely not the intention of those theorists, like Locke, who originally worked out the idea of tacit consent. For them the alien was only a convenient example of a group of men in fact much larger than the population of aliens, who had yielded nothing more than a silent acquiescence to the polity, and this larger group included native-born men and women. I should think that for Locke it included all those men (the poor and the landless, for example) who were not required to take oaths of allegiance, and if he thought of them at all, it included most women since they also were generally not sworn. It would also include all young men, whatever the economic condition of their families, for a young man below the "age of discretion" clearly cannot be thought to have expressed consent in any binding way and " 'tis evident there is no tie upon him by his father being a subject of this kingdom, nor is he bound up by any compact of his ancestors." [15] For Locke the population that has expressed its consent is thus likely to coincide with the population of adult, male property owners. Of course, he would almost certainly have conscripted young men without regard to the quality of their consent, since he distinguished the two kinds of consent, as we have seen, in a different way. But this leads him into a very curious position: he requires express consent for taxation, in fact, he requires a double consent, since property owners are individually sworn to the king and then collectively represented in Parliament, but he would require men to fight who are neither sworn nor represented. Perhaps he would have been willing to call this draft what it so obviously is, a simple impressment. [16] In any case, Locke's view of tacit consent suggests the existence

[15] Locke, *Second Treatise,* par. 118.

[16] Locke writes explicitly only of the obligation of soldiers, and says nothing of the obligation of citizens or subjects to become soldiers. I am here assuming what seems most likely, that he accepted contemporary recruitment practices. See *Second Treatise,* par. 139.

of a kind of moral proletariat whose members have nothing to give to the state—neither advice nor consent—except their lives. Such a proletariat did in fact exist in Locke's time. Does it exist in our own?

This is not an easy question to answer, because it requires that one suggest first what consent and citizenship mean or what they ought to be taken to mean in a modern democratic state—a state in which oaths have neither the social currency nor the moral weight that they had in the seventeenth century. It seems to me that the best expression of consent available to the resident of a democratic state is political participation after coming of age. Perhaps I should add, meaningful participation, for a man clearly does not incur the obligations of citizenship through actions about whose effectiveness and significance he is deceived. Meaningful is a vague word and one much abused, but for the moment it will have to serve. Just as the oath of allegiance in a monarchy was a pledge to acknowledge and abide by the commands of a sovereign lord, so meaningful participation in a democracy is a kind of pledge to acknowledge and abide by the decisions of the sovereign people. I doubt that this is a pledge often given without some awareness of what is being done. Actual participants in a democratic political process are generally not surprised to be told that they have committed themselves to abide by its results (or to refuse to do so, if they think they must, in a civil fashion, accepting whatever punishment their fellow citizens impose). War is simply one of the possible results and the obligation to fight one of the possible commitments.[17] Surely no one need feel hesitant about telling citizens this if they ever act as if they do not know it.

What of nonparticipants? I think we must say that resident nonparticipants have refused this express consent (and those whose participation is not meaningful have simply failed or been unable to give it) and have yielded only tacit consent to the political system. Though such persons have no legal

[17] The argument holds only if the decision to go to war is in fact made democratically; this is obviously not always the case, even in formally democratic systems.

status, their moral situation is not in any significant way different from that of resident aliens who could, but do not, apply for naturalization papers. The same applies to young men, especially if we assume with Locke that they are not commited by the commitments of their parents (and leave aside the question whether their own political activity can be called meaningful while they are below voting age). Native-born young men are not obviously different from young aliens. Before they are conscripted, then, they ought to be asked, as aliens traditionally were, whether they "intend" to become citizens, that is, whether they intend to exercise their political rights. If they say no, then we must at least consider the possibility that they be allowed, like aliens again, to avoid the draft and continue their residence, that is, to become *resident aliens at home*, acknowledging their obligation to defend society against destruction, but refusing to defend or aggrandize the state.

Now this may be taken as a monstrous suggestion. Even to talk of resident aliens at home, it may be said, is to misunderstand the meaning of "home." A man has enormous debts to his native land and to his polity. He receives from them both not merely physical security but moral identity. *Extra patria, nullum nomen.*[18] It is surprising how quickly we are back to Blackstone, for arguments of this sort necessarily suggest obligations akin to those we have to our parents. I do not want to deny the value of living permanently in one's native land and enjoying a secure political membership there, but I do want to deny the relevance of either of these to the question of ultimate obligation to the state. There is more than one reason for arguing irrelevance here, but I think it will be useful to stress a distinction that I have already made: the society into which we are born is not the same entity as the state that governs us, and neither of these is adequately described by the Latin word *"patria."* That word blurs the distinction between

[18] The psychological importance of "having" a native land is stressed by Sebastian de Grazia, *The Political Community: A Study of Anomie* (Chicago, 1948), but his argument helps to explain only the *sense* of obligation, not its reality. Exactly what arguments of this sort imply about being as distinct from feeling obligated is unclear to me.

state and society and is thereby faithful, perhaps, to the world of the polis, but radically divorced from the experiences of modern men. Liberalism from its beginning has emphasized the distinction, not merely in order to subject the state to certain sorts of social control, but also in order to free society and its individual members from the restraints of active citizenship and patriotic fervor. Liberal society is conceived as a voluntary association of private men, egotists and families of egotists, a world not of friends and comrades but of strangers. And the liberal state, though it permits a limited kind of membership and solidarity, really has another purpose. With its impersonal administration, its equality before the law, its due process, it represents the triumphant solution to the problem of governing a society of strangers. There is a sense, then, in which no one is at home in the modern state; we are all nameless aliens, *extra patria.*

That is an exaggeration, of course, even a gross exaggeration, though just how gross I really do not have to say. The modern liberal state is most often a democratic state, and through the mechanisms of mass self-government it seeks, with some success, to integrate and obligate its citizens. Nevertheless, that vivid sense of cooperating with one's fellows and governing oneself, which is so crucial to democratic legitimacy, has in fact been lost to many of those citizens. Whatever the reasons for that loss, its effects are fairly clear: an indeterminate number of men and women "drop out" of political life; a larger, but equally indeterminate number never join.[19] It is not the case that they simply do not vote, nor do I believe that nonvoting can be taken as anything but a very rough indication of political withdrawal or nonparticipation. Something more is involved: these people never have "Roman thoughts." They do not join in any of the actions available to democratic citizens; they do not participate in parties, sects,

[19] Some people never join because they are prevented from doing so, or from doing so in any meaningful way; they are excluded from citizenship by one or another form of oppression. Oppressed minorities in a democratic state may perhaps be regarded as alienated residents, but more needs to be said about them than I can say here; see the third of these essays.

or movements; they do not take part in political debate; they do not inform themselves on public issues. In all these ways they refuse or neglect or proclaim their inability to consent to the political system and to the various purposive actions it generates. These are the alienated residents of the modern democratic state, and they are probably far more numerous than are the resident aliens. I should stress that what these people suffer from (or endure or enjoy) is political and not, or not necessarily, moral alienation. They are strangers only to the state, and it does not follow from this either logically or psychologically that they refuse or neglect the obligations produced by their silence.

Liberal theory knows nothing of an alienation more profound than political alienation, but that is a condition it seems almost designed to specify. The politically alienated man has incurred social obligations by his residence, by the everyday contacts he maintains with other men and women, and by the benefits he accepts. But these obligations do not involve what the ancients called political "friendship" and do not bind him to share the political purposes or the political destiny of his fellow residents, or of those of his fellows who are active in state affairs. He has incurred limited, essentially negative duties to the state that regulates and protects his social life. He is bound to respect the regulations and to join at critical moments in the protection. But that is all he is bound to do. His only politics is the everyday politics of his personal life.

There is no established right to yield only tacit consent to the state. A resident alien need yield no more, but no state is bound to permit aliens to live permanently or even temporarily under its protection. Even the right of asylum might be qualified by the requirement that all refugees become citizens as soon as the law permits. A declaration of intention to become a citizen might well be made a requirement for admission. But if the legal status of resident alien could thus be eliminated, the moral condition of the alienated resident probably cannot be, at least not in the modern state. Nor can alienated residents simply be asked to leave; their condition is, after all, not their own "fault." It is some reflection on the quality of the state in which they find themselves. Yet, so far as I can discover, there are no states willing to admit the reality of ·alienation among their inhabitants or to recognize the alienated resident as a moral person. Just what this refusal means, what its reasons are, is not entirely clear to me. There are a number of possibilities. First, the rulers of the state may be claiming, with Blackstone, that obligation in fact derives from birth and upbringing and that the voluntary actions or inactions of adults have no significance in the formation or destruction of moral bonds. Or, second, they may be assuming express consent on the part of all native-born men and women in the absence of express dissent—perhaps on the grounds that such consent would probably be given were it somehow required, though the requirement itself would be administratively and politicaly difficult to enforce. Or, third, they may be denying that there is any moral difference between tacit and express consent and no special value to be assigned to the exercise of political rights. The first of these reasons is simply a denial of consent theory, and while I appreciate its consistency and force I am not going to discuss it here. The second and third quietly replace the notion that government is legitimized by consent with another notion: that government is legitimized by the absence of active and express dissent. People who hold this second view would, in effect, force all residents to choose between full-scale commitment on the one hand and emigration or revolution on the other. And when large numbers of men and women refuse to choose, as in fact they do, and rest, so to speak, in a position of tacit consent, they would allow the authorities to assume the commitment and to act accordingly. But surely this is to deny to those men and women their moral weight in the community and to treat them as children, that is as persons whose choices are not morally or politically effective.[20]

[20] Joseph Tussman has argued that there is no significant difference between express and tacit consent so far as their moral consequences go. He does believe, however, that there are many citizens who have not consented at all: "They are political child-brides who have a status they do not understand and which they have not acquired by their own

115

How might the force of tacit consent be recognized? It would of course be possible, as I have suggested, to allow native-born young men the same choice that young aliens have, or have had in the past. They could be invited at age nineteen or twenty either to declare their intention of becoming citizens, thereby accepting conscription, or to become resident aliens at home, losing forever their political rights and avoiding military service except in specified conditions of social emergency. There is, however, an obvious objection to this: it imposes a very difficult choice on very young men. Though it is true that we do this already, and by denying the possibility of voluntary alienage at home make the choice even more difficult, that does not make it a good thing to do. There may be nothing wrong with forcing young men to make hard choices, but forcing them to make permanent choices, with no possibility of reconsideration, places a burden on them that is clearly unjustified. On the other hand, the possibility that, if reconsideration were permitted, few men would choose citizenship until they were past the age for military service may be sufficiently strong to warrant the harshness of perpetual alienage. If this is so, another objection follows: perpetual alienage means the division of the members of state and society into two classes, with different rights and obligations. The whole tendency of modern legislation and of contemporary social struggle, however, is to establish a single class of citizens with precisely equal rights and obligations. A two-class system is not necessarily incompatible with democratic government, as the Athenian case demonstrates, but there is something repugnant in the spectacle of a group of men denied political rights because of a decision made in their late adolescence or very early manhood. The spectacle becomes especially repugnant when it is realized that not all

---

consent" (*Obligation and the Body Politic* [New York, 1960], p. 37). I am made uneasy by the presumption here that large numbers of adults can be passed off as children, and I doubt very much that these people have no understanding at all of their status, though they may have a different understanding of it than Professor Tussman does. I should add that Tussman is by no means content with his child-brides; he would prefer adult marriages. But what if the adults fight shy?

men will face the same choice when it comes their turn to decide. Women will presumably not have to decide at all, nor will men who reach the age of military service during years when conscription is not thought necessary, and the choices of men in peacetime and wartime will be radically different. So the division of the classes will be as arbitrary and unjust as such divisions have always been in the past.

It seems clear to me that tacit and express consent must be regarded as producing different degrees of obligation, and yet it seems equally clear that any legal recognition of these differences, or rather any recognition that makes them permanent, is undesirable. There is one way out of this dilemma, and that is to suggest that the state, while not legally establishing or perpetuating the differences, must do nothing to override them. That means, above all, that it cannot simply assume the express consent of its citizens and press them into its service, as it does today. For some of its citizens at least, and perhaps many of its citizens, have never yielded or will never yield such consent. For them conscription, except in cases of social emergency, is nothing more than impressment; it has no moral basis at all. But the group of alienated residents or silent citizens neither has nor ought to have any determinate membership. There are degrees of alienation, and even if the state were determined to recognize and measure these degrees, it is hard to see how it could do so. Nor does the group of alienated residents have a stable membership. In a democracy, at least, there is always the possibility of rejoining the polity. Individuals move, and should certainly be allowed to move, in and out of the political system.[21] Hence the principle "respect the differences between tacit and express consent" must establish a presumption against any conscription at all, except when the country as a whole or some part of it is threatened with devastation.

I am inclined to think that the presumption is very strong indeed and that military conscription at any other time or

[21] But note Rousseau's qualification in Jean Jacques Rousseau, *The Social Contract*, bk. III, chap. 18. It is generally easier to incur obligations than to renounce them.

for any other purpose—for political crusades, foreign inter-
ventions, colonial repressions, or international police actions—
is virtually certain to be unjust to many individuals, even if
the war itself is entirely justified. Conscription, then, is morally appropriate only when it is used on behalf of, and is
necessary to the safety of, society as a whole, for then the
nature of the obligation and the identity of the obligated persons are both reasonably clear. But the state must rely on
volunteers and can only hope (a genuine and vital democracy
might expect) that commited citizens, whether they can readily be identified or not, will choose to come forward.[22] Clearly,
they are obligated to come forward, though they may have
other obligations as well.

The myths of common citizenship and common obligation
are very important to the modern state, and perhaps even
generally useful to its inhabitants, but they are myths nonetheless and cannot be allowed to determine the actual commitments of actual men and women. These commitments depend upon their own actions, and their actions, presumably,
upon their previous moral experience: both actions and commitments are bound to be diverse in character. If the whole
gamut of possible commitments cannot be specified in law,
it can be understood in theory, and law can be adjusted on
the basis of that understanding. I have argued that the notion
of alienage provides a useful theoretical parallel to the moral
experience of alienation and to the commitment or lack of
commitment that follows from that experience. It suggests a
way of recognizing the political strangers among us and of
doing them justice as moral persons. I do not mean, once
again, that justice will or can be done by assigning a legal
status or creating a determinate class of individuals exempt

---

[22] There is one way of making this distinction in law that I want to
notice, but not necessarily to endorse. In Australia during World
War II, young men were conscripted for home service, while only volunteers were sent overseas. It is not the case, of course, that the defense
of Australian (or any other) society could never require overseas service.
Still, this is a rough and often acceptable way of guaranteeing that conscripts never be forced to wage a political war.

from certain obligations and deprived of certain rights. So far is this from being the case, that whenever conscription is enforced in the absence of social emergency, alienated residents (or those of them sufficiently self-aware to make claims on account of their alienation) should probably be treated as conscientious objectors are at present—exempted but not deprived, so as not to create a second-class citizenship. Perpetual alienage would be almost as bad as permanent exile, the only alternative to conscription available today to these same people. It can be argued, of course, that estrangement from the day-to-day self-government of society ought not to be tolerated in a democracy, for in the long run it undermines the sense of political obligation altogether and endangers the everyday mutuality and peacefulness of social life. Alienation is not a desirable human condition. That is no reason, however, for refusing recognition to those men and women whose condition it is.

6 Conscientious Objection

When a democratic state goes to war, there are two sorts of people whose refusal to fight warrants special consideration: those who have taken no part in the decision to go to war, and those who oppose that decision (or who oppose the conscription law that follows it) because they believe war itself or this particular war to be immoral. I am inclined to think that the refusal of the first group is easier to justify than that of the second. However, in the U.S., we make provision for people in the second group, or rather for some of them, and none at all for people in the first group. That provision is the legal right of conscientious objection, specified in each of the Selective Service Acts, which makes it possible for individuals with religious scruples against fighting or killing to avoid military service. The exemption does not extend to those who oppose some particular piece of fighting or killing, whether for religious or any other reasons, nor to those who oppose war in general, but cannot claim religious scruples. Still, conscientious objection, however restricted, is of great practical and theoretical importance—for it frees citizens, or some citizens, from the most serious obligation that citizenship is usually said to entail: the obligation to fight for one's country. I want to inquire into the grounds for this extraordinary freedom, and then to ask whether, given those grounds, it ought to be restricted to the small group that presently enjoys it.

It is, on the surface at least, a little strange to find a democratic state allowing conscientious objection at all, and even more strange to find a secular state allowing it on religious grounds *only*. For democracy implies a commitment to share the benefits and burdens of political life in some equitable fashion—the (occasional) need to kill is surely the most awful of the burdens—and secularism implies an absolute refusal to permit religious belief to affect the distribution. Yet the Selective Service Acts have uniformly worked so as to create a privileged class of citizens, the class of the conscientious, narrowly defined in religious terms and freed from burdens that anyone else can be obliged to bear. I say privileged class deliberately, though I know and respect the moral heroism with which those privileges have been won. It has always taken courage to win privileges: the rights of priestly castes and aristocracies were also vindicated by the self-sacrifice of heroic individuals. If most of us would agree that claims made on behalf of conscience have far more justification than the same claims made on behalf of aristocratic blood or priestly magic, this certainly has nothing to do with the heroism of the claimants. With what does it have to do? What is this conscience of which we are so tender? And do all of us have consciences of the same order?

The word "conscience" originally designated a kind of internal court where God's writ was thought to run, a faculty for moral judgment divinely created and implanted. Thus Milton's God in *Paradise Lost:* "And I will place within them as a guide/My Umpire Conscience . . ." Since this umpire was assumed to know the rules, conscience implied what the word itself means, a *shared knowledge* of good and evil, a moral science to which God and man were privy. Until the Protestant Reformation, however, the precise content of this knowledge was mediated by the church, and hence conscience, despite its internal character, had a public existence. Casuistry, or the application of conscience to its cases, was not in practice left to the internal court; it was an important priestly function. By denying the need for mediation, whether by priests or anyone else, Protestant radicalism profoundly altered the sense of the word. Conscience came to designate a knowledge shared by God and particular men, or rather, by a particular man and *his* God, a knowledge which had and could have no determinate social expression and no public content. A man's conscience was that inmost thought or feeling by which he knew himself to be in touch with something divine. It was a peculiarly precious and peculiarly private resource, and anyone who made conscience his guide walked confidently with his God even when, in the eyes of men, he walked alone. Indeed, he often walked alone (or in very small groups) since the Protestant conscience tended to be more proficient in refusing than in enjoining social tasks. By the early seventeenth century, the word had begun to be identified with "scruple," that is, it suggested inner doubts and hesitations as to the propriety of this or that conventional practice. Though conscience was sustained and passed on to the young in a great variety of sects and movements, it also tended to disrupt and fragment such groupings as soon as their practices began, as they invariably did, to look or feel routine. During the great creative period of Protestant reform, conscience was profoundly separatist in character.

Certainly it was as an agent of separation that conscience passed into liberal thought. Modern individualism had and probably required the support of this religious idea: that there was in each man, and not simply in man in general, an inner presence of divinity, or of something divine. A conscientious man was one who paid attention to this presence and sought to manifest it in his outward behavior—sought to manifest it, I should add, not occasionally, but all the time. Such a man deserved respect, not because his behavior was right in terms of some socially accepted standard, but precisely because it was conscientious, because it was the acting out of his inmost mind or heart. God worked in secret ways and revealed Himself inwardly only, through the introspections and personal decisions of individual men and women.

He provided no public revelation (for Scripture was subject among Protestants to an infinity of interpretations) by which the mind and heart might be guided, or judged. The individual could thus set himself against all that had hitherto been called true and lawful, orthodox doctrine, the wisdom of the ages, the rules and regulations of the state, and justify himself by referring to nothing more than the sincerity of his inward searching. And so long as men believed in something like a Protestant conscience, that was at least some justification, whatever else might be said about the idiosyncratic actions of particular men. I do not mean to suggest that the principles of individualism had no other justification than the idea of conscience. But we can judge the crucial role of that idea by the fact that even today we justify certain individual choices only insofar as we can bring ourselves to regard them as the acting out of a personal religious conviction.

To accept the Protestant idea of conscience, then, is to acknowledge the divine ratification of individualism, and that acknowledgment leads necessarily to the political practice of toleration. Historically, it leads to the establishment of two specific areas of tolerated actions (or of tolerated refusals to act). The first of these is the worship of God: the liberal state has come to accept all refusals to perform orthodox rites and all performances of unorthodix rites—short, of course, of such rites as human sacrifice or of performances which violate rules thought necessary for the general safety of the community. For all practical purposes, the state has simply yielded the world of religion to the scruples and injunctions of conscience. Liberal theorists like John Locke believed that nothing more would be needed to satisfy the conscientious. In his *Letter Concerning Toleration*, Locke reassured his readers on this point: "nobody ought to be compelled in matters of religion . . . The establishment of *this one thing* would take away all grounds of complaints and tumults upon account of conscience." [1] Locke was wrong, however, because the Protes-

[1] John Locke, *A Letter Concerning Toleration* (Indianapolis: Library of Liberal Arts, 1950), p. 52.

tant conscience resisted compulsion also in matters of politics —and because matters of politics were not so easily distinguishable from matters of religion as he thought. Above all, there was the matter of fighting and killing for the state. Significant numbers of conscientious men, most of them members of one or another Protestant sect, refused to participate in the military life of their country. They accepted all the benefits of the state, but they announced in advance of any particular domestic or international crisis that they would never bear arms in its defense. Over the years the obvious moral integrity and the extraordinary heroism of their persistant refusal won them a grudging respect and a limited legal toleration. But their toleration had other reasons also: first and most important was the general acceptance of the private conscience as a divine presence, its special theological status, which the heroism of conscientious individuals merely confirmed; second, there was the long-standing Christian aversion to killing, which had somehow survived an infinity of slaughters; and finally, there was the general respectability, piety, self-limitation, and sectarian discipline which marked most of the men who claimed the rights of conscience. The last of these should be especialy noted—I will return to it below—because it helps explain the readiness even of state officials and professional soldiers to make their peace with Protestant scruple.

These two great achievements, religious toleration and conscientious objection, differ from one another in one very important respect. The toleration of religious diversity quickly undermined all state-supported churches, but conscientious objection coexists, as time goes on, with greater and greater military establishments. I will suggest a reason for this difference later on; it is enough now to make the obvious point that the state has found it can survive, and particular rulers of the state have found that they can survive, without religious support but not without armed force. As a result of this discovery, the security of the conscientious objector has never been so great as that of the religious sectarian, nor have the two been equally free to indulge or express their inmost mind and heart.

In the United States, conscientious objection has been permitted since the earliest days of the republic—though it was then a matter chiefly for the several states to regulate. The New York constitution of 1777 declared, "That all such of the inhabitants of this State being of the people called Quakers as, from scruples of conscience, may be averse to the bearing of arms, be therefrom excused by the Legislature; and do pay to the state such sums of money, in lieu of their personal service, as the same may, in the judgements of the Legislature, be worth." In a rather more liberal vein, the New Hampshire constitution of 1784: "No person who is conscientiously scrupulous about the lawfulness of bearing arms shall be compelled to do so." [2] This last is a clause closely akin to the no-establishment-of-religion rule in the federal constitution: both are protections for tender conscience, the one against compulsory worship, the other against compulsory warfare. The requirement of a fee in lieu of personal service by New York and most other states (and by New Hampshire from 1792 on) is something like the recusancy fee in lieu of church attendance once required in England, and testifies to the imperfect toleration of refusals to fight. Even so, these were liberal provisions. In his original proposal for a Bill of Rights, James Madison included a clause of the same sort: "no person religiously scrupulous of bearing arms shall be compelled to render military service in person." [3] For some reason, it was not adopted by Congress, though a majority of the original states had, I believe, some such rule. Perhaps it was not adopted because a national draft was not yet envisaged. In any case, these provisions and proposals suggest that conscientious objection was no strange or frightening thing to early American statesmen—who were, of course, Protestants and Lockeian liberals. But I wonder whether these statesmen

[2] F. N. Thorpe, *The Federal and State Constitutions, Colonial Charters and Other Organic Laws of the States, Territories, and Colonies Now or Heretofore Forming the United States of America* (Washington, 1909), vols. IV (New Hampshire) and V (New York).

[3] Madison's speech to the House of Representatives, June 1789, is reprinted in *Conscience in America*, ed. Lillian Schlissel (New York, 1968), pp. 45–48.

would have responded in the same way if they had sensed the full potential of conscience or anticipated its secular forms.

In fact, the Protestant conscience as it confronted eighteenth century legislators was not the anarchic conscience of the Reformation period. It virtually invited a narrow construction of its own rights and privileges, though conscientious men insisted on these fiercely enough. I want to try to specify the social and historical features of this invitation and of the narrow construction it allowed—without, however, derogating in any way the moral seriousness and liberality of the men who wrote the early state constitutions. They certainly acknowledged the sanctity of individual conscience and the horror of war, but there were also practical considerations in their decision to tolerate conscientious objection. First of all, though the possibilities of Christian scrupulousness were (and are) logically unlimited, it was not necessary to worry about the infinite extension of claims. As long as the conscience was Protestant, it moved within a limited historical tradition, and this was a tradition with which the legislators were entirely familiar. There were a number of things besides war-making that certain Christians scrupled at (the taking of oaths, for example), but not an infinite number.[4] The ferment of the Reformation was long over, and the Protestant conscience had lost much of its radical *élan*. Its claims were increasingly stereotyped and could be anticipated—as in these cases, where the anticipation took the form of constitutional provision. Nor was it necessary to worry (as it is today) that some men might be averse to bearing arms in this war but not in that one. For a variety of reasons, no Protestant tradition of refusal had developed out of the old Christian distinction between just and unjust wars. The scruples of Quakers did not depend on whether war was being waged against In-

---

[4] In 1777 a Protestant group called the Schwenkfelders, living in Pennsylvania, explicitly declared: "We can not . . . take part in the existing militia arrangements, though we would not withdraw ourselves from any other demands of the government." For this and other early declarations and memorials of conscientious objectors, see *Conscience in America*.

dians or Englishman, whether for conquest or for what is now called national liberation.

Second, the making of these stereotyped claims against the state did not constitute any sort of political judgment on the state. Sometimes, of course, conscientious men urged that the state should not use force at all and should have no army. More often, I think, they urged only their own exemption, adopting an attitude toward war something like that of a monk toward sex.[5] The state could grant "freedom of conscience," then, without feeling that its own policies were being challenged or a judgment made that reflected in any specific way on its character. Even when Christian sectarians refused the specified money payment, as they frequently did, they were not condemning the state's war-making, but only maintaining the greatest possible distance from it.

Third, the state could assume that the number of people conscientiously refusing to fight would be fairly small. By the time toleration for such refusal was written into American law, the size of the relevant sects had been stable for some years, and any significant growth in their numbers, barring a second Reformation, seemed highly unlikely. The decision of the New Hampshire legislators not to name the sects whose members they meant to exempt was an easy gesture, because in fact the sects were well known, all of them were tiny, and the fragmentation of the larger Protestant groups had pretty well stopped. Finally, the identification of particular conscientious individuals posed no serious political problem. Given, once again, the decline of Protestant fervor, the signs of Christian scrupulousness were conventional and easy to discern: a

---

[5] I intended this only as a rough analogy and was surprised to find it argued explicitly recently by a Catholic writer, with support, he says, from the hierarchy: "a Catholic may claim that the will of God for him, as he has been able to discern it, forbids him to participate in war . . . There can be an analogy made to the vocation of celibacy. A man has the right to accept these paths to perfection, regarded as counsels . . . rather than precepts" (statement by Tom Cornell in Alice Lynd, ed., *We Won't Go: Personal Accounts of War Objectors* [Boston, 1968], p. 34). For a Catholic view opposed to this, see G. E. M. Anscombe, "War and Murder," in Walter Stein, ed., *Nuclear Weapons and Christian Conscience* (London, 1961).

certain pattern of sectarian membership, pious carriage, and stereotyped claims was an entirely satisfactory indication. For all these reasons, the accommodation of the Protestant conscience and the liberal state was relatively easy, even if it was sometimes shattered (when it was most valuable) by eruptions of patriotic nationalism, and all-to-often marred by the callousness and stupidity of particular state officials.

I have stressed the historical character of conscientious objection because the current disputes about the rights of conscience represent the first major effort to break with its religious history and to challenge the limits that history has imposed. Contemporary conservatives are, in effect, defending the privileges first won by radical sectarians in the seventeenth and eighteenth centuries. They are not necessarily wrong to do so, even if they have no more admiration for those radicals than for the ones they encounter in their own time. They merely argue what the rest of us may have to admit: that once we leave the safe harbor the sectarians long ago won, we are likely to find ourselves utterly at sea.

Let me ask again: what is conscience? There are two descriptions that do not require any reference to a divine presence and so enable us to approach more nearly the feelings of modern men and women. We can describe conscience as "a merely personal moral code." This is the formula that the U.S. Congress has most recently adopted in order to distinguish secular from religious scruple. The Supreme Court has called that distinction into question by suggesting that any "sincere belief" can be called religious if it "fills the same place" in the life of the individual who holds it as belief in God fills in the life of an orthodox Christian, Jew, and so on.[6] This is to suggest what is certainly true, that a moral code can be upheld as fervently as a religious code, that a man's life can be built around the one as easily as around the other. Nevertheless, it has the effect of turning the adjective "reli-

[6] *United States vs. Seeger*, 1965; for the text of Justice Clark's decision and Justice Douglas's concurrance, see *Conscience in America*, pp. 260–270.

gious" into a virtual synonym for "intense" or "strongly felt"—an identification which suggests forcefully how irreligious we have become. For what is lost when morality becomes "merely personal" is surely not piety or fervor, but the sharing of moral knowledge, the sense of Another's presence, the connection of the individual to a universal order. That is a real loss, not to be underestimated, because it calls the status of conscience itself into question. The phrase "merely personal" points to the possibility of moral egotism, which is surely very different from self-dedication to God's law—even if it can be argued that a secular state has no business judging the difference.

The description of secular conscience can, of course, be shaped so as to avoid the implicit disparagement of the statutory phrase, but I am not sure that solves the problem. In a recent and helpful article, Carl Cohen has called conscience "our blanket name for the personal governing principles to which a man is ultimately committed." Cohen argues that we all in fact believe that a man ought to act in terms of these personal principles: "When a man does what he honestly and deeply believes he ought not to do, we think him unprincipled and a hypocrite." [7] But surely we call a man unprincipled when he has no principles or no principles that govern his action, but not *whenever* he fails to act in accordance with principles he deeply believes in, for he may do that out of humility and in anguish, deferring to the judgments of his family, comrades, or fellow citizens. Then, it might be said, the man's ultimate principle is to defer to the judgments, and so forth. Perhaps that is true, and, if so, we can always discover a man's ultimate principles by what he finally does. But that is no reason to honor him for doing it. Before we honor him we want to know what it is he has done, and we want to know too how he reached his decision, how honestly he confronted his obligations, how seriously he weighed alternative courses of action and considered their likely consequences for others as well as for himself.

[7] Carl Cohen, "Conscientious Objection," *Ethics*, 78:270 (July 1968).

For the same reason, it is not clear that we owe any special respect, as Cohen suggests, to a man who "defies his community rather than be untrue to himself." That depends, surely, on the character of the man, the character of his community, and the relations that obtain between them. Polonius's famous lines, "to thine own self be true /And it must follow, as the night the day/ Thou canst not then be false to any man," are themselves true only if the self has some intrinsic or necessary connection with other men. If it does not, if conscience is not shared, then a man cannot simply be true to himself and win our respect; he must also try to be true to his fellow men. That is why the phrase "merely personal" is so disturbing. It points to the terrible dilemma of the individual who chooses to stand alone: how can he be certain he is right? What if the principles for which he spends his courage and stakes his life turn out to be silly, trivial, or fanatic? And what about the men and women he lets down by his willful isolation and defiance? At some point, indeed, he may have to stand alone and defend his personal integrity against his fellow citizens. But this is hard to do, and we ought not to pretend that it is (morally) easy; nor ought we to make it easy.

It is to the credit of many conscientious objectors that they do ask themselves hard questions and worry far more about the moral than about the physical risks they run. Their letters and memoirs are often marked by rigorous self-examination—though I think this is most often true of objectors who come out of a religious (or political) tradition that encourages self-examination or are actually members of religious (or political) groups that practice it. And this suggests that the description of conscience as "merely personal" may be inadequate or simply wrong in precisely those cases where conscientiousness is at its highest pitch. Men who continually worry that their objection is a piece of self-indulgence, or who ask over and over again whether they are "really helping the Movement," or "working effectively to stop the war," or "hurting their families," are obviously not acting on the basis of a "merely personal" code, however lonely they may feel while they worry. There is a difference between personal decisions and the moral code on which such decisions are based. The decisions we may finally make alone; the code we almost certainly share.

Thus conscience can also be described as a form of moral knowledge that we share not with God, but with other men—our fellow citizens, for example, or our comrades or brethren in some movement, party, or sect. Insofar as the group of men who share knowledge is coterminous with the group that shares citizenship, conscience takes the form that Hegel called "true conscience" or, simply, patriotism. Then conscientious objection is neither necessary nor possible. But the very existence of religious sects suggests that moral knowledge is often shared among much smaller groups, and surely all of us, religious or not, are capable of feeling conscientiously bound to principles we share with only some of our fellow citizens. And then conscience may well lead individuals like ourselves to challenge the state and refuse to play the patriot.

Any state that permits such groups to form and work out their common principles freely is bound to find itself challenged by conscientious individuals. These challengers will not make their claims on the basis of "merely personal" codes, but on the basis of shared principles and mutual engagements. They will most often say that they are pledged to these principles, committed to their fellow members (and not simply to themselves, to maintain their own integrity, or to do, as Thoreau wrote, whatever they think right). I do not mean to suggest that the principles to which groups of men commit themselves are necessarily or even probably better than the principles to which individuals commit themselves. I do think, however, that conscientious objection has and probably ought to have greater weight in the eyes of the larger community when it has as its basis a smaller community, within which some degree of responsibility, mutuality, and social discipline is likely to exist. Conscience is supposed to represent (it is one of the things we mean by the word) an inner alternative to the ego, a motive beyond self-interest. I do not doubt that it can play this role whenever a man discovers a principle for which he is ready to risk his comfort and even his life. But it is most likely to do so, and to do so in some stable and dependable way, when a man first discovers his fellow men, and works out with them (or with some of them) the principles for which he is ready to take risks.

Whatever judgment we make of conscience as a secular sharing of moral knowledge, I think it is clear that this is the conscience that we (and the political authorities) most often encounter. In a totalitarian system, such encounters might be minimized. A tyrannical state can force individuals to stand alone, or to draw on their memory of shared principles and hope that other men, as lonely as they, but with the same memories, will join them. But freedom of association virtually guarantees that certain laws will be met with demands for exemption, or for repeal, from groups of associated individuals. As conscientious objection in its Protestant form is the natural product of religious pluralism, so conscientious objection in its secular form is the natural product of political pluralism.

It is interesting to speculate that the secular conscience may undergo a development similar to that of the religious conscience—appearing first in anarchic, radically separatist forms, the product of an inchoate and fragmented group life, and then becoming more stable in character, its demands increasingly stereotyped, with the growing coherence of the relevant associations. In highly developed pluralist settings, it might even be possible to make judgments about the sincerity of an individual's objection by referring to (though not only to) his previous participation in some oppositional political grouping, just as contemporary judgments take into account sectarian membership. All that is necessary to make this plausible, or more plausible than it may at first seem, is to imagine long-term processes at work in the state similar or somewhat similar to the processes at work in the church in the early modern period.

The pluralist state need not grant all conscientious claims; conceivably, it need not grant any of them. But it cannot grant or deny them on the basis of the character or constituency of the groups that make them. It must consider the claims themselves, weigh their content and their likely effects. There is no other way to distinguish among the groups except on the basis of the claims they make. These may be incompatible with one another or with the general framework of rights and obligations that makes associational life possible. Given the secular description of conscience, however, it is simply not the case that one group is more, or more truly, conscientious than another. I do not mean that the state cannot make such judgments; I mean that there are no such judgments to be made. The conscience of members of The Society of Friends is no more real than that of members of The Resistance or, for that matter, of the White Citizens' Council. All that the pluralist state can do is to judge the claims made by each group in the light of the pluralist system itself and its security.

But perhaps the state should distinguish between groups which demand a general exemption from certain of its uglier activities, such as war-making, and groups which set themselves against one or another of its particular policies, for example, *this* war? It should be said that that is not quite the distinction presently made in the U.S., for we accord legal recognition only to religious demands for general exemption or, given the Supreme Court's new definition, to moral demands which "fill the same place . . ." and so on. These do not include, in the words of the Selective Service Act, demands made for "essentially political, sociological, or philosophical" reasons.[8] Of course, men can and do share moral knowledge by sharing political, sociological, or philosophical reasons. The effort to distinguish "being committed to a political doctrine" from "being committed to a moral (religious) doctrine" is utterly hopeless and futile, unless politics is defined in some very limited way (as political science, for example) in which case no one is ever likely to be a conscientious objector for its sake. So the distinction is either impossible to make or, if made, irrelevant. I suppose that what is wrong with political, sociological, and philosophical commit-

[8] Selective Service Act as amended in 1948.

ments, in the eyes of the state, is that they usually require us to distinguish degrees of ugliness and to make judgments about the relative necessity under these or those conditions of going to war. Certain sorts of otherworldly religious and absolutist moral doctrines (not all sorts) enable us to dispense with such difficult judgments, and while it is absurd to suggest that only adherents of these doctrines have consciences, it is by no means absurd to suggest that the claims made by such men are more safely tolerated by the state than any other claims can be.

If this toleration were actualy extended to groups which demand general exemption on other than religious grounds, the exclusion of political objectors would not necessarily be discriminatory. State officials might argue, with some plausibility, that they were willing to grant exemptions from the law, but not in cases where the demand for exemption was in fact a means of political protest against the law. Exemption, they might say, was designed as a way of protecting "tender" and otherworldly sorts of people (whose withdrawal from certain aspects of political life posed no threat to the state), while active opposition bespoke a toughness and a worldly commitment to which (precisely because it might pose a threat) other sorts of protection were more appropriate. Not that the state ought to judge such qualities as tenderness and toughness, but it can and must evaluate the consequences of granting the different claims of different groups.

The major consequence of granting exemption to political opponents, these same officials might continue, is that the very capacity of the state to carry out its policies—even policies democratically decided upon—would be called into question. Why bother having a political process if its determinations are subject to the conscientious objection of anyone who loses out? Why bother struggling to develop (what we do not yet have) a democratic way of deciding when to go to war and when not, if we leave it up to the members of every particular sect, party, or movement to decide whether or not to fight? Such individual and group decisions seem, in fact, to nullify the decisions of the larger political community, and if that is so, then the same arguments might be made against conscientious objection to particular policies or laws as were once made against the doctrine of nullification by the several states.

Nevertheless, I think conscientious objection by political opponents can be defended against these criticisms, if we begin by specifying carefully what we mean by a political decision and what follows from arriving at such a decision. When the state adopts a law, it does two things. First, it requires all citizens to obey, to stop doing what is prohibited, to start doing what is enjoined, to pay the relevant taxes, and so on. Second, it appoints particular men to enforce the law and to advance its particular purposes, inspecting, administering, and policing the activities of their fellows, and it gives to these men control over whatever public resources are necessary to their jobs. Every law—and I should add, every settled state policy—creates two sets of men, subjects and servants, and while all servants are also and necessarily subjects, it is never the case that all subjects are required to be servants and only occasionally that any are required. Citizens often find themselves forced to obey a law or give indirect support to a policy that they deeply dislike and have actively opposed. But they are rarely forced to administer such laws or policies. Subjection, once laws have been democratically adopted, is compulsory; state service, except in times of emergency and war, is a voluntary activity.[9] This is not an absolutely clear distinction, and it is especialy troublesome in wartime. But it

[9] In a democracy, according to Aristotle, the citizen rules and is ruled in turn, and presumably is morally bound and perhaps is legally bound both to obey and to serve. But "ruling" is not necessarily the same thing as holding office (it can include all sorts of political activity short of that), and it is official action that I want to separate out here. I am inclined, however, to think that there can be no obligation on the citizen as citizen to be politically active at all. Citizenship of some kind, indeed, of the kind we know in the United States, is obviously compatible with passivity. Jury duty is the only public activity other than fighting for which we regularly conscript people, but it is made so easy to opt out that this can hardly be called conscription. See the last two of these essays for further consideration of this point.

is a plausible distinction, for we do conceive differently the roles and obligations of citizens and officials (and of civilians and soldiers). It is also an important distinction because it enables us to make another: between two sorts of conscientious objection which have very different consequences for the state.

Conscientious objectors may refuse to obey, or they may refuse to become instruments of, the state. These are different refusals, even though men may lawfully be commanded to become instruments, as when they are conscripted into the army. The refusal to obey, but not the refusal of conscription, is a sort of nullification, and even though it may be justified on the part of particular individuals or groups, it is hard to see how the state can tolerate it. Refusal of this sort can only take the form of civil disobedience. Perhaps the state should respect the civility of disobedient citizens by punishing their actions more mildly than it would punish the same actions committed for other reasons; perhaps it should (sometimes) avoid punishment altogether.[10] But it cannot extend legal toleration to persons who refuse the ordinary duties of citizenship—especially not once it has been agreed that all consciences are equally tender and that no particular membership and above all no religious affiliation entitles a man to be treated differently than his fellows. To tolerate disobedience of this sort is simply to announce that the state's decision-making process is not a process for making *decisions*.

If the state in some sense requires universal obedience (I do not mean that it would collapse if men occasionally disobeyed its laws), it does not in any sense require universal service. The refusal of groups of men to become state servants, officials or soldiers, does not prevent the state from carrying out its policies. The state can always find other servants. It is not my purpose to deny that conscientious objectors are obligated, along with everyone else, to obey a conscription law, though they may have conflicting obligations as well. I do want to argue that the state can tolerate refusals of "personal

[10] See Ronald Dworkin, "On Not Prosecuting Civil Disobedience," *New York Review of Books*, 10, no. 11 (July 6, 1968), 14–21.

service" without permitting or opening the way to general nullification. Conceivably, if it does tolerate such refusals, it ought not to conscript anyone at all and rely entirely on volunteers. But surely no injustice is done if laws are enforced and wars fought by citizens who are in favor of the laws or the wars and also by citizens who are indifferent to them or only weakly and hesitantly opposed. The state cannot proclaim such citizens specially obligated; they are not in fact specially obligated; but it can exempt the others from their obligations. And it can do so without calling into question the democratic decision-making process. Indeed, it might add greater weight to that process, and guarantee its moral seriousness, if participants agreed that they were "declaring their consciences" and that these declarations would have effects later on for themselves as well as for the political community as a whole.

I suggested earlier that religious toleration undermined all established religion, but that (limited) conscientious objection had not had the same effect upon the military establishment. This difference follows from the two different demands that governments can make. The refusal to pay tithes or to obey church attendance laws is a refusal of ordinary subjection, and when it is tolerated the subjection is simply nullified, even if the laws remain on the books. The refusal of conscription, on the other hand, is a refusal of service, not of subjection (though it may be defended in the name of freedom), and its toleration does not interfere with the general recruitment of state servants nor with the allocation of state resources. It is possible, of course, to imagine a case in which there is such strong opposition to a war that the state can only recruit a sufficient armed force by coercing political opponents to fight, but any such example must call into question the democratic character of the previous decision to go to war. Given a democratic decision, and given a toleration limited to *conscientious* objection, the state, for better or worse, will not lack soldiers. I find it very hard to believe that "The effectiveness of a government, if not its very survival, could well depend on its success in coercing conscientious but recalcitrant minorities." [11] That is likely only if the word re-calcitrant is taken to mean rebellious, that is, if it suggests a refusal of ordinary subjection and not of state service alone.

The only possible exception to this argument is a genuine war of national defense against an invading army, when the state may well call on everyone to serve (women and children too, as in the *Levée en masse* of 1793) and actually need everyone's service. In such a case, I would be inclined to ad-mit that the toleration of conscientious objection has a spe-cial quality of magnanimity about it—which means, it may not be compatible with the safety of the state. "Forcing con-scientious objectors to fight and kill *may* be justified," Arnold Kaufman has written, "if there is a clear and present danger to the survival of all national values. The threat must be more than a mere possibility, or even a probability. There must be a very high probability of national destruction." [12] But this is the description of a limiting case, and it serves chiefly to highlight the real possibilities for toleration present at all other times.

I have so far argued only that conscientious objection for political reasons can be tolerated by the state; I want to argue now that it ought to be. To do this it is not necessary to in-sist that conscientious objectors have *rights* against a demo-cratic state, though this is what religious objectors have gen-erally insisted. Conscience takes precedence over the state, they say; the political authorities must never require a man to deny his God. This claim has considerably less force when it is translated into secular terms: the state ought never re-quire any of its citizens to contradict their deepest convic-tions. Surely the state should do this sometimes, for example, when it requires a man deeply opposed to public welfare to pay his taxes or when it requires citizens committed to racial segregation to support integrated schools (and even, if they

[11] S. I. Benn and R. S. Peters, *The Principles of Political Thought* (New York, 1965), pp. 224–225.

[12] Arnold Kaufman, "Selective Objection to War," *Dissent* 15:312 (July–August, 1968).

are too poor to afford a private education, to send their children to integrated schools). And though we would feel more uneasy about forcing such citizens to administer a welfare office or to teach in an integrated school, I doubt that they have any absolute right to refuse these services if the community ever decides, democratically, that conscription is necessary to insure their performance. It can be argued, however, that the refusal of such services should be tolerated by the state, not because of the quality of the convictions on which it is based, but rather to sustain the quality of the state within which such convictions can be freely acquired.

A democratic state is enormously dependent on the willingness and ability of its citizens to commit themselves to political values and to act consistently in their name. (There are political scientists who would say: "on the willingness and ability of *some* of its citizens," arguing that there can be too much of a good thing; but whether many or few committed citizens are needed is not relevant to my argument.) These commitments are generally made in groups, where values are collectively worked out and the strategy and tactics of political action debated. I am not speaking simply of interest groups, though obviously individuals can be morally committed to group interests as well as to group values and these are not always easy to distinguish. But it is chiefly in ideological sects, parties, and movements that commitments are made that later lead to conscientious objection. These associations, though relatively small, play a major part in determining the shape of political discourse and political action. They raise issues which the nonideological parties have tried to ignore; they translate interests into principles; they focus politics on the moral problems with which it is ultimately concerned; they teach their own members, and others as well, how to argue about such things as justice, obligation, means and ends, human rights—whatever their ideology encompasses and explains.

Life within an ideological group (like life in a religious sect) is very intense, partly because of the group's relative size, partly because of the steady focusing on moral issues.

Members become strongly committed to the values they share and to the other members because of the sharing. Sometimes such commitments consistently override the obligations of citizenship; then we call the group revolutionary. Most often, in a democratic state, they do not, and one or another sort of accommodation is possible between the group and the state. So long as channels for open disagreement and political struggle are available, the members generally submit to laws they dislike; they pay taxes, for example, even when they disagree with some of the ways in which the money is to be spent. But imagine the moral anguish of these same members when they are asked to play an active and official role in implementing laws or policies which contradict their most intense commitments. They are put in an impossible situation, though it may well be that no injustice is done them. Democratic states which insist on their performance, however, are doing an injustice, or at any rate an injury, to themselves. Such a demand undermines either the moral or the legal basis of the pluralist system on which democracy depends.

It undermines the moral basis of pluralism if the members perform as demanded, violating their consciences and selling out their fellow-members. For pluralism requires the integrity of conscience—at least, genuine pluralism does. I do not doubt that secondary associations of some sort can survive an infinite number of breaches of faith. But what kind of associations will they be? What moral relations can their members sustain? Surely no group life of intensity and value is possible if members of the various groups are repeatedly driven into what must seem to them morally degrading performances. It is just not the case that the only obligations on which a democracy rests, and which its citizens ought to respect, are obligations to itself.

The legal basis of pluralism is undermined whenever the required performances are refused. Refusal will most often, of course, take the form of civil disobedience, and that means that it will not be a refusal of all duties to the democratic system. But the conspiracy laws work so as to make associations within which even the most narrowly conceived forms of civil disobedience are planned or mutually recommended effectively illegal. They are not banned, but the normal activities of their members are turned into criminal actions.[13] Even if the prosecution of these actions is intermittent and arbitrary and does not aim at the systematic destruction of the dissident groups, it nevertheless has or is likely to have the effect of driving the groups outside the pluralist system (and, conceivably, of driving many of their members out of the country).

Democratic states suffer whenever conscience is coerced, whether the coercion is, in its own terms, successful or unsuccessful. I conclude that it is better to tolerate refusals of state service so long as the refusals are conscientious, that is, so long as they follow from some more or less consistent pattern of interpersonal commitment and group action. Since the persons involved are often likely to be young, however, this criterion cannot be strictly applied, and any coherent statement of personal convictions likely to lead to group action must be taken as a sufficient sign of conscientiousness. Young men called up for military service may have had no previous occasion to declare their consciences, but their silence or inaction cannot be taken to mean that they have no consciences to declare.

The argument for pluralism, then, not only suggests a wider range of toleration than has previously been accorded, it also suggests a somewhat less strict standard of conscientiousness than the present "religious training and belief." It is, first of all, harder to pay attention to political than to religious training, though that might still be worth doing, since men and women in political sects, parties, and movements certainly try to pass their values on to their children, just as religious believers do, if with less success. Second, it has to be admitted that political belief does not in practice have anything like the specificity that religious belief has. Even when no particular religion is legally specified, even when nothing

---

[13] Thus the recent trial of Dr. Spock and his associates in Boston (1968): the defendants were charged, in effect, with conspiracy to commit or encourage civil disobedience.

more than piety is required, the toleration of religious scruples, as I have already argued, accords special recognition to a particular religious tradition, with which we are all familiar, and to a particular way of describing personal scruple. (That is why the political authorities have such difficulty adjusting to groups outside the tradition, like the Black Muslims.) The toleration of political conscience, on the other hand, does not and cannot point to any single tradition of political commitment and zeal or even to a single vocabulary in which different traditions might be articulated. For these reasons, twentieth century legislators will not find it so easy to accommodate conscience as did their eighteenth century counterparts—and conscientious men ought to recognize the difficulties they pose. At the same time, however, they can reject the notion that these difficulties are insurmountable. Given a genuinely open politics, it will never be the case that the authorities are surprised by refusals to serve, or by the men who refuse, or by their reasons. The reasons will be typical in form, if not stereotyped, the men clearly marked, and their actions (within limits) predictable. For conscientious objection will always be preceded by visible and articulate opposition, the intensity and extent of which the democratic system ought to register.

There is one further difficulty to be considered, and its consideration will cast doubt not on the tolerability of conscientious objection, but on the tolerability of the system that makes objection necessary, conscription itself. If it is broadened in the ways I have suggested, conscientious objection will almost certainly introduce into the draft (for military service and conceivably for any other state service as well) a pronounced class bias. I have already argued the extent to which conscience is a social product, but it must also be said that it is the characteristic product of a particular segment of society. Rates of group membership and participation climb startlingly as one climbs the social scale, and this is especially true of rates of membership in groups that make more than minimal demands on the men and women who join. This means that while all men and women have scruples, some have more scruples than others—or, at least, the scruples of some are more subject to collective stimulation and reinforcement. These especially scrupulous men and women are likely to be selected or self-selected from the middle and upper classes. (Obviously, I am not making any judgments as to the relative worth or moral standing of different persons or social groups. Having scruples is not the same as being good. One can easily imagine a man conscientiously opposed to the performance of benevolent, useful, or necessary actions. This man too is likely to be middle or upper class.)

There are important exceptions to this general rule, such as the Jehovah's Witnesses and the Black Muslims, and the first of these has provided a substantial proportion of conscientious objectors to military service in the recent past. Still, it can hardly be doubted that the immediate effect of opening up the possibility of political objection would be to excuse large numbers of middle and upper class young men from the draft. The social basis of opposition to the war in Vietnam makes it especially clear that this would be the case today, and insofar as conscription is used in the future for similar sorts of wars, the effects are likely to remain the same.

If this is true, then any extension of conscientious objection would almost certainly generate class resentment of a very bitter sort—and a justified resentment, even though its focus would probably be on the objectors rather than on the war they are opposing or on the system of conscription. For it is surely not just that a nation should wage war with drafted soldiers, while exempting from the draft significant numbers of the children of its most influential citizens. It is not just even if the grounds of the exemption have nothing to do with social standing. Exemption is only justified if it is more or less equally available to all social groups. But this would be the case only in a classless society. Conscription without exemption is the democratic response to social inequality, and those of us who oppose the class bias introduced into the draft by such devices as student deferment ought surely to be wary of a more liberal provision for conscientious objection—which, whatever the intentions of its proponents, would almost cer-

tainly be another such device. On the other hand, the reasons
already given for tolerating refusals of state service seem to
me very good ones, and I do not see any way of balancing
the moral and political value of toleration against the injustice
it would involve and the social resentment it would stimu-
late. There is an important sense in which conscientious objection can neither be defended *nor* condemned in any finally
persuasive fashion.

I do not believe that the same thing can be said of conscription itself. It can be condemned, and precisely because
it poses an impossible choice between conscience and justice.
As a response to inequality and as an effort to distribute a
terrible burden as fairly as possible, conscription requires us
to reject the claims of conscience, repress the activities of the
claimants, and strain and distort the pluralist system. Adjusted
to accommodate conscience, conscription is no longer just.
The best solution to this difficulty, I think, is to avoid conscription whenever possible, that is, except in cases of national emergency. A volunteer army would also, of course,
display significant class bias. But the end of coercion would
at least open the way for political opponents of a particular
war to function freely in competition with army recruiters
and perhaps to extend their support across class lines. I do
not think there can be any doubt as to the inability of conscientious objectors to do the same thing; they are trapped
between government toleration and social resentment and are
effectively isolated. If toleration protects the pluralist system,
it also neutralizes it for the duration of the war: neutralization
is in fact the form of the protection.

Perhaps what conscience most requires in the modern world
is freedom and not toleration, the ability to act with minimal
restraint in the political arena and not mere exemption from
state service. If conscience is nothing more than scrupulousness, however, this is a distinction without a difference, for
then freedom *is* exemption. And there is probably no better
way to guarantee that this be the case, and also to facilitate
the premature stereotyping of the secular conscience, its sec-

tarian enclosure, and its effective isolation from political action, than to legalize conscientious objection. Toleration may be desirable at some later date, in some more nearly equalitarian society, when the pluralist system has a broader social base than it has at present. Today, it seems to me, the development and articulation of conscience would best be facilitated if compulsory state service (though not legal subjection) were simply abolished. But I do not want to predict what the consequences of such an abolition would be; it is enough to argue, as I have done, that they would not be such as to endanger the political community. The state can survive without a conscript army (as it survives without a conscript bureaucracy), and it will not be a worse state for making itself a testing ground of the quality and reach of the contemporary conscience.

7 Prisoners of War:
Does the Fight Continue After the Battle?

Just beyond the state there is a kind of limbo, a strange world this side of the hell of war, whose members are deprived of the relative security of political or social membership. Different sorts of people live there, mostly for indefinite periods of time, people who have been expelled from their state or otherwise deprived of legal rights, people whose state has been defeated in war and occupied or who have been separated somehow from its jurisdiction. Among the residents, two groups endure conditions paradigmatic for all the others: refugees, deprived of their rights by persecution; and prisoners of war, separated from their state by captivity. The two are very different, since refugees are stateless persons, radically dependent on their hosts and unable to look backward to any protecting authority, while prisoners remain citizens still and receive such protection as their states can provide. However distant and isolated they may be from their home country, their captivity is (hopefully) temporary; both captives and captors may one day be required to account for their behavior. Nevertheless, prisoners and refugees belong alike to the limbo world. They cannot expect effective help from any organized society; they do not know when, if ever, they will be "at home" again; they are compelled to reconstruct or redefine their obligations without reference, or without clearcut reference, to authoritative laws and commands.

Refugees face their hosts with a special kind of helplessness and pathos, but also with an unaccountable and peculiar freedom. They are men free of all allegiance except to other men, without political obligations, at least without obligations to any state in the world of states, and their condition testifies to the wretchedness of such freedom.[1] Frightening as it may be to the authorities (at least, the authorities generally profess to be frightened), it is far more so to the refugees themselves. Until they are given a home, they have a right to do whatever they can to save themselves, within limits imposed only by their humanity and the relations they form with particular other people. But in fact they can do painfully little, and theirs is a freedom any of us would speedily exchange for membership and protection, despite the restraints these impose. The value of the state as an inclusive community, the importance of even the most minimal kinds of social solidarity and legal definition—these are never more clear than when we regard ourselves as possible participants in the limbo of statelessness.

The prisoner, on the other hand, is doubly unfree, since he is not set loose from his former allegiance, or so he is told, by his captivity. If he is forced to face his captors, bound or at gunpoint, he must also look over his shoulder to the authorities of his own state. He is required continually to balance the obligations he knows he once had, and may still have, as a citizen and soldier, against the more immediate threats and coercions of his captors—and perhaps also against his new obligations to the society of prisoners. What should he do? It is never easy to say. If the statelessness of a refugee is frightening, so is the citizenship of a prisoner of war. To regard ourselves as possible captives is to learn how oppressive political obligations can be. Even limbo, as we shall see, has its temptations.

[1] For a brilliant discussion of the problem of statelessness, see Hannah Arendt, *The Origins of Totalitarianism* (New York, 1958), chap. 9.

Captivity can be conceived in two different ways: first, as the termination of combat for an individual soldier, the imposition by the captor and the acceptance by the captive, of a total quarantine for the duration of the war; second, as the termination of one sort of combat and its replacement by another sort, where the fighting is relatively circumscribed and its conditions radically unequal.[2] Both of these are modern conceptions; both depend on the recognition of the prisoner as a moral and legal person, possessed of certain rights, entitled at the very least to be kept and provided for by what the lawyers call "the detaining power." The prisoner is "detained," and that means that whatever else is done to him or with him during his detention, he cannot be killed or enslaved. Not so very long ago, a prisoner was thought to have forfeited his life by his surrender. And then his slavery was justified as the result of an exchange made possible solely by the benevolence of his captor, an exchange of life for perpetual service. In that view, captivity was in no sense a status within which a man might be more or less secure even if impotent. Prisoners were rapidly converted into dead men or living slaves, and the choice between these two conditions was only secondarily their own.[3] (In practice, during the early modern period, prisoners were often required simply to join the army of their captors, common soldiers being little more than chattel anyway.) Today, a prisoner can expect to remain a prisoner for as long as the war lasts, and then he can expect to be released. In the interim between capture and release, he is forced into a relation with his captors unlike that of slave and master, though not entirely unlike it, and into a relation with his fellow prisoners unlike that of any

[2] See G. S. Pugh, "Prisoners at War: The P.O.W. Background," *Dickinson Law Review*, 60:123–138 (1956), and "The Code of Conduct," *Columbia Law Review*, 56:678–707 (1956). The best book on the nature and laws of captivity is William E. S. Flory, *Prisoners of War: A Study in the Development of International Law* (Washington, 1942).

[3] Hugo Grotius, writing in the early seventeenth century, still defended the right of enslavement, *De Jure Belli ac Pacis*, bk. III, chap. 14, section 9. The decisive theoretical critiques of this idea are by Montesquieu, *The Spirit of the Laws*, bk. IV, chap. 2, and Jean Jacques Rousseau, *The Social Contract*, bk. I, chap. 4.

normal political (or military) association. The prison or prison camp is the scene of a new society, which exists precariously in the shadow of the detaining powers and whose members feel the pull of their previous political commitments, not least because these are likely to be their future commitments as well.

This new society of prisoners exists by virtue of, or at least in accordance with, international law. Its members have even been called, by a serene theorist of the nineteenth century, "citizens of the world." [4] The world is, unfortunately, not so organized that citizenship in it is much of a benefit—as stateless persons have learned over and over again in the past thirty years. But the name does suggest something very important, if true: that prisoners are no longer at war. It presses us toward the first of the two conceptions of captivity. For the war is being fought by citizens of this state and of that one, and citizens of the world, even if they hold dual citizenship in one of the belligerent states, are presumably exempt from the compulsions of the struggle. The rules of quarantine replace the code of battle, and this replacement is not merely legal, but moral as well; it frees the prisoner from all obligations to continue the war.

The same replacement would seem to be implied by the conventional practice of "surrendering" or "giving up," though this has sometimes been denied. In the *Code of Conduct* for U.S. soldiers issued by President Eisenhower in 1955, it is said that soldiers must never surrender "of their own free will." [5] If it were possible for soldiers to surrender in any

[4] James Lorimer, *Institutes of the Law of Nations* (London, 1884), II, 72. The whole passage is excellent and should be consulted.

[5] *The Code of Conduct* is the most important official statement on how U.S. soldiers are to behave when overpowered by an enemy, and I will refer to it frequently below. At the time it was issued, its legal status was unclear (see Pugh, "The Code of Conduct"), but it has recently been described, in the aftermath of the *Pueblo* incident, as "only a guideline." Violations of the articles of the *Code* do not constitute a criminal offense: *New York Times*, December 29, 1968. It is presumably still the opinion of the authorities that they constitute a moral offense, and the *Code* continues to play a very important part in the training of U.S. soldiers.

other way, the act might indeed have no moral consequences. But unless the *Code* is intended to bar surrender altogether—and then its subsequent provisions, which deal with the conduct of prisoners, would be superfluous—the phrase "of their own free will" is very odd. The authors presumably want to say that only extreme duress and the threat of imminent death are acceptable reasons for surrender, but that does not mean that the act of surrendering can never be a decision of the men who surrender or an agreement between them and their captors.[6] It most often is a decision, and it is probably always an (implicit) agreement. Even when no decision seems possible, as when the sailors of a sunken ship are simultaneously rescued and captured, it can probably be assumed that the prisoners agree to their captivity, if only for the sake of their rescue, and that they approve of the general practice of taking prisoners. In battle or in the aftermath of battle, surrender usually involves a more explicit judgment and choice on the part of the men surrendering, a judgment of their own continuing effectiveness as soldiers and of the risks they face, a choice to fight on or not. This is in some sense a free choice, though it is made under varying degrees of duress, since soldiers can and have been known to accept enormous risks and even fight to the death. Surrender is precisely a way of choos-

---

[6] Something must be said here about the difficult problem of coercion, though to deal with it in even a minimally adequate way would require another essay. The common and plausible view is that no man is morally bound to fulfill a contract or commitment he was coerced into making. Since the word "coerced" is usually taken to mean "forced by violence or the threat of violence," surrender would appear to have no moral validity. But it might be argued against this that the definition of coercion depends or ought to depend on the situation of the individual said to be coerced, and that in the context of war, violence exercised in accordance with the laws of war is not coercive. Surrender is a social practice designed to accommodate the human difficulties of war; it cannot be judged by conventions appropriate to other, and very different, settings. This calls into question the dictionary definition and ordinary usage of the word "coercion." There are only two alternatives, neither of them attractive: either to suggest that no morally binding agreements are possible in wartime, or to accept Hobbes's argument that "Covenants entered into by fear . . . are obligatory" (an argument Hobbes explicitly applied to prisoners of war—see Thomas Hobbes, *Leviathan*, chap. 14).

ing not to take enormous risks and not to fight to the death. It takes the conventional form of an agreement not to fight at all, to "give up" fighting, in return for life itself and then benevolent quarantine.

This agreement obviously requires a second party; surrender must be accepted as well as offered, and armies can refuse, though no longer lawfully, to take prisoners. Clearly, there would be a positive incentive to refuse if surrender were thought to involve no commitment to cease (and not to resume) fighting, just as there would be a positive incentive to fight to the death if the acceptance of surrender were not viewed as a commitment to one or another form of quarantine. Surrender as a social practice is only possible in the absence of these two incentives, that is, it is only possible when it is conceived as a mutual engagement with moral consequences. This conception is clearly reflected in international law, which requires benevolence of captors and simultaneously deprives a prisoner of all combatant rights.[7] If he kills a prison guard, for example, the act is murder and not war, for he has given up fighting and thereby reassumed some of those civilian obligations which are suspended for soldiers in the face of an enemy.

The essence of surrender is the agreement not to fight, and this agreement may not require quarantine at all. In the days when officers were also gentlemen and aristocrats, it was perfectly normal to release a prisoner on parole, that is, to accept his word that he would not rejoin the fighting and then to permit him personal freedom of movement, even to permit him to go home. This is only possible on a very strict view of surrender, which holds the captives temporarily free of political allegiance and so able to make arrangements on their own behalf: "separated for the time being from any political community, they . . . belong to humanity and to themselves." [8] Eighteenth and nineteenth century lawyers argued—

[7] See the discussion in Pugh, "The Code of Conduct," pp. 682–683, 690n., and Eric Williams's introduction to *The Escapers* (London, 1953), p. 15.

[8] Lorimer, *Institutes,* II, 72.

and their arguments were for a time widely accepted—that if a prisoner did return home on parole, his home state could not force him to fight again or in any way require him to violate his faith.[9] This clearly implies that the prisoner did not break faith when he gave parole in the first place; it grants that he belonged at that moment in time "to himself." Perhaps that is a status which aristocrats resume more readily than other men; nevertheless, its recognition is, I think, an extraordinary tribute to the liberality of eighteenth and nineteenth century states, or of some of them, and of their lawyers and philosophers. Modern states, whether liberal or not, are not inclined to grant a similar recognition. Most of them, including our own, deny prisoners the right to give their parole (except under very restricted circumstances and for short periods of time) and international law has been adjusted so as to deny validity to any parole arrangement contrary to the laws or regulations of the prisoner's home state.[10] Very occasionally the old ethic is rediscovered. Thus, a small number of captured American soldiers gave their parole to the Japanese in the Philippines during World War II, and "these paroles were recognized by the U.S. as prohibiting military and other resistance to the Japanese on the part of the individuals concerned."[11] But such agreements are rare in this century and today the *Code of Conduct* explicitly declares that prisoners must not give their parole to their captors. Prisoners, it would appear, never belong, or are never admitted to belong, merely "to humanity and to themselves."

It is perfectly understandable that the state should continue to claim the allegiance and support of prisoners. It is even in the interests of the prisoners that it should do so—up to a point. They have no wish to be abandoned, however un-

---

[9] See the British *Manual of Military Law* (1884): "A State has no power to force its subjects to act contrary to their parole." Quoted in Flory, *Prisoners of War*, p. 123.

[10] Geneva Convention I, Article 21; for a discussion of contemporary law on parole arrangements, see Morris Greenspan, *The Modern Law of Land Warfare* (Berkeley, 1959), pp. 108–110.

[11] Pugh, "The Code of Conduct," p. 683n.

easy they may be about their "obligations." Nor does the state make its claims very effectively, since it has no immediate control over the persons of the prisoners and is unable to offer any but the most minimal guidance as to their everyday behavior in the radically new society of the prison camp. The claims of the state are still enormously important; they point toward the second and at present (in our own country and more clearly in some others) the official view of the status of captives and the moral meaning of captivity. In this view, prisoners of war must regard themselves as combatants even after their capture, full-fledged members of a state at war, a state in trouble, needful of all the men it has, unwilling to yield the services of anyone except to death itself. The prisoner, so the *Code of Conduct* tells him, is an "American fighting man" (Article I). He must refuse any sort of cooperation with his captors and seek continually to escape. By implication, he must also help whenever he can to organize mass escapes, to maintain a resistance network in the camp, to harass the enemy, spy on him and sabotage his behind-the-lines operations. He must always act so as to require as many guards as possible. It is a little hard to see why any state at war would maintain prisoners who actually did or tried to do all these things, and insofar as the *Code* requires them, it is not entirely consistent with the idea of benevolent quarantine. This is partly because it was designed as a response to North Korean and Chinese captors who paid little regard to that idea, but it also reflects, as did the actions of the North Koreans and Chinese, an extension of state sovereignty and an attempt at ideological control which amount to a denial that individuals can ever move, even partially, out of the range of political action and supervision. There simply is no space, it suggests, that might be called limbo, where quarantine is possible and a certain human passivity morally justified.

Contemporary international law, as codified in the Geneva Conventions (1949), does not require the passivity of prisoners; indeed, it provides carefully and at considerable length for attempted escapes, though not for any other kind of resistance.[12] Nevertheless, the most humane provisions of the present code—for example, the rule that prisoners captured while trying to escape cannot be punished, but only detained more strictly, and that only for a short time—are rooted in the expectation that the vast majority of prisoners will not resume or make any attempt to resume their combatant roles. And that is an expectation most often realized in practice, despite the wishes of the governments whose citizens are imprisoned. The erosion of the idea of benevolent quarantine has come largely from the other side, from captors and not from captives, as one might expect; for if combat is resumed, it is the captors who have every advantage. Still, prisoners have chosen to fight on, sometimes in response to the coercive acts of the enemy, sometimes on their own initiative, and it is worth asking whether there is any justice at all in the increasingly strong presumption of their home states that they ought to do so.

Article III of the U.S. *Code of Conduct* requires that American soldiers, if captured, must "continue to resist by all means available." This is its most extreme provision, though the ambiguous word "resist" was carefully chosen. Carter Burgess, Assistant Secretary of Defense, argued at the time the *Code* was adopted that physical resistance (which is barred by Geneva Convention I, article 82) was not required of prisoners, but only mental resistance to political indoctrination.[13] That is hardly made clear by the *Code* itself, and the lack of clarity was presumably intentional, since the wording was long debated. One legal critic of the *Code* has pointed out that unless it is read as a call for resistance "by all *legitimate* means available," prisoners "would be encouraged to commit acts that may be war crimes or at least contrary to the spirit of the Geneva Conventions."[14] Needless to say, their captors would be similarly encouraged.

The *Code* was adopted in the immediate aftermath of the

[12] Geneva Convention I, Articles 42, 91–93; see Greenspan, *Modern Law*, pp. 135–137.

[13] Carter L. Burgess, "Prisoners of War," *Columbia Law Review*, 56:676–677 (1956).

[14] Pugh, "The Code of Conduct," p. 690.

Korean War, a struggle in which the noncombatant status of prisoners was undermined by both sides, though most dangerously and cruelly, judging from the available evidence, by the North Koreans and Chinese.[15] In prison camps north and south of the battleline, a new kind of war went on for the minds, that is, for the loyalty and political commitment, of the prisoners. To some extent, this was a war that could be fought within the limits set by the Geneva Conventions. But one of its most ominous results was that in the American-run camps, where the Conventions were fairly rigorously observed, and in contrast to the Communist camps where they were not, resistance was amazingly successful. At one point, major sections of the camp on Koje Island were entirely controlled by North Korean prisoners, who even captured and for several days held the American commander of the camp. It quickly became clear that "measures permitted under the Geneva Conventions would not completely destroy the Communist organization within the compounds." The North Korean prisoners could no longer be regarded, or treated, "as passive human beings in need of care and protection." [16]

General Mark Clark's comment on the Koje mutiny suggests what American officials learned from this incident: "My experience," he wrote, "had been with *old-fashioned* wars in which prisoners were people to be fed, housed, clothed, and guarded, nothing more. Never had I experienced a situation in which prisoners remained combatants and carried out orders smuggled to them from the enemy high command." [17] Only a few years later President Eisenhower brought American policies up to date by issuing the *Code of Conduct*, recommended to him in a Defense Department report entitled *P.O.W.—The Fight Continues After the Battle*.[18] The *Code*

---

[15] But see W. Burchett, *Koje Unscreened* (Peking, 1953).

[16] Pugh, "Prisoners at War," p. 131, citing UN Command Reports. A complete account of the Koje mutiny, from the American point of view, can be found in Hal Vetter, *Mutiny on Koje Island* (Tokyo, 1965).

[17] Quoted in Vetter, *Mutiny*, p. 10.

[18] Report by the Secretary of Defense's Advisory Committee on Prisoners of War, *P.O.W.—The Fight Continues After the Battle* (Washington, D.C., August 1955).

was explicitly intended to provide a secure moral basis for resistance to the indoctrination of prisoners as this had been practiced by the North Koreans and Chinese. But its careful ambiguity suggests that it was also intended to encourage action on the scale of the Koje mutiny. What happens then to the "old-fashioned" notion that prisoners must be maintained and guarded and nothing more? I am inclined to think that there would be some value in reiterating that notion, rather than merely conceding its antiquity.

On the other hand, when serious pressure is put on prisoners to collaborate with the enemy, either by supplying military information or expressions of political support, we do want "our" soldiers (at least) to refuse and resist. It is important to understand just what is involved in such refusals: they do not represent a continuation of the war so much as an unwillingness to enlist or be enlisted on the other side; they are a defense of all that is implied by the idea of quarantine. Prisoners refusing to collaborate are also, of course, refusing to "sell out" their comrades or their recent comrades and to betray their country, but the obligations which they thus acknowledge and sustain are minimal in character. They can most readily be expressed in the negative: not to inform, not to confess, not to collaborate, and so on. I do not mean to suggest that they are for that reason easy to sustain. Whether they are easy or hard (or impossible) to sustain depends on the actions of the enemy. They are significantly different, however, from obligations that lend themselves to positive statement: to try to escape, to harass, to sabotage, and so on. In practice, most states attempt legal enforcement only of negative obligations. Prisoners who collaborate with the enemy may be charged after the war with misconduct or even with treason, but not prisoners who refuse to join escape organizations.[19] Treason obviously requires some overt act of "aid and

[19] Rebecca West reports on the trials of several British prisoners of war for treason in *The Meaning of Treason* (London, 1947). For a complete review of judicial treatment of prisoner misconduct, see "Misconduct in the Prison Camp: A Survey of the Law and an Analysis of the Korean Cases," *Columbia Law Review,* 56:709–794 (1956).

comfort," so mere refusals to participate in escape or harassment attempts do not qualify. But the inability or unwillingness of states to enforce positive obligations has other reasons, which call into question their very status as obligations.

Negative and positive obligations (I mean the two adjectives merely as rough indications of certain sorts of actions and refusals to act) are mediated very differently to the individual soldier. Negative obligations are his as an individual, a member, let us assume a willing member, of a particular state or of its army, and they clearly survive temporary separation from either. In captivity (as out of it) these obligations may be overridden, or they may be violated in extenuating circumstances. Refusals to collaborate, for example, may endanger the society of prisoners as a whole or some of its individual members, and then the man who is being pressed to perform this or that service must weigh relative evils and make a difficult and painful decision. I would stress the word "must," for whatever decision he comes to, he is faithful only if he takes into account his obligation not to act so as to injure his country or endanger his comrades-in-arms.

Similarly, in those cases where a prisoner collaborates under duress, he is later judged, and rightly so, by the integrity of his resistance as long as it lasts, that is, by his own manifest sense of his obligation. I cannot say, and I am not sure any free man can say, what constitutes an adequate manifestation.[20] Once a prisoner has done what he can on behalf of his home state, by refusal, evasion, or deceit, and can resist no more, his fellow citizens can only mourn with him, and not condemn, the disloyal or degrading acts he is driven to perform. Some manifestation of resistance there must be, however, so long as the prisoner regards himself and hopes to be

[20] The courts must say something, however, and what they have said is discussed in "Coercion: A Defense of Misconduct While a Prisoner of War," *Indiana Law Journal*, 29:603–621 (1954). In passing judgment on prisoners who have given military information, it is worth noting the finding of army experts after World War II: "It is virtually impossible for anyone to resist a determined interrogator." Cited in *P.O.W. —The Fight Continues After the Battle*, p. 61. For a full discussion of this problem, see Albert D. Biderman's careful study of the behavior of American prisoners in Korea, *March to Calumny* (New York, 1963).

157

regarded as a citizen. Negative obligations survive every separation except explicit renunciation, which is only possible under certain conditions and which terminates citizenship. They are paralleled, it should be added, by the obligations of the home state to provide protection whenever it can, to protest every breach of the rules and agreements that make for benevolent quarantine, and to do nothing and demand nothing of its soldiers that might prompt or seem to excuse the coercion of prisoners.

Positive obligations belong to the individual as one of a group of citizens or soldiers. This can be a group of conscripts, whose members are designated as falling under one or another law or legitimate command, or a group of volunteers mutually engaged in some enterprise of value to the larger society. It seems most unlikely, in either case, that positive obligations survive clearcut (even if temporary) separation from the group. The prisoner is alone and on his own or he is a member of a new society, and while he remains in an important sense a citizen, he no longer be regarded as a servant of the state. For he is cut off from the group support and organizational structure that once made his service possible. Positive obligations can be reinstated by joining an escape organization or a resistance network in the prison camp. But such reinstatements are actually commitments to a new group, and the precise relation of the new group to the larger society, the state or the army, is radically unclear. It seems unlikely that the state's right to conscript, for example, can ever devolve to an association of prisoners, though such groups have sometimes claimed that right. A kind of rough and ready conscription may, of course, be effective in a camp where an escape organization has widespread support. There are many examples of this sort of thing in prison camp literature: certain kinds of minor helpfulness have often been required of prisoners who have no personal interest in escaping. It is less their patriotism that one appeals to at such moments, however, than their loyalty to fellow prisoners.

This appeal to the others may or may not be successful. Success will depend on the nature of the society of prisoners as a whole (which may in turn depend on the nature of the state and army from which the prisoners come) or on the character of the personal relations involved. But it is clear that no prisoner has a positive obligation *to the state or army* to work and take risks for the escape of himself and others or for the harassment of the enemy. Unless he actually commits himself to such purposes, he has what must be called a perfect right to "enjoy" his quarantine and to sit out the war—so long as doing so involves no conflict with his other obligations.

There are obligations, however, in addition to those positive and negative duties owed or said to be owed to the state, despite the prisoner's separation from the state. Captivity is not only a separation; it also brings men together and does so under conditions that make their cooperation both vitally necessary and extremely difficult. It cannot accurately be said that anyone joins the society of prisoners willingly, even though there is a sense, as I have already argued, in which their surrender is a voluntary act. Yet, once formed, that society can be organized on a consensual basis, and probably ought to be, either by intelligent officers who recognize that their own authority survives in a tenuous way, if at all, or, in the absence of officers and in accordance with the Geneva Conventions' provisions for enlisted men's camps, by the election of representatives.[21] The political organization of the prison camp, whatever form it takes, considerably simplifies the moral life of the prisoners. It makes possible, for example, the rationing of available food, clothing, and medical supplies. It also permits communal decisions on whether or not to support escape attempts, when these involve, as they often do, predictable reprisals against the whole society.[22]

[21] Geneva Convention I, Article 79. Resistance groups within the camp can also be organized democratically; thus an American group in Korea, one of whose members is quoted in Biderman, *March to Calumny*, p. 171: "We . . . agreed there would be no such thing as a leader. Before we would do anything, it would go before a vote and the majority would rule."

[22] These decisions can be informally made, as in the camp described by A. J. Evans in his memoir of World War I, *The Escaping Club* (London, 1922), pp. 180–181: "Escaping came before everything, and was an excuse for any discomforts which one or two members might

Even when the society of prisoners cannot be politically organized, obligatory ties are likely to develop between a particular prisoner and each or any of his fellows. Shared suffering is a powerful bond among men and seems to entail—though I cannot specify the method of the entailment—very strong positive obligations to mutual assistance. These bonds seem to arise among groups of men assembled with or without regard to their previous citizenship, though they may be stronger or given practical effect more quickly among prisoners with common political and social commitments.[23] There may be some sense, that is, in which the new society is parasitic on the old. Nevertheless, these new obligations are owed to other prisoners and not to the state from which they come. When the U.S. *Code of Conduct* requires captured soldiers to "keep faith with their fellow prisoners" (Article IV), it does little more than point to the specific context within which obligations have to be negotiated. It does not strengthen the ties, nor determine their precise character. Insofar as the obligations of prisoners to each other are enforced, later on, in state or army courts, this must be by virtue of a kind of proxy from the (now dissolved) society of prisoners.[24] Such enforcement can be justified, at least in part, by the need to prevent acts of private revenge, but not by the unqualified assertion that the state's writ runs in limbo.

We do admire prisoners who actively resist their captors, and such men were thought admirable even before the ideological struggles of the present day provided new motives for continuing the fight after the battle. There is a large literature, dating chiefly from the two World Wars, which documents and celebrates the efforts of prisoners of war to escape

---

bring on the rest of the community. If you wished for help, almost any man in the fort would have helped you blindly, regardless of consequences."

[23] P. R. Reid discusses some of the problems that arose in the multinational camp that the Germans ran for confirmed escapers at Colditz in World War II, in *Escape from Colditz* (New York, 1956).

[24] Sometimes prisoners set up their own courts in the camp, but these are not encouraged by the authorities. See Pugh, "The Code of Conduct," pp. 683n. and 702.

and harass the enemy. This literature does suggest that such efforts have been felt as obligations, at least by some of the prisoners. Moreover, the detaining powers expect (some) prisoners to try to escape; their military authorities often regard the attempt as honorable and clearly accept the necessity of establishing a secure quarantine. Thus General Clark's statement of the "old-fashioned" view: that prisoners must be maintained "and guarded." The same sense has worked itself into international law, as I have already indicated. But I want to stress again that the security of the right to try to escape (which is implied by the rule against punishing escapees and obviously does not include a right to succeed in the attempt) is dependent on the relative infrequency of its exercise. If attempts to escape are common, if whole camps are organized for the sole purpose of facilitating escape, as were many British officers' camps during the two World Wars,[25] then benevolent quarantine will almost certainly break down. Its cost to the captors will simply be too high, and they can argue that they had reckoned on a much lower cost when they accepted the surrender of the men in question. Thus the attempts of states like our own to require soldiers to "make every effort to escape" (Article III of the *Code of Conduct*) might well be disastrous for the soldiers, if they took the requirement more seriously than in fact they do. When we admire the men who "make every effort," we are really admiring heroes. It seems best to say of them, whatever they say of themselves, that their efforts are above and beyond the call of duty.

Escape is heroic only in part because of the physical risks involved, though these can be considerable, as a famous incident from World War II makes clear. In 1944 some eighty British officers escaped through a tunnel from the German camp at Sagan. All but three were eventually recaptured, and fifty were shot, apparently on direct orders from Hitler. Under the international laws of war, these executions constituted

[25] ". . . nearly everyone was working in some way on the X (escape) organization" (Paul Brickhill, *The Great Escape* [New York, 1967], p. 42); ". . . we pooled our knowledge. The camp was nothing less than an escaping club" (Evans, *Escaping Club*, p. 68). The best books on escape are almost invariably written by British officers.

murder, and after the war the men who carried them out were tried and, some of them, executed in their turn.[26] That surely was justice done, yet it is hard to imagine a detaining power that would not go to considerable lengths to deter such mass escapes—for they tie down large numbers of troops, demoralize the civilian population, and, if successful, supply valuable information to the enemy. Hopefully, prisoners will not again have to anticipate Nazi brutality, but something less than that (and how much less can never be known) must be regarded as a normal risk. There is more involved, however, in the heroism of escape. Once a prisoner gets out of the camp, he is likely to have to spend weeks behind enemy lines, hiding or in disguise, constantly in danger, expecting discovery and arrest at every moment, able to trust no one, often without adequate food and shelter. For many men the strain must be unbearable, worse than anything that happens in battle. No prisoner can be obligated to undergo such an exacting test of his nerves and his endurance. Escape is precisely the sort of action that a man must choose for himself.

But perhaps this is not always true. In one of the best of the many books on escape Aidan Crawley, an RAF officer captured during World War II, later a Labor MP and Under Secretary of State for Air, argues "that should a prisoner see a reasonable chance of escape, it [is] his duty to take it. Suppose a prisoner had been abandoned by his guard and deliberately sought captivity again, he would have been the equivalent of a deserter." [27] Perhaps so, but in this example, it should be noted, captivity is ended without any effort by the prisoner himself. Whether he then resumes his former military role is hard to say. It is certainly possible, but if we imagine such a man seeking refuge in the home of a friendly farmer and remaining there for the rest of the war, I doubt that we would have to say, or want to say, that he had deserted. Crawley attempts to argue that there was a duty to attempt escape even when a prisoner was securely held in a camp, but he fails to argue this with much conviction. Despite

[26] Brickhill, *Great Escape*, pp. 211–223.
[27] Aidan Crawley, *Escape from Germany* (New York, 1956), p. 8.

the military ethic, the sense of an obligation to escape does not seem to have been widely or deeply felt in the World War II camps, though it is almost always acknowledged in the memoir literature. "I am sure," writes one of the bravest of British escapers, "that the majority of the men who sought to escape did it for self-preservation. Instinctively, unconsciously, they felt that resignation [to an indefinite imprisonment] meant not physical, but mental death." [28] But what of the men who did not feel this way, who decided that they could make a worthwhile life even in the prison camp?

Crawley provides one of the most sympathetic accounts of these men and he is worth quoting at length:

> From the first moment of captivity . . . there began in every prisoner's mind a conflict which lasted often until the day of liberation. Should he, or should he not try to escape? Ought he to spend his time in what would almost certainly be fruitless endeavor, or should he use it to equip himself to be a better citizen later on? There were many who from the start decided on the course of self-improvement. With great force they argued that, however heroic escape might appear, the odds against success [were] so enormous that the realistic and truly patriotic thing to do was to put the idea out of their minds . . . To every thinking man, the wisdom of spending years in hopeless effort must at some time have seemed questionable and no one could blame those who decided escape was not worthwhile. Provided they stuck to their guns and held their point of view with tolerance, they were often most valuable members of the community. [29]

To call such refusals "patriotic" is, I suppose, to put a good construction on them, but not necessarily the only good, or the best, construction. Refusal to escape might also express a man's sense of belonging, now, "to humanity and to himself," or his sense of personal obligations to family and friends.

[28] Reid, *Escape from Colditz,* p. 35.
[29] Crawley, *Escape from Germany,* p. 7.

It might express his solidarity with his fellow prisoners, or with some of them, doomed to remain in the camp for the duration of the war and in need, perhaps, of his help in the building of a decent community.[30] It might also express his human fear or his relief at finding himself relatively safe and far from the battlefield. Surely, if a man makes himself "a valuable member of the (prison) community," even these latter reasons need not be judged any more harshly than the others.

Curiously enough, one of the best arguments on behalf of escape, even mass escape, is that the attempt is itself of value to the society of prisoners. Crawley has once again put the argument very well:

> Most important of all, the effort to escape preserved the morale of the prisoners themselves. One of the great difficulties of prison life was that almost all effort, apart from the business of feeding and existing, was directed to goals which could be achieved only in the indefinite future. The mere fact that in preparing for a mass escape hundreds of people were co-operating in an enterprise which held the prospect of an immediate result was the best tonic a prison camp could have. In building a tunnel, making clothes, forging papers, or preparing maps, men took part in a common effort and once again got the feeling of serving a community.[31]

It may be that this new community is parasitic upon the old: that escape can be a common enterprise of the prisoners only because it is an enterprise of value to the state and army from which they commonly come. But this is not necessarily so. In

[30] Exactly what this means and how such a community can be built are the main concerns of J. Davidson Ketchum's fine sociological study, *Ruhleben: A Prison Camp Society* (Toronto, 1965). In his postscript to this book, Robert MacLeod argues that the "prevalence of the idea of escape" may be a sign of group disintegration (or, presumably, of social underdevelopment), p. 353. But it is important to note that Ruhleben was a camp for enemy aliens, not soldiers.

[31] Crawley, *Escape from Germany*, pp. 9–10.

Pierre Boule's novel (and in the better film by David Lean), *The Bridge over the River Kwai,* the common enterprise of the prisoners is not of value to their state.[32] On the contrary, it poses a serious threat and even requires a military response. Yet it has an effect, and a plausible effect within the novel and the film, identical to that which Crawley describes. In the River Kwai case, the obligations that may arise to work on the bridge, and to work strenuously, are owed to one's fellow prisoners and to no one and nothing else. There is a certain absurdity in the spectacle of hundreds of men working with such zeal on a bridge that they "really" (as members of the conventional world, citizens and soldiers) do not want built. Yet this is an absurdity always possible in limbo, and it is the achievement of the novel and film to have evoked it. Nor is it clear that enterprises of more conventional value are very much less absurd. The extraordinary discipline and skill, the zeal and the sheer genius, that went into the British escape from Sagan were surely out of all proportion to its salutary effects upon the British war effort. George Harsh nicely summed up "the great escape" when he wrote of the prisoners involved that "they proved for all posterity that men, working together, can dig a damned deep hole in the ground." [33] Yes, they did prove that, and that hole was their triumph over captivity, their human triumph, as was the bridge for another group of men; and they dug it first of all for each other.

In limbo obligations are, by and large, not given, not established by any sovereign state, not waiting for discovery; they must be improvised. Attempts to specify them that go beyond those negative obligations which all citizens share are likely to be impositions on the freedom of the men involved and sometimes a cruel threat to their security. That is why they are largely ignored by the prisoners. Citizens and soldiers, safe or relatively safe among their comrades, have every

[32] They are forced, in violation of the Geneva Conventions, to build a bridge which is of military value to the enemy.
[33] "Introduction" to Brickhill, *Great Escape,* p. 9.

right to hope that prisoners will form some sort of society, find an effective way of making collective decisions, and remain faithful to one another. Armies have every right to train their soldiers to behave in that way. But to insist that this is what prisoners ought to do is to say nothing more than that they owe this much to one another, and finally it is up to the prisoners to say that themselves. Citizens and soldiers, and presidents and generals, may also hope that some of the prisoners will be heroes, that they will discover uncommon resources of courage and endurance, and unilaterally re-establish obligations that in fact have lapsed. But such heroism, it must be recognized, is also a denial of captivity, perhaps even a refusal of benevolent quarantine, and so a potential threat to the status of all those prisoners who do not choose to be heroes. All the more reason, then, that heroism should not be demanded by those of us who cannot expect to feel its consequences.

The fight does not continue after the battle, not for the men who have been captured, unless they choose together to fight on and accept the risks that choice involves. They have every right to choose differently, and this is what most of them do, opting for benevolent quarantine whenever it is offered. It is the responsibility of civilized men to insist that it always be offered and to repudiate decisively and without compromise the very idea of a "total war" to be fought within as well as without the bounds of the prison camp. The requirements of humanity are clear enough: detaining authorities must assume, and the prisoners' home states must give them reason to assume, that prisoners are not combatants and are no longer required by their citizenship to fight. Then they may safely be treated, and then they ought to be treated, if not like "citizens of the world," at least like men entitled to rest for a while in limbo.

Part Three: Citizenship

8 *The Obligation to Live for the State*

La république se passera très bien de mois après ma mort . . .
—VOLTAIRE

Tout homme est utile à l'humanité par cela seul qu'il existe.—ROUSSEAU

In wartime, soldiers are sometimes asked to take suicidal
risks, "to march up to the mouth of a cannon, or stand in a
breach, where [they are] almost sure to perish." [1] If they accept such risks and then die, their deaths are very much like
those suicides that Émile Durkheim called "altruistic." This
is the only sort of suicide that the state encourages. Throughout history, and even into the modern age, the state has vig-
orously opposed self-slaughter of every other sort, and the
laws of the state have visited upon the corpse of the successful suicide the most strange and horrifying mutilations. This
extraordinary hostility has sometimes had a religious basis in
the belief that a man's life belongs to God alone. Hence the
taking of his own life with his own hands can only be described as an insurrection against divine authority. Whenever
political officials conceive of themselves as representing that
authority, they seek to punish the insurgent. Since they must

[1] John Locke, *The Second Treatise of Government,* par. 139.

169

leave the living soul to God, they do what they can with the lifeless body.

Suicide has also been opposed by the state for political reasons, and this opposition involves a claim that must be of enormous interest to anyone concerned with the meaning of political membership. The claim is that the individual citizen, by virtue of his citizenship, has an obligation to live for the state. That does not mean an obligation to serve the state every moment of his life, for the same man also has, presumably, a right to live for himself. The argument is rather that a citizen is not entitled to die merely for his own reasons or at a time of his own choosing. The political community has an interest in his life, even his everyday life, and this is not an interest the individual can unilaterally deny. I do not think this argument has ever been made on behalf of the United States, at least, I have never seen it made, though most Americans would agree that the burdens of political life should be shared by all the members of the political community. Suicide, whatever else it is, is a way of not sharing these burdens. But it may also be an appropriate, as it surely is a conclusive, way of renouncing them, and so it seems to be in the United States today. If we object to suicide, it is generally not for political reasons. The liberal state does not require its citizens to live, though it encourages them to do so, so long as they have reasons of their own. I want to examine three cases in which it has been argued with considerable force that men are required to live and that suicide is not an appropriate way of renouncing political obligations. These cases will seem alien to our experience, or to the experience of most of us. It is worth asking why this is so and whether or not anything of value was lost when we gave up the idea that citizenship makes suicide morally impossible. I will begin by listing the three cases, so that their distance from our own case is immediately apparent.

A. In the *Nichomachean Ethics*, Aristotle takes up the question of whether a man can treat himself unjustly (which is similar to the question of whether a man can have obligations to himself) and then considers the problem of suicide.

170

He who through anger voluntarily stabs himself does this contrary to the right rule of life, and this the law does not allow; therefore he is acting unjustly. But towards whom? Surely towards the state, not towards himself. For he suffers voluntarily, but no one is voluntarily treated unjustly. This is also the reason that the state punishes; a certain loss of civil rights attaches to the man who destroys himself, on the ground that he is treating the state unjustly.[2]

I am not sure what is entailed in saying that a man cannot treat himself unjustly. Perhaps Aristotle means that no man can possibly believe his own (voluntary) actions to be unjust to himself, else he would not commit them. His self-slaughter is not unjust, then, because he does not regard it, or experience it, as murder. Now if he were obligated only to himself, this view of the matter might well constitute the only judgment that could be made of his action. He is not, however, obligated only to himself, but also to the political community; there are other judges in his case; other men than himself have expectations as to his behavior. The state, or rather, the body of magistrates or citizens, believes that he owes it something more than his voluntary death or that he owes it his voluntary death only at times of its choosing. So it calls his suicide, and Aristotle agrees, an injustice to itself, hence a criminal act.

B. Sir William Blackstone, in his *Commentaries on the Laws of England,* treats suicide as a special sort of homicide, in which the victim is not, for obvious reasons, the man who is killed.

The law of England wisely and religiously considers that no man hath a power to destroy life, but by a commission from God, the author of it; and, as the suicide is guilty of a double offense, one spiritual, in invading the prerogative

---

[2] Aristotle, *Nichomachean Ethics,* trans. David Ross (London, 1954), bk. V, chap. 2, p. 134. I am not sure what force to assign to the phrase "through anger." Perhaps Aristotle intends to indicate some special heedlessness of civic responsibilities, but I do not believe it is the anger that makes the injustice.

of the Almighty, and rushing into his immediate presence uncalled for; the other temporal, against the king, who hath an interest in the preservation of all his subjects; the law has therefore ranked this among the highest crimes.[3]

The power of the king, presumably, is enhanced by the sheer number of his subjects, and this is certainly one source of his interest in their preservation. Blackstone may also believe that he is responsible to God for their safety—even though he must also have a commission from God to destroy them when he believes it necessary. He stands in God's stead as benevolent father and angry sovereign. In another part of the *Commentaries*, Blackstone argues that subjects owe a "debt of gratitude" to the king for preserving them in their infancy and, indeed, up to the very moment when they contemplate death or some other form of desertion.[4] Their status as subjects, then, is a permanent bar to suicide; self-murder is a crime not against the self, but against God and the king.

C. In December 1964 a man named Augusto Martinez Sanchez, an official of the Cuban revolutionary government, committed suicide. Fidel Castro issued the following statement:

> We are deeply sorry for this event, although in accordance with elemental revolutionary principles, we believe this conduct by a revolutionary is unjustifiable and improper . . . We believe that Comrade Martinez could not consciously have committed this act, since every revolutionary knows that he does not have the right to deprive his cause of a life that does not belong to him, and that he can only sacrifice against an enemy.[5]

I know nothing more about Comrade Martinez, though it seems fair to assume, from the tone and contents of the statement, that his act was in fact conscious, that he was neither

---

[3] William Blackstone, *Commentaries on the Laws of England*, bk. IV, chap. 14.

[4] *Commentaries*, bk. I, chap. 10.

[5] Fidel Castro in *New York Times*, December 9, 1964.

insane nor delirious at the time he committed it. In that case, Castro tells us, his act was a crime against the revolution, a movement or a cause or a band of men to which Martinez was fully committed. Like a soldier, he had a right to die only when he had an obligation to die or to risk death, that is, when he stood face to face with the enemy. A twentieth-century revolutionary is to the revolution as an eighteenth-century Englishman is to the king and a fourth-century Athenian citizen to the polis: bound up in a political relation which, whatever its other characteristics, precludes suicide. What can we say about these three relations? Can any political bond stand as a morally effective bar to suicide?

The three relations described by Aristotle, Blackstone, and Fidel Castro are obviously not the same (though later on I will suggest some similarities among them). They refer to very different sorts of political allegiance and association, and they do not by any means exhaust the range of difference. Now surely we can say of some of the possible sorts of allegiance and association that they are not a bar to suicide. Any political bond that can legitimately be broken by rebellion, withdrawal, or departure, for example, can also be broken by suicide. Thus, in the case of the Athenian polis, if the Laws are right when they tell Socrates (in Plato's dialogue *The Crito*) that he could have left the city at any time before his trial, if the departure of a citizen is always legitimate, then it is hard to see why suicide could ever be called illegitimate. From the point of view of the polis, its officers, and its citizens, there cannot be much difference between a dead and a departed citizen (though death might be preferable to departure since it adds no strength to a potentially hostile neighbor). The Greeks generally regarded exile as a kind of civic death, and it is not implausible to regard suicide by analogy as an ultimate expatriation.

Apparently the Athenians did not recognize the same parallelism, not, at least, if departure was as easy as the *Crito* suggests. Suicide was not easy, or rather, it was not easy to commit a legal suicide, though it is important to note that there were procedures for doing so. "At Athens," Durkheim reports, "if [a man] asked authority of the Senate before killing himself, stating the reasons which made life intolerable to him, and if his request was regularly granted, suicide was considered a legitimate act." [6] This sounds very much like applying for a visa from a modern state, but it is impossible to guess at the solemnity with which the question was treated. We are probably wrong to imagine any sort of bureaucratic intervention between the unhappy citizen and the political community. Given the size of the polis, the Senate (actually the Council of the Areopagus) must have been more like "a little group of neighbors" than a contemporary draft board is, and its members, or some of them, probably knew something about the individual who petitioned them. They were concerned about his possible death because they were involved with him in "civic friendship" and not only because of their magisterial responsibilities.

Durkheim does not tell us what reasons were regarded as legitimate by the Athenians or whether or not the would-be suicide's civic obligations were taken into account. It seems likely that they were, and permission denied if it were thought that the polis required, or if it urgently required, the services of the man in question. For then his suicide would entail, as Aristotle says, an injury to the city. It was the clear implication of the citizen's petition that he had no right to injure the city and no right to decide for himself whether his death would constitute an injury. A passage in Libanius, a very late classical writer, suggests that permission was generally granted by the Athenian Senate, at least in the latter days of the city.[7] This may mean only that men urgently needed by the political community are not the sort of men who want to kill themselves. Or it may indicate something more important: that the Athenians (or the latter-day Athenians) believed the moments when communal membership overrides individual

[6] Émile Durkheim, *Suicide,* trans. John A. Spaulding and George Simpson (New York, 1951), p. 330.

[7] *Ibid.;* see also K. A. Geiger, *Der Selbstmord im klassischen Altertum* (Augsburg, 1888), pp. 59–60.

wretchedness to be very rare. They must be very rare, I should think, if the political community claims, as Athens did, to be based on the free consent of its citizens. On the other hand, there must be such moments if the body of citizens imagines itself, as the Athenians did again, to be a group of friends, mutually bound to certain common purposes, responsible to one another. Or rather, there must be such moments if the citizens are what they imagine themselves to be. We have (rightly) grown skeptical of such imaginings, but none of us has ever lived in a polis.

We are probably even more skeptical when confronted with the claim that some moral quality is inherent in the relation of a subject and his king. Yet this morality too has seemed real enough in the past and has given rise to a sense of commitment similar to that of an Athenian citizen—as in the case of the Stoic philosopher Euphrates who sought the permission of the emperor Hadrian before killing himself. (Hadrian gave his permission.) I do not think that I can specify the force of such commitments. Often they have had a genuinely personal quality, issuing in a peculiar kind of friendship between the king and at least some of his subjects, compounded of deference on the one side and *noblesse oblige* on the other. Whatever one wants to say about friendships of this sort, and however much they are conditioned by prevailing ideologies and distributions of power, they clearly can be and often have been voluntary relations. Men have chosen to found their lives on personal loyalty to other men no different from themselves, except for the crowns they wore, and have pledged their faith in the most solemn ways. But this same relation can also have a more attenuated form, to which the personal pledge is far less crucial. In this case, friendship is unlikely, and the king is more often described as a political father, his subjects as children whom he protects even though he does not know their names. He preserves their lives for their sakes, presumably, as well as for God's and his own, but without reference to their feelings in the matter and certainly without reference to their merely personal misery and despair. The king stands above the mass of his subjects, a distant, imposing figure of

175

paternal rigor and compassion, and saves them from their own willfulness. If he saves them for their sakes, they ought then to live for his; they owe their lives to him, and he, it might be said, owns their lives.

It is this second relation which Blackstone describes in legal language, and it is against this relation and all it implied legally and morally that the eighteenth-century revolutions were directed. In France the laws declaring suicide a criminal offense were immediately repealed; in the United States the same result was obtained more gradually in one state after another.[8] Though these were marginal acts in the history of the two revolutionary republics, I do not think it is unfair to suggest that the defense of suicide (against Blackstone's arguments and conceivably also against Aristotle's) was central to the intention of the revolutionaries. Patrick Henry would not have been proclaiming nihilist doctrine had he shouted, "Give me liberty *and* give me death!" In fact, the right to commit suicide is what many eighteenth-century writers meant— or rather, it is part of what they meant—by the right to life.[9] They meant to put a man's life entirely in his own hands. They meant to deny that his life belonged or ever could belong to the king or the state. They claimed instead that he could live as he liked (so long as he did not injure or threaten others) and that he could die if he liked. For many of them, the fact that men are actually capable of self-slaughter was the best proof of their standing as free and rational creatures. It was an advantage, Hume suggested, that mankind possesses even over God himself.[10] Surely the right to commit

---

[8] The French laws against suicide were repealed on January 1, 1790, on a motion by the famous Dr. Guillotin, who seems to have had a sustained interest in death. The Napoleonic Code of 1810 does not mention suicide. In the United States, attempted suicide remained a criminal offense in some states. See Helen Silving, "Suicide and Law," in E. S. Shneidman and N. L. Farbarow, *Clues to Suicide* (New York, 1957), p. 84.

[9] See Lester G. Crocker, "The Discussion of Suicide in the Eighteenth Century," *Journal of the History of Ideas*, 13:47–72 (January 1952), for a useful survey of both radical thought and the traditionalist response.

[10] David Hume, "On Suicide," in *Essays* (Oxford, 1963), p. 596.

suicide could never be surrendered to kings—or fellow citizens.

The revolutionaries and their intellectual predecessors thus insisted that allegiance was subject to abrupt terminations, though only through physical acts like emigration and suicide. Individuals could not disobey whenever they pleased, but they could escape their obligations altogether if their desire to do so was sufficiently strong. In the eighteenth century, that was a very radical claim indeed, as it suggested that political associations could have no other foundation than the consent, even the daily and weekly consent, of the associated individuals. This claim was soon challenged by the assertion, or, perhaps, the discovery, that there existed a moral bond between the revolutionaries and the revolution, which required a long term commitment and precluded suicide. Nevertheless, it is still an important claim, and so widely accepted today, so intimately bound up with our sense of ourselves and our politics, that it requires close analysis.

The political justification of suicide can take two forms as it is related either to specific sorts of oppression or to unhappiness in general. Both of these are very old; both were reaffirmed and strengthened by eighteenth-century writers. The first involves a description of suicide as the rightful self-assertion of a persecuted or tortured individual. The life of such a man may in fact be in the hands of the state, but it is surely not legitimately there. He can always resist, flee, or kill himself without doing wrong, at least, without doing wrong to the state. Blackstone refers to this sort of suicide (and also to the voluntary deaths of old or sick men) as "the pretended heroism, but the real cowardice of the Stoic philosophers, who destroyed themselves to avoid those ills which they had not the fortitude to endure." [11] Even he would hardly have argued, however, that the would-be suicide restrain his hand for the sake of his torturers. Any man has a right to insist that he does not belong to them.

[11] *Commentaries*, bk. IV, chap. 14.

The same argument can be put more generally, on behalf of men enslaved or oppressed, but not subject to immediate physical duress. As they are not obligated to live for their masters, so they are free to die for themselves. It is not difficult to imagine a slave for whom voluntary death represents not only a free choice, but the only possible free choice, hence freedom itself. In its most extreme form, this position has been stated by Kirollov, a character in Dostoevsky's novel *The Possessed*, who announces that he intends to commit suicide as the supreme act of self-assertion and so of rebellion against a tyrannical God. Kirollov makes the usual claim: my life is my own! But he believes this is the equivalent of saying: I am God! [12] I can think of no political analogue to this kind of theological rebellion. Suicide is at best a desperate and unsatisfactory way of making oneself sovereign—and, in contrast to Kirollov's case, it is not the only way.

The second defense of suicide is cogently argued in David Hume's essay on the subject, an essay unpublished during his lifetime because of its radicalism.

A man who retires from life does no harm to society: he only ceases to do good; which, if it is an injury, is of the lowest kind. All our obligations to do good to society seem to imply something reciprocal. I receive the benefits of society, and therefore ought to promote its interests; but when I withdraw myself altogether from society, can I be bound any longer? But allowing that our obligations to do good were perpetual, they have certainly some bounds; I am not obliged to do a small good to society at the expense of a great harm to myself: why then should I prolong a miserable existence because of some frivolous advantage which the public may perhaps receive from me? [13]

[12] Fyodor Dostoevsky, *The Possessed*, trans. Constance Garnett (New York, 1961), part 1, chap. 3, section 8.

[13] *Essays*, pp. 593–594. Crocker, "Discussion of Suicide," notes that Holbach's views were essentially similar (p. 57). See also the same argument put by Ibben in *The Persian Letters*, 76, which probably represents Montesquieu's opinion (Montesquieu, *The Persian Letters*, trans. J. Robert Loy [New York, 1961], pp. 156–157).

Hume's argument amounts, I think, to a justification of suicide whenever it is committed. All citizens, he is saying, are citizens for the duration of their enjoyment or for as long as they can avoid misery. At any moment when they feel utterly miserable, certain that their prolonged life would be a great harm to themselves, they can renounce their civic obligations and withdraw altogether from society—without reference to the circumstances of their fellow citizens. The only evidence that they do feel utterly miserable, of course, is that they actually do commit or attempt to commit suicide. Assuming a strong love of life, as Hume does, this is conclusive evidence. The motives that drive a man to suicide are *always* reasons sufficient to justify the act.

This is not an implausible position, especially if its other assumption is granted: that political association is an exchange of benefits. For it would be hard to argue that a man who does not believe his life worth living has received any significant benefits from the association. Surely he owes no gratitude to the king for preserving so wretched a life and, given the exchange system, any benefits he provides for others seem entirely gratuitous so long as he receives none for himself or none that please him. Even if the benefits he provides for others are not frivolous, as Hume cruelly suggests they will be, how can their social value be weighed against the private misery of a man who came into society only in order to be happy? No political association committed solely to that happiness, or committed solely to the pursuit of that happiness, can maintain much of a grip on a man who is wretched. In a sense, wretchedness and despair play a part in Hume's argument similar to that played by fear in Hobbes's. They set a precise limit to political obligation. As a man cannot be bound to die for the state if he is afraid, so he cannot be bound to live for the state if he is desperately unhappy.

The difficulty with both these limits is that they are subject to unilateral interpretation. It is not possible to argue with a man who announces that he has reached his limit, or at least it is not possible to argue with him in political terms. No official of the state can tell someone who refuses to fight that he is not sufficiently fearful to justify the refusal; nor can he tell someone preparing to kill himself that he is not unhappy enough. It can never be said that an individual's private feelings just do not matter when compared with some other social or political value. Yet state officials do want to say this sometimes, and other sorts of political leaders want to say it at other times, and one or the other or both may even need to say it. If they cannot refer to any stable structure of values, then they are likely to seek in public emotion an antidote to private feeling and stir up a kind of loyalty and patriotism that has no basis in day-to-day political experience. Hume's radical individualism may even have this as its necessary practical consequence: that the moral life of the community, which cannot be sustained by the exchange system, comes to rest instead on temporary but recurrent fits of patriotic exhilaration.

The inadequacy of Hume's argument is most dramatically illustrated by the fate of the men who refused, so to speak, to put their opinions in their desk drawers, but began to fight for them. They quickly found themselves locked into a political movement that denied to its own members certain of the freedoms they were fighting for. One of the first among these was the right to commit suicide.[14] Castro is entirely correct to insist that his denunciation of Comrade Martinez represents a long tradition of revolutionary thought. Nor does it obviously belong to that part of the tradition that heralds the betrayal of the revolution. It may well be one of the healthiest, and it is certainly one of the best grounded, forms of revolutionary discipline. It derives directly from the revolutionary's commitment. For the pledge he makes to his fellow militants and to the movement or party as a whole is in no sense a

---

[14] An interesting sign of this shift is the following Napoleonic "Order of the Day": "A French soldier ought to show as much courage in facing the adversities and afflictions of life as he shows in facing the bullets of an enemy. Whoever commits suicide is a . . . soldier who deserts the battlefield before victory" (quoted in Silving, "Suicide and Law," p. 83). The new theoretical attitude is clear in William Godwin's *Enquiry Concerning Political Justice* (London, 1798), I, 138–140.

promise to exchange benefits. Working for the cause may well make him happy, but he does not work in order to be happy, and his continued happiness cannot be regarded as the condition of his continued work. He cannot quit the movement or withdraw from the struggle whenever he feels like it, that is, whenever he is frightened or unhappy. He has joined up for the duration and accepted a kind of military discipline (though just what kind and who the officers are may be matters of dispute). Castro's reference to soldiering is appropriate, even when revolutionary work involves none of the immediate risks of battle. Like soldiers who fight side by side, revolutionaries come to count on one another's performances; they require of their comrades a pattern of cooperation and systematic activity that is morally coercive and cannot readily be terminated by any of the individuals involved. The revolutionary movement does not and cannot depend upon the momentary consents of its members.

Yet there must be some morally acceptable procedure by which a revolutionary who has changed his mind about revolution in general or about this particular revolution can escape his previous commitments, giving due warning to his fellows and acting in such a way as not to endanger them. This is so because of two serious ambiguities in the theory of revolutionary commitment and perhaps of political commitment in general: what does it mean (in Castro's words) to "belong to the revolution"? What does it mean (in my own paraphrase of Castro's intention) to "join up for the duration"? As for the first, I suppose Castro actually believes that the life of Comrade Martinez belonged to the revolutionary *state*. But that is not what he said, and what he said is subject to as great a number of interpretations as there are ideas of revolution. Every man has his own revolution. Even when he joins with others in a party or movement, he does not wholly surrender his own sense of what a revolution is. Rather, he and his comrades together commit themselves to an idea they all share, and that idea must exercise some control over their future actions and obligations. No man can bind himself to be, as Brecht argues in *The Measures Taken*, "a blank page

181

on which the revolution writes its instructions." [15] Blank pages are not moral persons and cannot be conceived of as making promises or having obligations. Revolutionaries can and of course do commit themselves to some decision-making procedure within some particular organization. But this commitment is limited by the agreed-upon purposes of the organization—though not, in this case, by the fear or unhappiness of the members since their private security and delight are not the agreed-upon purposes. It would be difficult to deny absolutely the right of withdrawal or suicide to a man who comes to believe that those purposes have been forgotten or replaced with others to which he never agreed. He undoubtedly owes an explanation to his comrades; he must give reasons and refer to their original commitment, and he must listen to their response. But how can he belong to a revolution that no longer belongs to him? [16]

Perhaps Comrade Martinez committed suicide because he was disillusioned with the direction the Cuban revolution was taking and deeply pessimistic about his own power to alter that direction. I have no evidence that this was the case, but if it was, then Martinez was not an aberration in the world of revolutionary morality. There are many historical examples of what might be called Catonic suicides in the face of the failure or the betrayal of the revolution. One of the best known is that of A. A. Yoffe, Trotsky's friend and an old Bolshevik, who killed himself in 1927.[17] In a farewell letter, Yoffe described his suicide as "a gesture of protest against those who have reduced the [Communist] Party to such a condition that

[15] Bertolt Brecht, *The Measures Taken*, in *The Jewish Wife and Other Short Plays*, trans. Eric Bentley (New York, 1965), sc. 2.

[16] This is perhaps too strongly stated: his comrades may feel his reasons not sufficiently serious to warrant, or the situation too critical to permit, his departure—and (in any given case) they may be right. But that only means that when a man takes his physical, he also takes his moral life into his hands. The same thing is true, though less dramatically so, when he terminates his membership in this or that political association; we should, I think, presume a general right to withdraw, but a particular man acting at a particular time has no absolute right.

[17] The story is told in Isaac Deutscher, *The Prophet Unarmed: Trotsky, 1921–1929* (London, 1959), pp. 380–384.

it is unable to react in any way against this monstrosity [i.e., Trotsky's expulsion]." The revolution had been betrayed, and Yoffe, who for twenty-seven years had, as he wrote, lived for socialism and not wasted a single day, now felt his life to be useless and without purpose. It would surely be hard to argue that he was obligated to go on living for the sake of the Party as it then was, though there were probably members of the opposition, Trotsky among them, who felt let down by his suicide and excused it only because of his age and infirmity. At Yoffe's funeral, Trotsky addressed his followers in the clearest possible terms, not so different from Castro's: "The struggle goes on. Everyone remains at his post. Let nobody leave."

For how long does the struggle go on? Is it ended, and with it the obligations of the participants, by defeat? This is what Yoffe's letter suggests, and not implausibly, for men cannot be bound to go on living and fighting for goals that no longer can be won, however deeply they are committed to those goals. Perhaps the individual revolutionary should not decide for himself that defeat is final; nor, however, can he be bound to accept the decision of some tattered remnant of the movement he once joined. Is the struggle ended by victory? Presumably the victorious revolution issues in a state to which the revolutionaries happily commit themselves. But I think it is important to stress that a new commitment is necessary and that its terms may be as different from those of the earlier commitment as the state is from the movement.

One way of describing that difference is to refer back to the military analogy, which has been common in arguments about suicide since classical times, and which may deserve to be taken literally. The movement is in some real sense (if we ignore the rhetorical extravagance and posturing of radicals during nonrevolutionary periods) always at war. The state is only sometimes at war. This distinction divides also the obligations of their members, for men are required to live for the movement or the state, it might be said, only at those moments in time when they are also required to die or risk death. Only when they depend on one another in this ultimate sense, so that each man is necessary and knows himself to be

183

necessary to the safety of the others and all of them are necessary for the defense of the cause, can they be bound to live—
and to die, if they must—for one another but not for themselves.

In the state as distinct from the movement, however, such
moments are occasional and not continuous. There are long
periods of time when mutual dependency is nowhere near as
acute as it is all the time during the period of revolutionary
struggle. The political authorities may, and probably will,
seek to perpetuate the sense of danger and the militancy it
bred and so sustain something like the old obligations. But the
two situations are clearly different, and the individual militant
cannot be bound to carry over into the period of victory and
consolidation the obligations he incurred in and for a very
different time. "Joining up for the duration" is a meaningless
phrase if the duration is subject to repeated redefinition or if
it is, simply, forever. There may come a time, then, when a
man can act for himself, kill himself for himself, disregarding
a community that does not, in any very strong sense of the
word, need his services. Perhaps Comrade Martinez justified
his own suicide in this way. If we agree that there is a close
connection between the obligation to live and the obligation
to die, the only way to dispute such a justification would be to
insist that the state was actually at war or that it faced a danger as acute or imminent as that posed by war. For warfare
clearly does establish very strong bonds of mutual dependency, at least among the men who fight together (the movement is made up of men who fight together), and perhaps
more widely. This is probably what Hegel means when he
writes that only in time of war does the state achieve its true
universality. Only then are "the rights and interests of individuals . . . established as a passing phase." [18] The same
thing might be said, I suppose, of the polis and the king: only
in time of ultimate crisis are the private rights of citizens and
subjects entirely surpassed.

[18] G. W. F. Hegel, *The Philosophy of Right* (trans. T. M. Knox),
par. 324; but it should be noted that Hegel does not grant "an unqualified right to suicide" at any time: see par. 70 (Addition).

The problem with this argument is that the obligation to live and the obligation to die or risk death are not really commensurate. One can die for the state only when the state is at war, but it is always possible to commit or not to commit suicide. (I am not committing suicide right now, though unfortunately for my argument, this is not because of my citizenship.) It is always possible to live for the state, either in expectation of future emergencies or out of a day-to-day sense of closeness and commitment. To insist that war is the only occasion when it is necessary to do this, when the individual right to commit suicide is transcended or surpassed (or simply lost) may also be to insist, as Hegel does, that war is necessary to the "ethical health" of the state. The least that can be said in reply is that this is not obvious: if war is clearly a time when men know that other men are counting on them, that does not mean that at any other time they can know that other men are not counting on them. Surely there is some sense in Rousseau's dictum that man is never useless to humanity, and this recognition leads naturally to the attempt to describe a political community whose members can commit themselves or have committed themselves to be useful—even in time of peace—to help the poor, console the unfortunate, and defend the oppressed, as Rousseau suggested.[19] In such a community, the citizen would turn to his fellows, not only when it is obvious that they need him but when they might need him, not only when moral bonds are most vividly felt but whenever they are known to exist. He would refer himself to the community as a whole, as the citizens of Athens apparently did, before taking his life into his own hands.

Now clearly we (in the United States) do not act in this way. We neither make the reference nor do we ask it, not at least of men who are related to us only in some political fashion. Among us, suicides are mourned, but not judged. This is not because our state is not at war—at the moment I am writing it is at war—but because of the kind of state it is. The point, then, is not to distinguish the revolutionary movement

[19] Jean Jacques Rousseau, *La Nouvelle Héloise*, pt. III, letter 22.

from the successor state, or war from peace, but one sort of political community from another.

The associations that I have briefly examined, that stand, or so it has been said, as a bar to suicide, have several things in common. They are relatively small groups; they involve close, even intimate, relations; and they involve voluntary relations. (Blackstone, of course, denies the last of these, but it is true nonetheless of the association of the king and his "men," if not of the king and all his subjects.) Obviously, these common features have something to do with the force of the obligation to live. They tend to bring that obligation very near to another sort of bond that most of us understand much better and admit more readily, that arises from familial relations or personal friendship. But it is just these features that are lost, or usually lost, to political associations in the modern world. The groups expand; the members grow apart; the moral tie is steadily attenuated. The predictable insistence of the political authorities that nothing has really changed is, rightly, I think, resented. For the city has in fact been transformed in scale, and civic friendship replaced by more impersonal forms of union. The king has ceased to be a personal leader; he has laid claim to an equal allegiance from all his subjects and become a legal sovereign, the head of a bureaucracy. The revolution has triumphed and created a state within which little of the solidarity of the revolutionary movement survives. Our own lives are determined, in part, by all these processes, and it is not surprising that we no longer feel obligated to live for the political community. Nor is it merely a matter of feeling: there is no *reason* for feeling obligated and no reason for suggesting that we ought to acknowledge the obligation without regard to our feelings. "Whatever connection there may be between our daily tasks and the whole of public life," writes Durkheim, "it is too indirect for us to feel it keenly and constantly." [20] However useful we may be or want to be, our usefulness is not organized or given expression within the political community. Now these facts are clearly a reflection on

[20] *Suicide*, p. 374.

186

the moral quality of the modern state. They may well constitute an entirely sufficient argument for its radical reconstruction.

Durkheim makes a further argument: not merely that the modern state is a community unique in human history, whose members possess (without noticeable pride) the absolute right to kill themselves, but that they actually do and will kill themselves in greater numbers than ever before, precisely because they possess the right. Alienated men strain toward death. This is surely the strongest possible argument against political alienation, and it forms the basis for Durkheim's urgent insistence that new associations be created, "a cluster of collective forces outside the state." [21] It has to be said that the statistics assembled by Durkheim and those studied since do not by any means provide conclusive evidence for this argument. Suicide rates are higher in modern than in traditional social settings, but the considerable variations among modern societies seem to relate to factors other than those on which Durkheim focused.[22] It is, in any case, virtually impossible to measure the number of people driven to self-slaughter by a missing factor, an absent quality they conceivably could not name even if it were of the first importance to them: the absence of political meaning and associational responsibility. But I do not think it implausible to argue more simply, and without reference to statistical controversies, that insofar as men once found a reason to live or to go on living in political commitment (as I have tried to suggest they did), their alienation within the modern state deprives them of that reason and so produces or may produce a new and profound readiness to die.

The obvious response to this bleak view is to urge that the modern state fosters and protects private life as it has never been fostered and protected before, and that men can (or, perhaps, should) find their reasons for living in their private lives and, above all, in their families. This has considerable

[21] *Suicide,* p. 380.
[22] See, for example, Herbert Hendin, *Suicide and Scandinavia* (New York, 1965), and the references there.

force, for the differing structures and life patterns of the nuclear family clearly play a large part in determining the suicidal rates, perhaps especially so in the modern world. Nor is it irrelevant that those political associations thought to bar suicide are usually described in familial terms. Subjects are taught to regard their king as a father and revolutionaries call one another brethren—as if to emphasize that the best reason an unhappy man can have for refraining from suicide is his family connection. Perhaps this is true; I am inclined to think it is, even if the family connection has a great deal to do with the unhappiness. But surely it puts an enormous strain on that connection if a man has no other reference than his relatives in a time of despair. The very fact that we do extend the uses of familial imagery to all sorts of other associations suggests a need that many of us, at least, share: to supplement our most intimate bonds. That means, to incur other obligations to live and possibly to die for other men and women. I do not want to insist that wherever such obligations cannot or cannot easily be incurred, the suicide rates will rise; there are, after all, other forms of self-destruction. But it does make sense to say that if the state is to act, as it should act, to preserve our lives, it must do more than protect our privacy.[23]

This is the heart of the matter: to be obligated to live for the political community (or for the king, or for the revolution) is to have a reason for living; indeed, it is to have a very good reason, and that is a very valuable thing to have. It is valuable even when suicide is not the immediate issue, even in the case of persons so insensitive as to be incapable of imagining their own deaths. But the value of such a commitment cannot be demonstrated statistically or in any other way. I have attempted only to suggest it by examining the moral quality of the associations (or of some of them) within which it has been experienced. To do this is not to insist that all men should have moral experiences of this kind. That is up

[23] I have not considered in this essay the question of whether the state has an obligation to prevent suicide in particular cases (over and above its more general obligation to preserve life). This suggests what might be a good reason for laws against attempted suicide: they permit police to intervene against the attempt.

to them. I do think, however, that there are moral experiences of this kind to be had. The freedom to die whenever we feel like it is a freedom we can legitimately surrender, if not to the modern state, then to some other group, which we can invent if necessary.

There is something admirable, even if, for us, something slightly macabre, in those Athenian citizens who came to the Senate to tell their peers that they were thinking of suicide and something admirable too in the Senators who listened. Perhaps Camus is right when he says, in *The Myth of Sisyphus*, that such thoughts rarely begin with any reflections, however obscure, on the social system or the relations of citizens. "Society has but little connection with such beginnings. The worm is in man's heart." [24] This is the conventional view, but Camus gave it unconventional power by publishing his words in 1942, when he was already involved in the French Resistance. He never suggests the possible value of such an involvement, never explores the meaning of the heart's social connections. But surely the *résistant* ought to appear among those modern heroes whom Camus so much admires, who know the worm, who face death without illusions, who lucidly choose to live (to risk living). Camus's analysis admits of no political heroism, and I would not be surprised to discover that some of his fellow *résistants* resented his book. If so, they pointed to a truth of their own experience more impressive than his philosophy: when an individual commits himself to a community (like Athens) or to a cause (like the Resistance), he may not kill the worm, he does not kill the worm, but he resolves to fight it or repress it if he possibly can. That is at least sometimes a resolution men want to make and are able to make, and then it is a resolution they ought to keep.

[24] Albert Camus, *The Myth of Sisyphus and Other Essays*, trans. Justin O'Brien (New York, 1955), p. 4.

9 *Political Solidarity and Personal Honor*

I didn't think we ought to take the building; I opposed the plan at our meeting. But once some people went in, I had to join them. It was a question of solidarity.—a Harvard undergraduate, April 1969

Years ago I was taught never to cross a picket line. At college my fellow students and I sang "Solidarity Forever" at marvelous parties, never to be forgotten. We thought mostly of one another while we pledged our hearts to the working class. That sentimental identification pointed us toward a particular sort of politics, marked more, I suppose, by a sense of solidarity with the oppressed than by any actual alliance, but still providing a purpose that life would otherwise not have had. Afterwards we watched each other carefully for the first loss of purpose, the first signs of selling out. Some of us, no doubt, sold out, but I can say with confidence that none of us ever betrayed the working class: we knew no workers to betray and no workers had any expectations as to our behavior. We moved into, and some of us moved out of, one or another left intellectual grouping. There we found our real comrades, though we still sang of a greater union that would make us strong. And our relations with our real comrades were (sometimes) still mediated by our imaginary or wished-for relations with the working class.

There is a problem here that I would like to explore (without any further personal reference), that has to do with what the Italian writer Ignazio Silone calls "the choice of comrades." [1] This choice lies at the very center of our ideas about morality and obligation. Unfortunately, it is not always the case that comrades choose one another; sometimes the choice is entirely one-sided. Silone, for example, "went over to the side of the proletariat," that is, he joined the Communist Party, a movement led mostly by men like himself, though the Party at least included substantial numbers of workers, whom its officials both served and exploited. Many similar radical groups are made up entirely of men who have "gone over." These men have acted well, surely, for love of the oppressed is the finest of passions. But who are their comrades? To whom are they committed? Solidarity is the patriotism of the Left; often it replaces the sense of citizenship and even the love of country. Yet it is a strange emotion, relating us simultaneously to actual and ideal co-workers, to a real organization and a community only dreamt of.

The real organization is the Party or some such group that serves or claims to serve the oppressed and whose members are loyal to one another, presumably, for the sake of that service. They share an ideal, but that ideal has to do with other people. Their organization is not usually mandated by those other people, though it is sometimes said to have been mandated by an impersonal agency on their behalf—much as God is said to have given the Church to a fallen mankind. "We can only be right with and by the Party," wrote Trotsky, "for history has provided no other way of being in the right." [2] That means, the Party is the only effective instrument of working class emancipation; the cause of the working class can only be sustained through disciplined work, obedient performances, *law abidingness*, within the Party. In the particular case, the assertion is certainly wrong, and it is fair to doubt

[1] Ignazio Silone, "The Choice of Comrades," *Dissent* 2:7–19 (Winter 1955).

[2] Quoted in Boris Souvarine, *Stalin* (London, 1949), pp. 362–363. Trotsky wrote this in 1924; the heroism of his subsequent career is a denial of it.

that any agent has or can have such an absolute appointment. But I am inclined to grant the possibility of a moral obligation mediated in this way: I am bound (I bind myself) to this or that organization because it serves the cause of those men, who are not members, to whom I am not bound, but whom I want to help (I believe they should be helped).

The actual obligation is to the other members, and what I agree to when I join with them is, first, that we will decide together the ways in which our chosen cause can best be served, and second, that we will act together, sharing risks, once we have decided. This is a serious commitment; it may give rise to what I have elsewhere called "the obligation to disobey," that is, it may override commitments of a more conventional sort to the state. (In the case of an oppressed group or of men really acting on behalf of an oppressed group, there may be no commitments to override.) It clearly does override mere individual inclinations and preferences. A man may join because he believes that this particular organization actually does serve the interests of the working class or the oppressed generally. Once he has joined, however, his beliefs are not so simply determinative of his actions. Now he must take into account the beliefs of his comrades and abide by their decisions.

It is not merely the claim of his comrades that he has committed himself to them and through them to the "side of the proletariat." They also claim a kind of collective wisdom as to how that "side" can best be served. Thus Bertolt Brecht's hymn to the Communist Party:

> The individual has two
> The Party has a thousand eyes.
> The individual sees a city
> The Party sees seven states.
> The individual has his hour
> The Party has many hours.[3]

[3] Bertolt Brecht, *The Measures Taken*, trans., Elizabeth Hanunian, printed in U.S. House of Representatives, Committee on Un-American Activities, *Hearings*, Sept. 24, 25, 26, 1947, 80th Congress, First Session (Washington, 1947), p. 206.

Now any individual who hopes to serve the oppressed must recognize that there is some force to this claim. The chief reason he has joined the Party, after all, is that he knows he cannot act effectively alone; nor can he act effectively on his own terms. He must cooperate with his comrades if he is to deal with the rest of the world, and he can hardly cooperate unless he respects his comrades and weighs their collective wisdom above his own. On the other hand, he cannot simply stop using his own eyes; at least, he cannot do so without paying a price: henceforth his commitment, like the faith of a medieval Christian, will be blind. If he surrenders his critical judgment entirely, dulls his mind and if necessary his senses, abases himself before the Party—as men and even intelligent men have often done—he ceases altogether to be a moral agent capable of making commitments to other moral agents. He turns himself into an automaton, giving over his self-control to his comrades. There is a great deal that could be written about the self-abnegation and even the self-destruction of leftist intellectuals and militants, acting, or so they persuaded themselves, for the sake of the working class, but always at the command of the Party.[4] Of the moral quality of the persons involved, there is little to write: they have yielded their liberty, and "to renounce liberty," as Rousseau argued, "is to renounce being a man, to surrender the rights of humanity and even its duties."[5]

A theory of consent and obligation must include a view of

---

[4] It is perhaps worth citing one extreme example of this surrender, a statement of the ex-Trotskyist Pyatakov after his capitulation to Stalin's Party: "a true Bolshevik will readily cast from his mind ideas in which he has believed for years. A true Bolshevik has submerged his personality in the collectivity . . . to such an extent that he can make the necessary effort to break away from his own opinions and convictions . . . There could be no life for him outside the ranks of the Party, and he would be ready to believe that black was white, and white was black, if the Party required it. In order to become one with this great Party he would fuse himself with it, abandon his own personality, so that there was no particle left inside him which was not at one with the Party" (quoted in Robert Conquest, *The Great Terror* [New York, 1968], p. 128).

[5] Jean Jacques Rousseau, *The Social Contract*, bk. I, chap. 4 ("Slavery").

the consenting self: the person who incurs and carries the obligation has to be and continue to be a person of a certain sort, an autonomous and responsible man or woman. Rousseau means to suggest that a slave is no longer a person of this sort; hence he has, as a slave, no obligations whatsoever. Clearly, there have been (there are) political associations whose members have sold themselves into a kind of slavery, that is, have given up the use of their critical judgment and foresworn the very possibility of moral choice. Such men may not have surrendered "the duties of humanity," but they have incurred no new duties by becoming members. They are not comrades, and we ought to be brutally skeptical when they speak of solidarity. Short of this extreme case, however, are all the hard cases, where the renunciation demanded by the Party or the movement is of something less than liberty itself, where the discipline enforced by the others is not utterly destructive of the consenting self, where the danger involved is far more subtle than slavery—the loss of a kind of moral balance almost as difficult to describe as it is to maintain: between my comrades and myself, my two eyes and their thousand eyes, my obligations and my—what?

The citizen's point of reference is the political community, but as a man he has other memberships, other references, and these he sometimes sets against the state. When he challenges the state, he says, "But my oath, my order, my commitment!" He does so, that is, as the member of a smaller group or one differently based, as a priest, for example, or a comrade. The priest or the comrade refers himself to the Church or the Party, but he too may have still other memberships and other references. So Church members challenge the state, and sect members challenge the Church. All these groups, however, rest finally on individual men, who determine the shape of their moral lives by their comings and goings, so to speak, their acts of adherence, opposition, and resignation. What determines these? Only the individual men themselves, moved by whatever moves them, their prejudices and principles, hopes and fears. Now imagine a man who adheres to the Party for the sake of the working class (or to the Church for

God's sake), finds comrades, joins in a complex and long-term project, incurs serious obligations, but then decides that he and his fellows are not in fact helping the working class (not in fact obeying God's will). It is entirely his own decision; he sees things, with his own eyes, in a certain way; he may be wrong. His comrades remind him of his pledge: solidarity forever! It is a frightening situation. He can only stay or leave; there is no middle ground; and if he leaves, he must do so by himself. The state is (most often) resisted by organized groups whose members sustain one another's spirit, but men leave the Party (most often) alone. I do not want to ask, what should he do? That depends on the particular case, the issues involved, the man himself. But what is the nature of the conflict?

"It is a matter of personal honor," writes Silone, explaining why he left the Communist Party, "to keep faith with those who are being persecuted." [6] This is a very suggestive, but not a precise formula. Silone never in fact pledged his faith to the mass of the persecuted (or the oppressed or the working class). There is no ready way of doing that. He committed himself *because of* his love for them, *in front of* the whole world, but specifically *to* the Party. Now if he decides to leave the Party, he must do so in public, giving his reasons, showing "decent respect" for the opinions of mankind and more especially of his comrades. But he is not obligated to leave, whatever his reasons for deciding to do so, for in the case as I am imagining it, no one is calling upon him to leave.[7] His obligations, if anything, point the other way: his comrades are calling upon him to stay and using every possible form of moral suasion to hold him fast. It is his "honor" that demands that he "keep faith" with people he does not know and to whom he has no concrete political ties and that he break faith (or terminate his relations) with people who can plausibly say they are counting on him. The conflict is be-

---

[6] "The Choice of Comrades," p. 17.

[7] The case would be quite different if we imagine some organized group of workers calling upon members of the Party to join in this or that action barred by Party discipline or simply to come over to them.

tween political obligation and personal honor or, to put it in more paradoxical form, between his duty and his integrity.

Honor and integrity are complicated notions, and I am concerned here with only a small part of the whole range of meanings they can have—that part that suggests the possibility of making a formal judgment about the strength of a man's principles and the value he attaches to them and to himself as the man who holds them.[8] Honor, in this sense, is consistent with a great variety of principles; it is inconsistent with the surrender of principle or with any denial of oneself as a man capable of choosing principles and then coherent courses of action. A man has integrity, in this sense, if his conduct derives consistently from a core of deeply held ideals or if he makes the decisions that moral life requires with real attention to his possibly conflicting ideals. With regard to his comrades and associates, we say that he acts honorably if he always tells them what his principles are, what his judgments are, what he really thinks, with absolute honesty, even if this involves breaking off his association with them.

Consider the case of the seventeenth-century English radical, Robert Everard, who is supposed to have told Oliver Cromwell: "whatsoever hopes or obligations I should be bound unto, if afterwards God should reveal himself, I would break it speedily, if it were an hundred a day."[9] Everard's argument was put in terms of conscience, but of a conscience shared with no other man; it could as easily have been put in terms of honor. "It is a matter of personal honor with me," he might have said, "always to keep faith with my God." Nor is such a man dishonorable in his relations with his fellow men, so long as he has announced to them that these relations are subject to the extraordinary danger of divine intervention. On

---

[8] I am using these words to approach Jean-Paul Sartre's notion of "authenticity" or "good faith"—as, for example, in his *Existentialism and Humanism*, trans. Philip Mairet (London, 1948), p. 58: "The attitude of strict consistency is that of good faith." "Honor" and "integrity" have the great advantage of being in common use in the English language.

[9] A. S. P. Woodhouse, ed., *Puritanism and Liberty* (London, 1938), pt. I ("The Putney Debates"), p. 34.

the other hand, Cromwell's response is entirely justified: that engagements ought not to be broken or so readily broken whenever someone imagines his personal scruples to be warnings from God. "We may not give too much way," he said, "to our own doubts and fears." That is true enough, and if Everard were our fellow citizen, we would certainly expect the authorities (who enforce contracts) to be hard on him. Even men who accept the reference to God might well refuse to form associations with someone so ready to make that reference so often. Yet it is difficult to refuse entirely to admire him: one suspects he had, what he certainly needed, the inner strength to stand alone.

Silone's case is formally the same, though his external reference is different, and we are likely to take it more seriously and attach more credit to his doubts and fears; they are doubts and fears more like our own. He describes himself as a person who intends to work for the working class. That intention leads him to join the Party; later, increasingly skeptical of those "usurping bureaucrats who have climbed on the shoulders of the poor," it leads him to leave the Party. What is constant throughout is his intention, his personal project, and his critical intelligence enlisted in his project. His comrades must run the risks of his intelligence, and doubtless they have been forewarned. He will do what *he* thinks best for the working class, and though he will hesitate a long time before defying his comrades, he will not hesitate so long as he would if his comrades were the workers themselves. The external reference is obviously important here, but it is not and cannot be determining: what is crucial is Ignazio Silone's honor.

It might be said, he is really keeping faith with himself, maintaining his own sense of himself, whether through the Party or against it. But he is not obligated to himself any more than he is obligated to all those persecuted men and women with whom he cannot or does not form any concrete political alliance. Nor does he form any alliance with himself. There may be aspects of our mental life usefully described in the metaphor of commitment, as if we had two selves, one of them wayward and likely to lapse unless reminded by the other of "his" promises. In fact, however, moral actors are not so complicated (and moral action far more difficult) than this metaphor suggests. A man has principles that actually govern his conduct (like Silone's "matter of honor") or conflicting sets of principles that force him to make hard choices, or he does not have such principles at all. If he does not, he is not betraying himself, whatever he does, for in the sense of the word "self" here implied, he has no self to betray. He is perhaps a weak man, but he is not selling out his convictions, whatever he does, he is only expressing the minimal force with which he holds them or his lack of confidence in his own intelligence and judgment. He is perhaps a good man, but his goodness consists entirely in yielding to the wishes of his associates and not in applying for himself the principles he and they supposedly share. Hence he is without integrity, for to have integrity is to be aware of and to act upon a set of beliefs and ideals. Those hapless figures bobbing up and down in every political current are similarly men and conceivably good men, but they too are without honor. Not that they are morally bound, to themselves or to anyone else, to steer their own course: that is simply what honorable men do.

Someone might respond to all this: "I do indeed jump into the passing current, but only when my name is called. It is a matter of personal honor with me always to do what my comrades call upon me to do." Here is a man who will do anything, and though he always acts conscientiously, or at least sincerely, telling himself over and over again that his comrades are upholding his own convictions, freely choosing and choosing again their solidarity, his talk of honor seems to me only desperate vanity. The rest of us can talk only of his usefulness or his lack of usefulness, as we talk of hacks or sycophants or those perennial enthusiasts whose agreeableness we never confuse with integrity. His case is exactly the same as that of the (doubtlessly sincere) patriot who says, "My country right or wrong!"

These are easy examples, however, and I ought to distinguish two more complex sorts of agreeableness. Neither of these will be novel to anyone with some experience of political life; nor will my comments be novel, for I need only suggest what we commonly feel (or what I think we commonly feel) about them. First, there is the comrade or associate who tells us: "I think this action is wrong (it will not help, it may even harm oppressed men and women), but I will stick with you; I will go along this time for the sake of our solidarity and our long-term service to the oppressed." He can certainly say this so often that it seems insincere, a merely routine hedging of his bets. But it is not at all a dishonorable thing to say. It expresses his private scruples or his strategic judgments, without giving either "too much way." Second, there is the comrade or associate who says: "I thought this was wrong, but after all, there is this reason for doing it . . . and that one . . . and this other that never occurred to me before . . . and it can always be said that *they* did it first . . . and so on." He can be very clever in inventing defenses of actions he (really) does not like, but as we listen we come to doubt that he is arguing for himself. Of course, he may be arguing on his own behalf, that is, in his interests: his conduct is probably best described as a form of ingratiation. He wants above all to go along, to approve . . . and be approved. His own principles are not in evidence.

By whom does he want to be approved? The leftist militant is rarely in a position to play the part of a democratic politician and bow to the will of the masses. He is more often drawn into a competition in devotion and militancy unchecked by the cooling presence of the people to whom he thinks himself devoted. He must prove himself to his comrades, and they can invent the most extraordinary tests, driving one another on to a dangerous and adventurist politics (and building, whether intentionally or not, an elite of militants). I do not want to suggest that this is the only cause of political adventures that compromise the principles of their participants. But it is one of the mechanisms at work today in the politics of middle-class student radicals; at least, it is at work whenever they surrender their intelligence, their "sweetness and light," their sheer competence for the sake of a communion in action that has painfully little to do with helping oppressed people and a great deal to do with their relations to one another. Most of these young radicals would never endure the discipline or recognize the solidarity of a group like the Communist Party, but they are enormously susceptible to the demands of their peers. They need to be reminded—it is one of my purposes here—of Silone's "matter of honor."

Now every political association depends upon its members to do what their comrades tell them—most of the time—to go along, to seek approval. So every political association must challenge the personal integrity of its members (some of the time) and demand some repression of their sense of honor or, at least, of their pride. Pride is honor at its highest pitch, the arrogance and egotism of a moral man, and it is one of the most profound sources of our faithlessness to our fellow men. Hence it is a danger to the community—as Shakespeare's Coriolanus, an aristocrat "too absolute," was a danger to the Roman republic. A man like Coriolanus is dangerous because he can never be a citizen or a comrade; he denies the very possibility of solidarity. Nor is it necessary to be an aristocrat to have such a developed sense of pride. The Left has had its share of moral egotism and arrogance, of leaders, for example, who insisted on their own ideological position with a fanatical rigor and a reckless commitment to detail, dividing the labor movement and dividing it again. But it is important to distinguish such men from someone like Silone, who finds himself driven *sometimes* to resist the pressure (and the temptation) of solidarity and to leave the Party or movement. When spokesmen for the Communist Party describe departing members as "petty-bourgeois individualists," they are accusing them of pride (perhaps of petty pride), but they miss the distinction, and they do so, of course, deliberately and systematically. Theirs may occasionally be a useful description, but in cases like Silone's, and in other cases too, there are better ones, that account for a greater number of departures.

This essay has been an attempt to offer one such description and to justify the men whom it fits, who have seen, with their own eyes, that the Party or the movement no longer serves the purposes to which it is pledged. They may be wrong, and they surely ought to recognize this and never make their decision easily or complacently. But they have sensed something very important, that "solidarity with the oppressed," despite the numbers of the oppressed, is sometimes a lonely politics, in which all a man can hold fast to is his own judgment as to what ought to be done.[10] There may be moments of exuberance and passion when it is all too easy to surrender that judgment, when no personal loss seems too great to bear. There may be moments of crisis when no loss is so great but that it ought to be borne. I am not thinking here of a loss of life, but of that inner life that a man defends when he defends his honor. At some point, surely, we must hope that he defends his honor. It is not difficult to imagine a community whose members have no honor to defend: their solidarity would be extraordinary, beyond doubt, beyond testing. But this imagined community would not be a happy, nor for long a free, association. Dishonor is not the same as slavery, but it is well along the way to moral enslavement.

Politics at its best is the art of overcoming pride and every sort of individual caprice while still associating honorable men—comrades who fulfill their commitments whenever they can, who take their commitments very seriously, but who have reasons for committing themselves, which they also take seriously, and who may not fulfill their commitments if these reasons ever seem to them to lose their force. The solidarity of such men is fragile, for it depends not only on the principles they share, the promises they have made, and the respect they have for one another, but also on the respect they have for themselves, for their own intelligence and judgment. They will stand together for a long time, avoiding every form of self-indulgence, but there are limits to their exuberance and to their moral union and, above all, there are limits to what

---

[10] "Nor does this mean that I should not belong to a party, but only that I should be without illusion and that I should do what I can" (Sartre, *Existentialism and Humanism*, p. 41).

they will do, even at one another's behest. Yet theirs is the only solidarity worth having, and it is almost certainly the only solidarity that can serve the cause of the oppressed— and someday include them too as self-respecting men and women.

10 The Problem of Citizenship

We have a number of words in the English language that describe the act of breaking faith with our fellow men: treason, treachery, betrayal. But we have only one word, or only one in common use, that describes the man who breaks faith: we call him a traitor. Traitor has both a general and a specific meaning; it names the faithless man but also and more particularly the faithless citizen. We single out no other kind of treason, treachery, or betrayal except that directed against the state. We have no word, for example, that refers specifically to the faithless son, friend, lover, political ally, or comrade in arms. All these we name with a word that always calls to mind the "crime against allegiance." Once we also singled out the faithless churchman or religious brother with such words as apostate or renegade, but today these words are not often used in their strict sense and they have come to signify (in Leftist polemics, for example) a man who renounces his principles rather than one who betrays his fellows.[1] This suggests very dramatically the priority citizenship is thought to have, as religion was once thought to have, in the moral

---

[1] "Turncoat" has the same meaning: "one who changes his principles or party, a renegade . . ." but not, like the traitor, "one who betrays any person that trusts him." See the *Oxford English Dictionary* for this and related terms. I should also note the word "betrayer," which appears occasionally in melodramatic literature, but is rarely used in common speech.

hierarchy. I wonder, though, if this priority too is not fading (for language registers our past and not necessarily our present moral intuitions). Some of us at least have doubts: traitor remains a term of moral execration, but it is not so easy in the mid-twentieth century to identify the traitor with the faithless citizen. Citizenship itself has become a problem.

We must consider, for example, the citizen whose state requires him to perform monstrous acts or to fight in brutal and unjust wars: do we want to call his disobedience treason? Or the citizen whose state divides before his eyes into warring factions: how can he be faithful? Or the citizen whose state is seized by a revolutionary party or conquered and then reestablished by an imperial power: where does his allegiance lie? These are the most obvious cases in which the word traitor seems to lose its meaning or defy our efforts at application.[2] But there is another case, nearer our own, where the state has simply outgrown the human reach and understanding of its citizens. It is not necessarily monstrous, divided, or subjugated, but its citizens are alienated and powerless. They experience a kind of moral uneasiness; their citizenship is a source of anxiety as well as of security and pride, and if they are not traitors in the specific sense of that word, they are sometimes hard put to explain what holds them fast. This is the kind of citizenship I want to examine; I begin by doubting or at least worrying about its moral priority.

In the history of Western political thought, there are two common ways of asserting that priority, two ways of defining or explaining the word citizen (which parallel the two conceptions of liberty so widely discussed in recent years). Taken as descriptions of our own political experience, both are false or partly false or no more than partly true. I will try to suggest the precise ways in which the two definitions fail.[3] Doing

[2] Andre Thérive, *Essai sur les trahisons* (Paris, 1951), provides many more examples.

[3] I am not concerned here with the dictionary definition or the legal meaning of the word, but rather with two definitional formulas, each of which is really an argument about the character of our political life. The ways in which we use "citizen" in everyday speech obviously reflect this life, and I will have some occasion to refer to them.

this will not by any means resolve the uneasiness of contemporary citizens, but recognize it, characterize it, perhaps even grant its permanence. There is a way of living with that uneasiness that I also want to consider, heralded by contemporary political scientists under the name "pluralism." As it is usually pictured, pluralism is a pleasant illusion, a more comfortable way of life than we have any right to expect. But it can be pictured differently and then it suggests a hard politics indeed. For a pluralist, at bottom, is a man with more than one commitment, who may at any moment have to choose among his different obligations. Citizenship is one of his obligations, but only one. Before considering what it means to have more than one commitment, however, I must consider citizenship by itself and suggest why, when taken in either its negative or its positive sense, it is something less than one commitment.

The citizen can be regarded first and most simply as the recipient of certain benefits that the state, and no other social or political organization, provides. This view has its origin in imperial Rome, I think, but it becomes prominent in political theory at the very beginning of the modern period. It is not unfair to identify it with liberalism—the reasons for doing so will become apparent as I go along—though it has played a part in the work of men not usually called liberals. Thus Jean Bodin, the early theorist of sovereign power, suggests the typical formula: "a citizen is one who enjoys the common liberty and protection of authority." [4] The word enjoys is somewhat ambiguous here and perhaps deliberately so. Bodin may mean "rejoices in," but I do not think so, for it is an essentially passive relation that he has managed to describe in the active voice. He might better have said, a citizen is one who is provided with liberty and protection. The state is thus conceived

[4] Jean Bodin, *Method for the Easy Comprehension of History*, trans. Beatrice Reynolds (New York, 1945), p. 158. In *The Six Books of a Commonweale*, ed. K. D. McRae (Cambridge, Mass., 1962), pp. 46ff., Bodin offers a different definition, in stricter accord with the theory of sovereignty, but he moves toward the formula of the *Method* in the course of his argument against Aristotle, see esp. p. 53.

as an instrument which serves individual men (or families), but not or not necessarily as an instrument wielded by those men themselves. It is wielded on behalf of the citizens and the citizens are simply those persons on whose behalf it is wielded. The group of citizens may be marked out by birth or residence or even consent, but its crucial characteristic is that it, and no other group, receives protection from a particular state.

Given this view, liberty and protection tend to merge: "political liberty," writes Montesquieu, "consists in security or . . . in the opinion that we enjoy security." [5] To be provided with liberty is to be protected against various sorts of interference whether by other men or by agents of the state itself. It is to be made secure in one's life (Hobbes) or in one's family and home (Bodin and Montesquieu) or in one's conscience and property (Locke). I do not want to denigrate this security; it is enormously valuable and doubtless to be enjoyed; it makes possible all sorts of enjoyment. I do want to point out, however, an essential feature of security in general: we cannot call a man secure unless he is freed from the need to provide security, on every occasion, for himself. In the liberal myth of the state of nature, individuals are imagined to have come together and created the instrument of their own security. That mythical act of creation is or is intended to be their last creative act. The descendants of natural men have the great advantage of inheriting security; they have nothing to do except enjoy it, and this is widely thought to be all they want to do. When we say that a man is the citizen of this or that state, then, we say nothing about his characteristic activities; we mean merely that the authorities of that state (whoever they are and however they are chosen) acknowledge an obligation to protect his person and his private life.

In turn, he is supposed to acknowledge an obligation to obey the law and even to "protect his protection." It would be curious if this last were an obligation owed or said to be owed to the state—as if a man could be bound to risk his life

[5] Montesquieu, *The Spirit of the Laws* (trans. Thomas Nugent), XII, 2.

for his instrument (an artist for his brush, a carpenter for his saw, a citizen, in this view, for his state). The authorities may well expect gratitude from the citizens they protect, and insofar as they achieve some public personality, as in a monarchy, they may get it. But the protection they provide is by no means a piece of benevolence or a gratuitous act. They are authorities only because they provide protection, and it is hard to see that any gratitude is due them.[6] Social contract theory suggests more plausibly that the citizen is bound not to the authorities at all, but to his fellow citizens, bound, that is, to protect *their* protection because or so long as they protect *his*. The difficulty with this is that the description of the citizens as recipients of benefits suggests no relations among them, or no continuing relations once the contract is signed, that would warrant any such obligation. It suggests instead an indefinite number of distinct and singular relations between the individual citizens and the authorities as a body—a pattern that might best be symbolized by a series of vertical lines. There are no horizontal connections among citizens as citizens. Even a phrase like Bodin's "common liberty" does not evoke a liberty collectively enjoyed but only a liberty individually enjoyed by everyone. And that means that the status of political obligation (insofar, at least, as obligation depends upon the existence of a political community) is radically unclear.

But there is an obvious ambiguity in the description of the authorities as men who provide, the citizens as men who receive, protection. Who decides what precisely is to be protected? Who decides whether or not the protection is sufficient? Insofar as the state is the instrument of the men for whom it provides, it would be illogical in the extreme to allow the instrument and not the men to make decisions. Even a theorist like Hobbes, who gives enormous power to the authorities, recognizes that ultimately the individual citizen

---

[6] Gratitude is apparently what J. P. Plamenatz has in mind when he argues that the obligation to obey may be "a special case of the general obligation to help persons who benefit us" (*Consent Freedom and Political Obligation* [Oxford, 1968], p. 24).

must judge the sufficiency of his own protection. Locke says the same thing, and goes on to recognize, as Hobbes does not, the right of a number of individuals who feel inadequately served by the authorities to combine against them. In fact, however, if all these citizens do is complain to one another, they have established or begun to establish a political tie not readily encompassed by the first view of citizenship. This is the case even if they are exercising a "common liberty" to complain. Similarly, though the right to participate in political decision-making may be protected by the state, and even institutionalized in one or another kind of electoral process, its exercise by any considerable number of citizens points toward a view of citizenship very different from that urged by the theorists of security. The difference is hard to put precisely because of the real importance of political liberty in its negative sense, but it can be suggested if we ask again, who decides?

The answer must now be, anyone who chooses to exercise the protected right to participate (I will assume for the moment that everyone's right is equally protected). And the usual expectation of liberal theorists is that only men dissatisfied with the security they receive will choose to participate in any very active fashion. Indeed, there is a profound tension between private enjoyment (as they described it) and public activity—the vulgar parallel, perhaps, of the tension discovered by classical writers between philosophy and politics. Why should we be active in politics? asked Hobbes, and his sarcastic reply points to a central animus of liberal theory:

> to have our wisdom undervalued before our own eyes; by an uncertain trial of a little vain-glory to undergo most certain enmities . . . to hate and be hated . . . to lay open our secret councils and advices to all . . . to neglect the affairs of our own families.[7]

Locke, too, suggests that politics will be the activity of the few (authorities on trust), interrupted only when it becomes abu-

[7] Thomas Hobbes, *De Cive, or The Citizen*, X, 9.

sive by revolution, the activity of the many. Barring a "long train of abuses," ordinary men will enjoy the common liberty in their shops, churches, and families and have no political life at all. Nor will they seek any such life; they will not relish the distractions of committees, debates, mass struggles, or yearn (even secretly) for power. Or, the power for which they yearn will be found in wealth and not in office. Effectively, then, most of the time and in most of the cases, the authorities will decide.

Now this arrangement seems unsatisfactory for obvious reasons: because there is no everyday politics to which the authorities can refer themselves, they are all too likely to plunge into the cycle of abuse and revolution. Nor will they be able even between revolutions to claim the loyalty (though they may have the forebearance) of the citizens. So far as I know, there is only one solution to these difficulties within the confines of the first view of citizenship. That is to constitute the authorities as a random sample of the body of citizens, a picture of the whole and not merely of some leading class or caste or professional group. The relevant procedures, whether the ancient lottery or the latest scientific sampling techniques, have occasionally been discussed in the literature on representation.[8] But the idea has never been widely canvassed, and this is curious since it would have the happy effect of producing a government sensitive (presumably) to every nuance of private discontent—without ever requiring anyone to engage in political activity. The arguments against it, of course, are very clear: we would not want to be governed by citizens who knew nothing of the arts of government, who had no commitment to the general well-being, who conceived themselves and were commonly conceived to be private men, politically passive until they were randomly selected to be politically active. The lottery worked in ancient Athens (if it did work) precisely because the common view of the citizen and his own self-image were so very different from this. I am inclined to think the same argument holds for an elected gov-

[8] See Hannah Pitkin, *The Concept of Representation* (Berkeley, 1967), pp. 73–75 and references there.

ernment, where the candidates at least are activists: elections "work" best when the citizens are active, too. If we urge citizens to inform themselves about issues, to go to meetings, to join this or that political party or movement, however, we are talking to them in terms very different from those of writers like Bodin or Locke.

The description of citizens as passive recipients of benefits is inadequate because it tells us nothing about the political and moral dimensions of citizenship (I mean, of the word itself as we ordinarily use it and of our own experience as citizens even in liberal society). Or rather, it tells us something we are not, I think, ready to accept: that the life of the citizen is flat, two-dimensional, marked by private and social concerns, but never heightened or, in a less friendly phrase, puffed up by political aspiration. That description fits enough people to make it plausible, but it is wrong in three ways. It hides even from those people the latent politics of their passivity and acquiescence (which simply puffs up the authorities). It tells us nothing about who the authorities are and how they are chosen, and if they are elected, as in our own case, it does nothing to explain the role of citizens in the electoral process; nor does it account for the obligation we commonly feel to participate. It denies the lively interest in political power, in the well-being of men other than ourselves, in public action and renown, that many of us still have (in part, *because* we are citizens) and cannot altogether repress.

In brief, if the citizen is a passive figure, there is no political community. The truth, however, is that there is a political community within which many citizens live like aliens. They "enjoy" the common liberty and seek no further enjoyment. They are not traitors, in the specific sense of that word, and indeed there are professional students of politics quick to tell them, what the early modern theorists also believed, that the security of the state is improved by their passivity.[9] That is to put a great deal of trust in society's trustees, the everyday decision-makers of the liberal state, and perhaps that trust is

---

[9] See, for example, Bernard Berelson et al., *Voting* (Chicago, 1954), chap. 14.

justified. But there is another view of the authorities, well within the liberal tradition and sometimes dominant there, according to which the common liberty can be secured only by the "eternal vigilance" of the citizens. Not only occasionally, in moments of revolutionary outrage, but regularly and consistently over time, they must protect themselves and each other against their putative protection. I am afraid our citizen-aliens do not measure up to that, so they may well fail, if they do not actually betray, the political community. Though it is not without its pleasures, eternal vigilance is the very opposite of private enjoyment.

Bodin's formula is intended as a repudiation of Aristotle, whose views the French writer considers at some length. There can be no doubt that he was aware of what he was doing; he denies explicitly that citizenship entails any kind of political activity. This is what Aristotle had asserted: a citizen is a man who rules and is ruled in turn.[10] Aristotle is referring here to the practice of the Athenian polis where certain political offices were held in turn by all the citizens. In working out his definition he chose to emphasize the actual exercise of executive or judicial powers, the periodic holding of office, though he might equally well have emphasized the continuous exercise of deliberative powers, the regular meetings of the assembly. In any case, the spirit that lies behind "ruling and being ruled" must be ever present: it consists in the lively sense of oneself as a participant in a free state, concerned for the common good. Bodin aims at something different, not a sharing of power and concern, but an exchange (whose precise character was later made more explicit) between the powerful and the powerless, an exchange of obedience for security or the sense of security and of acquiescence for contentment: "there is no better proof of a good and effective

---

[10] Aristotle's formal definition is: "a man who shares in the administration of justice and in the holding of office." He later suggests, however, that this may describe only the citizen of a democracy and offers a more general formula: "he who enjoys the right of sharing . . ." (*Politics,* trans. Ernest Barker [Oxford, 1948], bk. III, chap. 1, pp. 106–109).

state than to . . . maintain the citizens in contentment."[11] This presupposes a spirit that might best be characterized as a lively longing for private pleasure. The contrast is clear enough, and I do not think I have overemphasized it. It was restated with special intensity by Rousseau, who sought to revive the classical view in the face of the latter day followers of Bodin and Locke: "As soon as public service ceases to be the *chief business* of the citizens . . . the state is not far from its fall. When it is necessary to march out to war, they pay troops and stay at home; when it is necessary to meet in council, they name deputies and stay at home."[12]

In the modern democratic state, an interesting combination of the two views of citizenship has been worked out: if contemporary citizens name deputies to deliberate on their behalf, they also march out to war, at least sometimes, themselves. Except for young men in time of war, however, it can hardly be said that public service is ever their chief business, and the second view shares in the combination, I think, chiefly as an ideal and an ideology. It is an ideal of the Left and of those modern liberals influenced by the Left, like John Stuart Mill. The demand for a more active citizenship is also, of course, a demand for a more equal protection of the right to be active. But that equality is sought primarily because of the belief that "ruling and being ruled" or self-determination is the proper destiny of the individual human being. Political activity, even eternal vigilance, is not the price of liberty; it is liberty manifest. Man the citizen, who obeys only the laws he has made, is man at his very best: free, virtuous, and powerful.

This imposing and difficult ideal becomes an ideology whenever we are told that we are already citizens, men at or near our very best, and that our country is a nation of citizens. We should all be more active, patriotic orators tell us, but they manage to say this without ever suggesting that we are so inactive as to render our citizenship inauthentic or the ideal suspect. They proceed to deduce our obligations (to

[11] *Method*, p. 278.
[12] *Social Contract*, bk. III, chap. 15.

participate, to obey, to fight, and so on) from that ideal. This is mystification of the worst sort, but it might be argued that it serves a useful purpose: it keeps the ideal uppermost in our consciousness. Ideology is the social element within which ideals survive, and this may well be true even when the ideology is perfectly hypocritical. For if hypocrisy is the tribute that vice pays to virtue, then it serves at least to sustain the social recognition of virtue.

The problem, however, is with the ideal as well as with the ideology. Aristotle and Rousseau are very clear about this. They argue that citizenship as they describe it is only possible in very small states (Athens, Geneva, possibly a federated Poland).[13] Here is one of the major differences between the two views of citizenship: the first can be extended indefinitely; the second, whether or not we accept the severe limits on scale urged by Aristotle and Rousseau, cannot. The quality of the protection offered by the state is not affected by the number of persons to whom it is offered. Or, if it is affected at all, it probably improves as that number increases (up to a point, at least) and economies of scale are realized. But the quality of participation and even the opportunities for participation of whatever quality almost certainly decline as numbers increase. It is not only that the actual efficacy of the individual citizen is reduced: this may be calculated, Rousseau suggests, as the fraction $\frac{1}{n}$, where n is the total number of active citizens.[14] The citizen's ability to act with whatever fractional efficacy he is presumed to have is also reduced, largely as a function of organizational complexity, itself made necessary by the problems of size and scale. The development of large-scale organizations progressively restricts the access points of individual citizens to the decision-making process and narrows or distorts the view any one of them can have of the process as a whole.

[13] Aristotle argues that the state must be small enough so that the citizens can "know one another's characters" (*Politics*, bk. VII, chap. 4, pp. 342–343).

[14] *Social Conract*, bk. III, chap. 1. Rousseau concludes, "the larger the state, the less the liberty," since the individual's power of self-determination declines as n increases.

Despite all this, and for reasons I will discuss a little later, the sense of efficacy among American citizens remains surprisingly high and large numbers involve themselves in public affairs, if only minimally. They do not make this their chief involvement, nor even a very important one in their lives; nor do they often act so effectively as the fraction $\frac{1}{n}$ suggests. If their number is large, it does not by any means include all those who can legally call themselves citizens. Hence, citizenship cannot be defined as an involvement even of this minimal sort. The relation of those who act politically to those who do not is unclear. I see no reason to grant even the plausibility of an argument recently made: "If all citizens have an approximately equal opportunity to act, there is a high probability that those who do act will be roughly representative of those who do not." [15] Surely those who choose to act will be unrepresentative by virtue of that very choice: they have political concerns that the others, for some reason, do not share. Once again, it seems desirable to be governed by citizens with public interests and it is hard to imagine being governed by anyone else. But if the nonpolitical citizens are neither present nor represented, what obligations can be deduced from their citizenship? Are they bound to obey laws they have not prescribed to themselves? Perhaps they are, but then they have none of the qualities of citizenship in the second sense: they are not free, or virtuous, or powerful.

It would not be difficult to increase the number of participating citizens, and some modern states, especially revolutionary states in search of obedience and legitimacy, have set themselves this goal. The techniques by which it can be reached are various—propaganda, bribery, coercion—and they do not necessarily require that participation be a meaningful form of "ruling." In states like our own, the same goal might be reached more simply by making political action even less time- and energy-consuming than it already is (putting a voting booth on every street corner, for example) and by drawing public attention even more than we already do to politics

[15] Robert A. Dahl and Charles E. Lindblom, *Politics, Economics and Welfare* (New York, 1953), p. 313.

conceived as a spectator sport. These possibilities are somehow unattractive, and so they invite us to re-examine the ideal. It might be said that the easier participation becomes, the less serious it will be and the less freedom, virtue, and power it will express. This is a puritanical objection, but all the more useful for that since citizenship in the second sense is a puritan ideal. "Chief business" implies hard work, and that requires a great deal more than a sporting interest in electoral competition. It requires an ethic of hard work, a commitment sustained over time, an attention to detail even in matters not of immediate relevance to oneself, a kind of "public spirit." None of this can be generated by patriotic oratory or by government *fiat* or by any sort of political huckstering. But there is another motive for participation that I have said too little about; politics in the absence of public spirit is sometimes, after all, as serious as we could want it to be. Citizens are driven into action by their particular interests, chiefly economic: they think they have been injured (they are usually right) or they anticipate injury or they hope for some sort of material advance. They are Lockeian men. Yet they are not driven continuously by their interest, at least, they are not driven continuously *into politics*, nor are all political questions matters of interest to them unless they have a sense of the whole over and above their sense of themselves as particular persons. It is upon some such sense of the whole that the ideal of citizenship rests. And so the ideal is not served by enticing or dragging citizens into the public arena who have no awareness of their business there and no commitment to the public business; only the ideology is served. Given the scale and complexity of action in the arena, however, and the extraordinary character of the commitment required, we might plausibly conclude that the ideal is unserviceable.

The truth about political activity in the modern state is that it does require hard work, that the citizens by and large do not do that work and probably cannot, and that the authorities can and do. As Hegel suggests in *The Philosophy of Right*, it is only the bureaucrats (we can add, the professional politicians) whose chief business is the public business and who "find their satisfaction in . . . the dutiful discharge of their public functions." [16] They are citizens in lieu of the rest of us; the common good is, so to speak, their specialty. What does "ruling and being ruled" mean, then, in the modern state? It is a special way of being ruled. It empowers the authorities, gives them a legitimacy different from and, perhaps, higher than the legitimacy they earn by providing protection on the exchange system. I do not mean to suggest that the activity of those citizens who choose to be active, even minimally so, is a fraud or a piece of self-deception. If the authorities can be empowered, they can also (sometimes) be removed from power, and that important possibility is what contemporary writers have in mind when they call one or another state democratic. But this is something less than self-government. In no state called democratic do the citizens actually exercise power; nor does that seem a lively possibility.

When the word citizenship is used ideologically, the claim is being made that citizens do exercise power—on the cheap, as it were, with little expense of spirit. That claim is simply wrong in the case of those men and women who do not participate at all. With regard to the rest, it is ambiguous: they are implicated in the exercise of power, since it is exercised with something like their consent. That implication is what the authorities have in mind when they urge citizens to participate. For the citizens, however, it must be a problem. The authorities may well involve them in actions of which they profoundly disapprove, and involve them, or so they are told, by their own choice. In some sense that is right, and the pressure is very strong to go along or to oppose such action with nothing more than their $\frac{1}{n}$ effectiveness.[17] War is the hardest case and one that I want to dwell on for a moment, not only because of its contemporary relevance, but also because it poses crucial issues in the clearest and most direct light.

[16] C. W. F. Hegel, *The Philosophy of Right* (trans. T. M. Knox), par. 294.

[17] A man can increase his effectiveness, obviously, by acting outside the system whose rules are constraints on all other actors—though he runs certain risks in doing so, not least that the others will join him outside.

Then the claims of the state are strongest, though there are also strong arguments to be made, as I have suggested elsewhere, for the toleration of conscientious objectors. But when the authorities commit the citizens to a war many of them believe to be profoundly unjust, their problem is not only whether to fight or not, but how to continue to live in the state those authorities govern, in whose politics they are implicated. Perhaps this is the problem of any minority in a critical time, but I am not thinking now of the citizens organized in this or that party or movement which may well be too small to elect new authorities or enforce new policies. I am thinking of the citizens as citizens, who are told they make decisions, who are implicated in the decisions made, but who do not in fact decide. Hence the portrait of a contemporary citizen (sketched from life): compromised, anxious, guilty, impotent. Treason must be a temptation for such a man: to break his bonds, to do what seems right, to help the enemy! But he is too hapless actually to become a traitor; he takes no firm political line at all. There is yet another temptation and an easier one; he can escape his guilt by denying his involvement, insisting that (or acting as if) he is a citizen only in the first sense of the word. Then he can say, "I am involved in this war only if it is being fought for my protection; but it is not (or I do not believe it is); so let the authorities hire mercenaries; I will do what I please." This frees him from all the mystifications to which the second view of citizenship is susceptible, but that is not all it does. It also denies whatever reality lies at the bottom of the mystery. Now there is no community with whose moral unity or participatory politics he can beguile himself.

Thus, on the one hand we have a definition of citizenship that simply misses the moral and political implications of the word and of our own lives *as citizens*. On the other hand, we have a definition that insists upon those implications and yet fails to describe any reality we know or can project for the future. The first is a statement, not quite straightforward, of our alienation from all that is public and common; the second is an ideological mask of that alienation or a vain (and possibly dangerous) fantasy of its transcendence. Many of us, at least, cannot manage to be good citizens on either definition: we are not sufficiently passive for the first, nor is it clear that our passivity would be compatible with equal protection; we are not sufficiently active for the second. The solution to this dilemma does not necessarily lie somewhere between the two. Both definitions have elements of truth, each is attractive in its fashion, and there is probably no way of resolving the contradictions between them. We can, however, reduce the force of the contradictions if we recognize that the ties between individual citizens and the political community are not only direct, as both definitions imply, but also mediated. The citizen stands to the state not only as an individual, but also as the member of a variety of other organizations with which the state must relate in relating to him.

Pluralism is a great comfort, at least, the doctrine of pluralism is a great comfort. It enables us to describe the citizen as a communal man and a participant at the very moment when citizenship by itself does not seem to permit either description. A citizen, we might say, is a man whose largest or most inclusive group is the state. Both the earlier definitions can be reinterpreted in the light of this one. First of all, the citizen is protected not only in his privacy but also in his associations and with his chosen comrades. I do not mean only that he shares in the "common liberty" of association—though that is an important liberty and one that the state sometimes must protect against coercive groups—but also that the groups themselves have standing with the state (or more informally, within the political process) so that citizens can make decisions about the quality of the protection they receive together. Moreover, and this is a point much emphasized in contemporary pluralist literature, the individual citizen is protected by his associations and by his comrades, so that their eternal vigilance and not simply his own is the price of his liberty. The costs of citizenship are dispersed and even shared.

Second, the citizen governs himself most actively in groups

218

other than the state, groups that sometimes play an informal, sometimes an official, role in determining state policy. Self-determination is an indirect process made possible by the participatory politics of church members, union members, party members, and so on. It has been argued by pluralist writers that participation in lesser groups prepares men and women for citizenship.[18] This is wrong insofar as it assumes that participation of the same sort is possible in the state. Yet members of lesser groups do have a considerably greater sense of their efficacy as citizens than nonmembers do, and they are probably more effective because of the training they receive in the techniques of political action. But in pluralist theory, groups are less important as training grounds than as alternate forums for "ruling and being ruled." They provide space and facilities for an important human experience that might otherwise be impossible. This argument is put very clearly by Hegel, who anticipates much of contemporary pluralism and suggests its compatibility with state power:

> Under modern political conditions the citizens have only a restricted share in the public business of the state, yet it is essential to provide men . . . with business of a public character over and above their private business. This work, which the modern state does not always provide, is found in the corporations.[19]

Thus the moral and political meanings of the word citizen find expression, and around these meanings grow up interests and concerns to which the authorities reach out, groups that they overlook and protect. "This is the secret of the patriotism of the citizens," writes Hegel, ". . . because it is the state that maintains their particular spheres of interest, together with the title, authority, and welfare of these." [20]

This is surely the great strength of a pluralist citizenship:

[18] See A. D. Lindsay, *The Modern Democratic State* (Oxford, 1943), for the argument in its classic form.

[19] *Philosophy of Right,* par. 255 (Addition). Hegel's "corporations" are simply the secondary associations of his own time: guilds, religious bodies, societies of scholars, and perhaps also local governments.

[20] *Philosophy of Right,* par. 289.

that it not only implicates the citizens in state policy, but generates real obligations and an authentic patriotism by recognizing a sphere within which they actually have scope for meaningful action. Still there is a difficulty here Pluralism builds loyalty not only toward the state but also against it. It builds moral and political conflict into the political system. I think it is worthwhile at this point to recall the earliest meaning of the word, which stresses just this conflict: pluralism once described a practice thought to be immoral, whereby a priest or minister accepted more than one benefice and committed himself to more than one set of pastoral duties. This was thought immoral because it was widely believed that one man could only fulfill the duties of one parish; the commitments were mutually exclusive. We do not generally think pluralism immoral because we choose to imagine the groups to which the citizen commits himself as complementary in some sense or at any rate not exclusive. We picture them as a set of Chinese boxes, one fitting neatly into the next, all contained within the state, or as a series of overlapping circles within the larger circle of the state. We stress the adjective "lesser" in the phrase "lesser groups," regarding these as secondary associations and the state as somehow primary.

This is often the case, but not always or for all men, and we must ask ourselves whether we want to justify pluralism only when it is the case. The view that the authorities will usually take is put with brutal frankness by Hegel: popular participation in lesser groups, he argues, "is all the more permissible, the more trivial, from the point of view of the universal affairs of state, is the intrinsic worth of the business which in this way comes to ruin or is managed less well or more laboriously." [21] There are two kinds of triviality involved here, and, since they can appear separately or together, they need to be carefully distinguished. The business itself can be

[21] *Philosophy of Right*, par. 289. The passage continues: "And further, it is all the more permissible, the more this laborious or foolish management of such trivial affairs stands in direct relation with the self-satisfaction and vanity derived therefrom." Note that civil servants derive "satisfaction" from their work (par. 294); ordinary men only "self-satisfaction and vanity."

trivial: then the groups are lesser in the strict sense of that word, that is, concerned with lesser things. Or, the business managed "in this way," that is, with popular participation, can be trivial. So far as the second of these is concerned, Hegel's statement might be revised for the sake of clarity: if the business is serious, as it often is, popular participation is all the more permissible the more trivial is *its role* in the actual management of that business. This preserves Hegel's central assumption that anything is better done if done by trained bureaucrats. It is not necessary, however, that these bureaucrats be civil servants in order for them to be sufficiently like civil servants so that the latter will not complain about the difference. Nor will citizens pay much notice to the difference. When bureaucrats share or compete for power among themselves, citizens neither share nor compete. They are twice-alienated, within the state and within the "lesser" group. And if the work they do is trivial (in either of the senses I have distinguished, one or the other of which seems to fit most examples of contemporary pluralism), so will the obligations engendered in the course of the work be trivial. Then the pluralist mediation loses its moral and political value; it becomes, like citizenship in the second sense, an ideal and, more important, an ideology—not a comfort but an illusion of comfort.

The demand for a more serious pluralism is pervasive in contemporary political science, but I am not sure that the writers who make that demand or echo it are always aware of the moral and political conflicts they are setting up. For if the business of the "lesser" groups is not trivial, then the "universal affairs of state" will lose their distinction. And the authorities in turn will lose their distinction: they will be challenged by a multitude of "lesser" authorities "dutifully discharging their public functions." These are the inevitable products of pluralist participation: a citizen whose largest or most inclusive group is the state is not simply a citizen of the state. He has other responsibilities, for there is no way to be a responsible citizen except to have more than one responsibility. That does not mean that he will not be a good citizen most of the time, protecting his protection (if only for the sake of his comrades) and sharing in the public business. In the sense of the word to which I have paid most attention, he will be the best possible citizen, free because he governs himself, virtuous because of his public spirit, powerful because his actions have significant effects. But if the authorities launch some action of their own of which he disapproves, he will be a dangerous man and he may find himself, whether he is happy about it or not, living dangerously. This is the meaning of Morton Grodzin's profound remark: "All patriots are potential traitors." [22] The secret of their patriotism is also the secret of their treason: they are committed to "business of a public character," but not always to the same piece of business or kind of business as are the authorities.

Grodzin intends to describe our own situation, and it is worth considering the possibility that his words are especially true now, when patriotism (for many of us) is inauthentic, the state seems out of reach, and citizenship is a hollow or a confusing and anguished experience. A man who commits himself elsewhere and discovers or creates a sphere of public action may also find himself forced into opposition, confronting the state with greater hostility than he would if the state were realized differently in everyday life. If it were realized differently, articulated in a genuinely pluralist way, then increased participation in organized groups might well reduce the tensions of political life and the strain toward treason. Certainly there are times (now) when it is perfectly consistent with their own view of the state for the authorities to foster voluntary association and even to decentralize state functions. They enhance their authority if not always their power by doing so. But it would not be entirely honest to rest the argument for a serious pluralism on such considerations. The reasons for pluralism lie elsewhere. They have to do with the sorts of protection that are necessary and the sorts of self-determination that are possible in the modern state. If we imagine a citizen maximally protected and maximally self-

[22] Morton Grodzin, *The Loyal and the Disloyal: Social Boundaries of Patriotism and Treason* (Cleveland, 1966), p. 213.

determining, we are not imagining a citizen maximally obedi-ent.[23] I can make this point especially clear by turning briefly to the connections between pluralist activity and class conflict.

Pluralism has often been described as the liberal (or the American) answer to Marx.[24] Multiple and overlapping mem-berships are said to dilute class consciousness and to weaken the force of its attendant struggles. There is certainly some truth to this argument. I do not doubt, for example, that pat-terns of ethnic and racial identification, even when these are not manifest in organized group life, cut dramatically across class lines and complicate politics in ways Marx did not fore-see. But two further points need to be made. First of all, class conflict requires class organization, even multiple organization. and is hardly possible without it. There is no reason to accept the old Wobbly notion that the class struggle can only be fought by "one big union." On the contrary, periods of in-tense struggle have been marked by an enormous prolifera-tion of groups (many of which clearly had overlapping mem-berships). Thus the "rise" of the bourgeoisie was expressed in the rapid and extraordinary expansion of its group life: churches, sects, clubs, parties, leagues, associations of all sorts played a part. Second, class quiesence is expressed in the ab-sence of group life or its failure to expand. It correlates, as one would expect, not with overlapping membership, but with nonmembership. For membership *is* participation, and participation breeds conflict.

Now in the United States, as in other countries, pluralist experience is closely related to socioeconomic status: the higher a man's status the more experience he is likely to have. Americans as a whole and on the average belong to a larger number of organized groups than citizens of other countries

[23] That pluralism may not promote "order" and yet still be socially and morally valuable is the argument, or part of the argument, of an important essay by William Leon McBride, "Voluntary Association: the Basis of an Ideal Model, and the 'Democratic' Failure," in *Voluntary Associations*, ed. J. Roland Pennock and John W. Chapman, *Nomos XI* (New York, 1969), pp. 202–232.

[24] See, for example, John W. Chapman, "The Political Theory of Pluralism," in *Nomos XI*, p. 98.

with whom they have been compared (hence our greater faith in our own political effectiveness). Yet most Americans, particularly those in the lower class, have very little experience with public business of any sort. A majority belong to no more than one "secondary" association; only 24 percent describe themselves as belonging to groups involved in any way in politics.[25] One might suggest, then, that the American answer to Marx is not pluralism, but passivity and privatization. Increased working class activity in any of a variety of organizations would almost certainly generate or intensify the sorts of conflict Marx meant to describe. It would have this effect even if it did not also have the effect of producing a group of people ready to say, with him, that "the working men have no country."[26]

What such people are likely to say, or to feel, is that they have more than one country (or more than one loyalty). That is the direct consequence of their organization into groups whose work is not trivial. Before they are organized, they have less than one country. For then they can be described as citizens only in one or the other of the first two senses of the word, and these, as I have argued, exaggerate or distort the moral significance of the protection they receive and the public business they transact. From the point of view of state power, I am not sure how to choose between these two conditions—something more than citizenship and something less—but I suspect, as do the authorities, that the second is safer. The state's is not, however, the only possible point of view, and I want to conclude this essay by speaking from the perspective of the individual citizen (though not on his behalf: that he must do for himself).

The citizen is safer, it seems to me, in his groups, safer from bureaucratic neglect or abuse, safer also, as the example of the working class suggests, from social oppression. He is more capable of judging the quality of the protection he receives

[25] This information is from Gabriel A. Almond and Sidney Verba, *The Civic Culture: Political Attitudes and Democracy* (Princeton, 1963), chap. 10.

[26] Karl Marx, *The Communist Manifesto*, intro. Harold Laski (London, 1948), p. 142.

and more capable of protecting himself. The citizen is more responsible in his groups, more responsible in the state which is the largest or most inclusive of these, but not only there. He rules and is ruled; he helps in the making of policies and he helps in carrying them out, and he does both these things in the state where his $\frac{1}{n}$ effectiveness is very small and in other groups where it is much greater. Now these two, protection and responsibility, are the substantive values implied by the word citizenship. Insofar as the individual "enjoys" (shares in) these values, he may well rejoice in them.

Not that his moral or political life will be easy: in the best of times, he will face difficult decisions; in the worst of times, he will have to choose his treason. I do not want to argue that citizens are obligated to say no to all those men who offer to relieve them of such choices, to make their lives easy and their work trivial. Some citizens, doubtless, have assumed obligations to say no, but that is not true of all or most of them. In the modern democratic state, citizens are bound to certain sorts of obedience, but not to eternal vigilance or to the hard work of "ruling." Pluralist participation is not a duty, but only a means to realize values that ought, perhaps, to be realized, values that are carried, as it were, by the word "citizenship" and that many of us want to uphold, but to which individual citizens are not necessarily committed. But we should be clear about our alternatives. If we are not willing to rule in our turn, other men (Hegel's civil servants, professional politicians and professional revolutionaries, corporate bureaucrats, and so on) will rule out of theirs. They will call us citizens, but we will be something less. Perhaps I should say, they do call us citizens, but we are something less.

Appendix: Three Kinds of Citizenship

In various of these essays, I have suggested that citizens come in kinds and degrees and that all of those men and women legally bound to the state are not in fact morally bound in the same way. It may be useful to list the three kinds of citizenship and obligation that I have distinguished. Obviously, the list is not exhaustive, nor can my brief characterizations do more than suggest the complexity of moral life in the modern state and the difficulties involved in recommending some particular course of action to one's fellow members.

First, the *oppressed citizen:* he counts for less than his fellows, sometimes for a great deal less, when it comes to the protection of life, liberty, property, and welfare, and he acts with less effect. But he is not entirely unprotected, else he would not be a citizen even in the legal sense, and he can join in political activity, though his path is hard and often dangerous. In his struggle against oppression, he has a wide range of moral options (which he can share, as it were, with other citizens working with him or on his behalf). His obligations depend upon the ways in which he chooses and manages to involve himself in the larger community.

Second, the *alienated citizen:* he receives whatever protection the state provides and lives every day with his fellows in the shadow of that protection. But he does not participate at all in political life; he chooses not to participate (for whatever reason). He thinks of the state as an alien though not necessarily as a hostile force, and he wants only to live in peace under its jurisdiction. He is bound to those actions necessary for the safety of the social life he shares, but not to actions dictated by "reason of state."

I should note that I have identified alienation here with

self-alienation, treated it as a kind of boycott of the political system.[27] However, the word is a confusing one, or it is used confusingly, and often in an entirely different sense. So there may be another kind of alienated citizen: the man who participates in political life but only in ways that fit the ideology, not in ways that fit the ideal, of citizenship. That is, he is active in essentially trivial ways (what is trivial and what is not remains, of course, a matter of argument). The alienated citizen (2) is not self-made, but a product of the system and its ideology. He is unlikely to experience conflicts of obligation, and for this reason he is widely regarded as a "good" citizen. If the state stands over him as an alien force, he does not know it; he thinks it is his own.

Third, the *pluralist citizen:* he receives protection and shares in ruling and being ruled, not in spite of his plural memberships but because of them. Citizenship (as a moral choice rather than a legal status) is possible only if there are other groups than the state within the state, and it is fully accepted only by joining other groups along with the state. This means that at any given moment, citizens fall into one of two categories. They belong to groups that are actually making claims against the state, and then they *may be* obligated to disobey its laws. The state in its turn may or may not tolerate their disobedience: if it does, they are conscientious objectors; if it does not, they are disobedient citizens and, in critical cases, traitors. Or, the citizens belong to groups that are not putting forward such claims (and whose work is not trivial), and then they are simply bound, bound without complications, to obey the laws they help in making.

In either of these categories, pluralist citizenship meets the specifications of leftist idealism. This is my own idealism too, and I have tried to defend it throughout this book. But I do not want simply to deny what might be called the opposite idealism: the acceptance of alienation, the love of a private life. Just as there is or can be an important moral tension between political solidarity and personal honor, so there is a

[27] On the extent of this "boycott," see E. E. Schattschneider, *The Semi-Sovereign People* (New York, 1960), chap. 6.

tension between political responsibility and personal privacy. Something must be said here of the rights of the ardent noncitizen: hence the last of these essays. I do not need to say much, for the noncitizen usually finds his own ways to escape the moralizing of political men.

11   A Day in the Life of a Socialist Citizen

Imagine a day in the life of a socialist citizen. He hunts in the morning, fishes in the afternoon, rears cattle in the evening, and plays the critic after dinner. Yet he is neither hunter, fisherman, shepherd, nor critic; tomorrow he may select another set of activities, just as he pleases. This is the delightful portrait that Marx sketches in *The German Ideology* as part of a polemic against the division of labor.[1] Socialists since have worried that it is not economically feasible; perhaps it is not. But there is another difficulty that I want to consider: that is, the curiously apolitical character of the citizen Marx describes. Certain crucial features of socialist life have been omitted altogether.

In light of the contemporary interest in participatory democracy, Marx's sketch needs to be elaborated. Before hunting in the morning, this unalienated man of the future is likely to attend a meeting of the Council on Animal Life, where he will be required to vote on important matters relating to the stocking of the forests. The meeting will probably not end much before noon, for among the many-sided citizens there will always be a lively interest even in highly technical problems. Immediately after lunch, a special session of the Fish-

[1] Karl Marx and Friedrich Engels, *The German Ideology*, ed. R. Pascal (New York, 1947), p. 22.

ermen's Council will be called to protest the maximum catch recently voted by the Regional Planning Commission, and the Marxist man will participate eagerly in these debates, even postponing a scheduled discussion of some contradictory theses on cattle-rearing. Indeed, he will probably love argument far better than hunting, fishing, *or* rearing cattle. The debates will go on so long that the citizens will have to rush through dinner in order to assume their role as critics. Then off they will go to meetings of study groups, clubs, editorial boards, and political parties where criticism will be carried on long into the night.

Oscar Wilde is supposed to have said that socialism would take too many evenings. This is, it seems to me, one of the most significant criticisms of socialist theory that has ever been made. The fanciful sketch above is only intended to suggest its possible truth. Socialism's great appeal is the prospect it holds out for the development of human capacities. An enormous growth of creative talent, a new and unprecedented variety of expression, a wild proliferation of sects, associations, schools, parties: this will be the flowering of the future society. But underlying this new individualism and exciting group life must be a broad, self-governing community of equal men. A powerful figure looms behind Marx's hunter, fisherman, shepherd, and critic: the busy citizen attending his endless meetings. "Society regulates the general production," Marx writes, "and thus makes it possible for me to do one thing today and another tomorrow." [2] If society is not to become an alien and dangerous force, however, the citizens cannot accept its regulation and gratefully do what they please. They must participate in social regulation; they must be social men, organizing and planning their own fulfillment in spontaneous activity. The purpose of Wilde's objection is to suggest that just this self-regulation is incompatible with spontaneity, that the requirements of citizenship are incompatible with the freedom of hunter, fisherman, and so on.

Politics itself, of course, can be a spontaneous activity,

[2] *German Ideology,* p. 22.

freely chosen by those men and women who enjoy it and to whose talents a meeting is so much exercise. But this is very unlikely to be true of all men and women all the time—even if one were to admit what seems plausible enough: that political life is more intrinsic to human nature than is hunting and cattle-rearing or even (to drop Marx's rural imagery) art or music. "Too many evenings" is a shorthand phrase that describes something more than the sometimes tedious, sometimes exciting business of resolutions and debates. It suggests also that socialism and participatory democracy will depend upon, and hence require, an extraordinary willingness to attend meetings, and a public spirit and sense of responsibility that will make attendance dependable and activity consistent and sustained. None of this can rest for any long period of time or among any substantial group of men upon spontaneous interest. Nor does it seem possible that spontaneity will flourish above and beyond the routines of social regulation.

Self-government is a very demanding and time-consuming business, and when it is extended from political to economic and cultural life, and when the organs of government are decentralized so as to maximize participation, it will inevitably become more demanding still. Ultimately, it may well require almost continuous activity, and life will become a succession of meetings. When will there be time for the cultivation of personal creativity or the free association of like-minded friends? In the world of the meeting, when will there be time for the tête-à-tête?

I suppose there will always be time for the tête-à-tête. Men and women will secretly plan love affairs even while public business is being transacted. But Wilde's objection is not silly. The idea of citizenship on the Left has always been overwhelming, suggesting a positive frenzy of activity and often involving the repression of all feelings except political ones. Its character can best be examined in the work of Rousseau, from whom socialists and, more recently, New Leftists directly or indirectly inherited it. In order to guarantee public-spiritedness and political participation, and as a part of his

critique of bourgeois egotism, Rousseau systematically den-
igrated the value of private life:

> The better the constitution of a state is, the more do public
> affairs encroach on private in the minds of the citizens.
> Private affairs are even of much less importance, because
> the aggregate of the common happiness furnishes a greater
> proportion of that of each individual, so that there is less
> for him to seek in particular cares.[3]

Rousseau might well have written these lines out of a deep
awareness that private life will not, in fact, bear the great
weight that bourgeois society places upon it. We need, beyond our families and jobs, a public world where purposes
are shared and cooperative activity is possible. More likely,
however, he wrote them because he believed that cooperative
activity could not be sustained unless private life were radically repressed, if not altogether eradicated. His citizen does
not participate in social regulation as one part of a round of
activities. Social regulation is his entire life. Rousseau devel-
ops his own critique of the division of labor by absorbing all
human activities into the idea of citizenship: "Citizens," he
wrote, "are neither lawyers, nor soldiers, nor priests by profession; they perform all these functions as a matter of duty." [4]
As a matter of duty: here is the key to the character of that
patriotic, responsible, energetic man who has figured also in
socialist thought, but always in the guise of a new man, freely
exercising his human powers.

It is probably more realistic to see the citizen as the product
of collective repression and self-discipline. He is, above all,
dutiful, and this is only possible if he has triumphed over
egotism and impulse in his own personality. He embodies
what political theorists have called "republican virtue"—that

[3] Jean Jacques Rousseau, *The Social Contract*, bk. III, chap. 15.
[4] Jean Jacques Rousseau, *Considerations on the Government of Poland*, in *Political Writings*, trans. Frederick Watkins (Edinburgh, 1953),
p. 220.

means, he puts the common good, the success of the movement, the safety of the community, above his own delight or
well-being, *always*. To symbolize his virtue, perhaps, he
adopts an ascetic style and gives up every sort of self-decoration: he wears sans-culottes or unpressed khakis. More important, he foregoes a conventional career for the profession
of politics; he commits himself entirely. It is an act of the most
extreme devotion. Now, how is such a man produced? What
kind of conversion is necessary? Or what kind of rigorous
training?

Rousseau set out to create virtuous citizens, and the means
he chose are very old in the history of republicanism: an authoritarian family, a rigid sexual code, censorship of the arts,
sumptuary laws, mutual surveillance, the systematic indoctrination of children. All these have been associated historically
(at least until recent times) not with tyrannical but with republican regimes: Greece and Rome, the Swiss Protestant
city-states, the first French republic. Tyrannies and oligar-
chies, Rousseau argued, might tolerate or even encourage li-
cense, for the effect of sexual indulgence, artistic freedom,
extravagant self-decoration, and privacy itself was to corrupt
men and turn them away from public life, leaving government to the few. Self-government requires self-control: it is
one of the oldest arguments in the history of political thought.[5]

If that argument is true, it may mean that self-government
also leaves government to the few. At least, this may be so if
we reject the disciplinary or coercive features of Rousseau's
republicanism and insist that citizens always have the right to
choose between participation and passivity. Their obligations
follow from their choices and do not precede them, so the
state cannot impose one or the other choice; it cannot force
the citizens to be self-governing men and women. Then only
those citizens will be activists who volunteer for action. How
many will that be? How many of the people you and I know?
How many ought they to be? Certainly no radical movement

---

[5] It is sympathetically restated by Alan Bloom in his introduction to
Rousseau's *Letter to M. D'Alembert on the Theatre*, in *Politics and the
Arts* (Glencoe, Illinois, 1960), pp. xv–xxxviii.

or socialist society is possible without those ever-ready participants, who "fly," as Rousseau said, "to the public assemblies." [6] Radicalism and socialism make political activity for the first time an option for all those who relish it and a duty—sometimes—even for those who do not. But what a suffocating sense of responsibility, what a plethora of virtue would be necessary to sustain the participation of everybody all the time! How exhausting it would be! Surely there is something to be said for the irresponsible nonparticipant and something also for the part-time activist, the half-virtuous man (and the most scorned among the militants), who appears and disappears, thinking of Marx and then of his dinner? The very least that can be said is that these people, unlike the poor, will always be with us.

We can assume that a great many citizens, in the best of societies, will do all they can to avoid what Melvin Tumin has called "the merciless masochism of community-minded and self-regulating men and women." [7] While the necessary meetings go on and on, they will take long walks, play with their children, paint pictures, make love, and watch television. They will attend sometimes, when their interests are directly at stake or when they feel like it. But they will not make the full-scale commitment necessary for socialism or participatory democracy. How are these people to be represented at the meetings? What are their rights? These are not only problems of the future, when popular participation has finally been established as the core of political and economic life. They come up in every radical movement; they are the stuff of contemporary controversy.

Many people feel that they ought to join this or that political movement; they do join; they contribute time and energy—but unequally. Some make a full-time commitment; they work every minute; the movement becomes their whole life and they often come to disbelieve in the moral validity of life out-

[6] *Social Contract*, bk. III, chap. 15.
[7] Melvin Tumin, "Comment on Papers by Riesman, Sills, and Tax," in *Human Organization*, 18:28.

side. Others are established outside, solidly or precariously; they snatch hours and sometimes days; they harry their families and skimp on their jobs, but yet cannot make it to every meeting. Still others attend scarcely any meetings at all; they work hard but occasionally; they show up, perhaps, at critical moments, then they are gone. These last two groups make up the majority of the people available to the movement (any movement), just as they will make up the majority of the citizens of any socialist society. Radical politics radically increases the amount and intensity of political participation, but it does not (and probably ought not) break through the limits imposed on republican virtue by the inevitable pluralism of commitments, the terrible shortage of time, and the day-to-day hedonism of ordinary men and women.

Under these circumstances, words like citizenship and participation may actually describe the enfranchisement of only a part, and not necessarily a large part, of the movement or the community. Participatory democracy means the sharing of power among the activists. Socialism means the rule of the men with the most evenings to spare. Both imply, of course, an injunction to the others: join us, come to the meetings, participate! Sometimes young radicals sound very much like old Christians, demanding the severance of every tie for the sake of politics. "How many Christian women are there," John Calvin once wrote, "who are held captive by their children!" [8] How many "community people" miss meetings because of their families! But there is nothing to be done. Ardent democrats have sometimes urged that citizens be legally required to vote: that is possible, though the device is not attractive. Requiring people to attend meetings, to join in discussions, to govern themselves: that is not possible, at least not in a free society. And if they do not govern themselves, they will, willy-nilly, be governed by their activist fellows. The apathetic, the

[8] John Calvin, *Letters of John Calvin*, ed. Jules Bonnet, trans. David Constable (Edinburgh, 1855), I, 371. Of all alternate communities, the family is clearly the greatest danger to the movement and the state. That is not only because of the force of familial loyalty, but also because the family is a place of retreat from political battles: we go home to rest, to sleep.

occasional enthusiasts, the part-time workers: all of them will be ruled by full-timers, militants, and professionals.

But if only some citizens participate in political life, it is essential that they always remember and be regularly reminded that they are . . . only some. This is not easy to arrange. The militant in the movement, for example, does not represent anybody; it is his great virtue that he is self-chosen, a volunteer. But since he sacrifices so much for his fellowmen, he readily persuades himself that he is acting in their name. He takes their failure to put in an appearance only as a token of their oppression. He is certain he is their agent, or rather, the agent of their liberation. He is not in any simple sense wrong. The small numbers of participating citizens in the U.S. today, the widespread fearfulness, the sense of impotence and irrelevance: all these are signs of social sickness. Self-government is an important human function, an exercise of significant talents and energies, and the sense of power and responsibility it brings is enormously healthy. A certain amount of commitment and discipline, of not-quite-merciless masochism, is socially desirable and efforts to evoke it are socially justifiable.

But many of the people who stay away from meetings do so for reasons that the militants do not understand or will not acknowledge. They stay away not because they are beaten, afraid, uneducated, lacking confidence and skills (though these are often important reasons), but because they have made other commitments; they have found ways to cope short of politics; they have created viable subcultures even in an oppressive world. They may lend passive support to the movement and help out occasionally, but they will not work, nor are their needs and aspirations in any sense embodied by the militants who will.

The militants represent themselves. If the movement is to be democratic, the others must *be represented*. The same thing will be true in any future socialist society: participatory democracy has to be paralleled by representative democracy. I am not sure precisely how to adjust the two; I am sure that they have to be adjusted. Somehow power must be distributed, as it is not today, to groups of active and interested citizens, but these citizens must themselves be made responsible to a larger electorate (the membership, that is, of the state, movement, union, or party). Nothing is more important than that responsibility; without it we will only get one or another sort of activist or *apparatchik* tyranny. And that we have already.

Nonparticipants have rights; it is one of the dangers of participatory democracy that it would fail to provide any effective protection for these rights. But nonparticipants also have functions; it is another danger that these would not be sufficiently valued. For many people in America today, politics is something to watch, an exciting spectacle, and there exists between the activists and the others something of the relation of actor and audience. Now for any democrat this is an unsatisfactory relation. We rightly resent the way actors play upon and manipulate the feelings of their audiences. We dislike the aura of magic and mystification contrived at on stage. We would prefer politics to be like the new drama with its alienation effects and its audience participation. That is fair enough. But even the new drama requires its audience, and we ought not to forget that audiences can be critical as well as admiring, enlightened as well as mystified. More important, political actors, like actors in the theater, need the control and tension imposed by audiences, the knowledge that tomorrow the reviews will appear, tomorrow people will come or not come to watch their performance. Too often, of course, the reviews are favorable and the audiences come. That is because of the various sorts of collusion which presently develop between small and co-opted cliques of actors and critics. But in an entirely free society, there would be many more political actors and critics than ever before, and they would, presumably, be self-chosen. Not only the participants, but also the nonparticipants, would come into their own. Alongside the democratic politics of shared work and perpetual activism, there would arise the open and leisurely cul-

ture of part-time work, criticism, second-guessing, and bur-
lesque. And into this culture might well be drawn many of the
alienated citizens of today. The modes of criticism will become the forms of their participation and their involvement
in the drama the measure of their responsibility.

It would be a great mistake to underestimate the importance of criticism as a kind of politics, even if the critics are
not always marked, as they will not be, by "republican virtue."
It is far more important in the political arena than in the
theater. For activists and professionals in the movement or the
polity do not simply contrive effects; their work has more
palpable results. Their policies touch us all in material ways,
whether we go or do not go to the meetings. Indeed, those
who do not go may well turn out to be more effective critics
than those who do: no one who was one of its "first guessers"
can usefully second-guess a decision. That is why the best
critics in a liberal society are men-out-of-office. In a radically
democratic society they would be men who stay away from
meetings, perhaps for months at a time, and only then discover that something outrageous has been perpetrated that
must be mocked or protested. The proper response to such
protests is not to tell the laggard citizens that they should
have been active these past many months, not to nag them to
do work that they do not enjoy and in any case will not do
well, but to listen to what they have to say. After all, what
would democratic politics be like without its kibitzers?

Index

Index

Index

Index